Can I Pay My Credit Card Bill with a Credit Card?

Also by Mary Hunt

Debt-Proof Living

Debt-Proof The Holidays

Live Your Life For Half The Price

Everyday Cheapskate's Greatest Tips

Debt-Proof Your Marriage

Cheapskate Gourmet

Debt-Proof Your Kids

Tiptionary

Tiptionary 2

Tiptionary Journals

The Financially Confident Woman

Cheapskate in The Kitchen

The Complete Cheapskate

Money Makeover

The Best of Cheapskate Monthly

Can I Pay My Credit Card Bill with a Credit Card?

And Other Financial Questions We're Too Embarrassed to Ask!

By

MARY HUNT

Cover Design: Steve Soto

For information regarding special discounts for bulk purchases, please contact: DPL Press, Inc., Special Sales: 800 550-3502.

First published in 2009 by DPL Press, Inc.

ISBN 978-1-9345080-4-6

"Don't be afraid to ask dumb questions.
They're more easily handled than dumb mistakes."

– William Wister Haines

Contents

Introduction

I'll never forget reaching into the mail and pulling out the first letter I'd ever received from someone who assumed I knew something about personal finance.

I'd just come clean, so to speak, to a reporter with the *Los Angeles Times*. My story, warts and all, had appeared above the fold on Friday, May 15, 1992—front page of the View Section. I will be forever indebted to stringer Lorelei Lachman and the *Times* for the story that launched my newly minted newsletter, *Cheapskate Monthly*, to the moon.

The U.S. was in the throes of a recession. Things were especially bad in California, where I live. Jobs were disappearing; businesses were dropping like flies. The governor was threatening to raise taxes and people were scared.

Almost overnight a sense of doom settled in as the topic of personal finances gurgled to the top of peoples' minds. How could they keep food on the table, pay their mortgages and credit-card bills, too? (Is anything here beginning to sound familiar?)

"Dear Mary," the letter began. "I've never told anyone what I'm about to tell you. I am so embarrassed ...."

She went on to recount her vast secret debt, her never-ever-reconciled bank account, her shame and fear about money. Her questions indicated that clearly she had more confidence in me than I had in myself.

My only claim to fame was that I'd dug my way out of a horrid debt situation and had dared to believe that anyone might want to subscribe to my newsletter. I never purported to be a personal finance expert, only someone who needed enough money to finish paying off a horrendous amount of credit—and was willing to share what she knew in exchange for a few bucks a year to buy a subscription.

Sure, my idea to publish a newsletter was, shall we say, brilliant; the timing fortuitous. But my plan was only to help readers cut their grocery bills and figure out how to make their own cleaning supplies, not to teach them to balance their checkbooks or venture into the finance part of personal finance.

The letter caught me off guard. What started out as a lark was getting serious. I felt like a fraud.

As inadequate as I felt, I responded by drawing on what I did know and the success I'd discovered on my journey out of debt. I offered her a few ideas for how she could stop her outrageous spending, devise a plan to get control of her money—and told her I had faith that she could do it.

No sooner had I mailed that letter (remember 1992? No email), two more arrived. Then four and before I could get my breath, the mail was coming packed in long U.S. Post Office trays.

For several years, I responded to every letter. First in longhand, soon after by computer-generated letters printed in dot-matrix. The advent of email became my lifesaver.

If there is a miracle in all of this, here it is: Rather than say I didn't know the answer, I promised to find out. I became a voracious "searcher." I subscribed to all the personal finance magazines; I read all the columnists. I waded into *The Wall Street Journal*, and pored over every book I could get my hands on that was remotely related to money management and personal finance. I pretty much devoured the IRS and Social Security websites, discovering that I possessed an insatiable appetite for the subject matter. I couldn't get enough.

The more I learned, the more I wanted to know. And if learning was a good thing, teaching it to others was even better. Whoever said, "Teaching teaches the teacher," sure got that right!

Over the years the "Dear Mary..." column in each issue of the newsletter—subsequently changed to *Debt-Proof Living* to reflect a much larger mission than just cutting costs—became the reader favorite. The more letters and responses I published, the more mail I got.

In time I would get letters from readers who recounted the number of years they'd been reading the newsletter, books, syndicated column, and *Woman's Day* magazine (yeah, things have grown a bit over these 17 years), telling me they feel like they've earned the equivalent of a degree in personal finance. That's what they get for peeking over my shoulder year after year as I have responded to every kind of money question imaginable.

Turns out that first letter writer was not the only embarrassed reader out there. And hopefully, not the last. My readers are free to ask any question without fear of being exposed, excoriated or embarrassed. They don't worry about revealing their deepest money secrets; they're safe with me.

Not a day goes by that at least a couple of people tell me this relationship has changed their lives. And that's nothing compared to what it has done for me.

In your hands you hold a very eclectic, random collection of questions and answers—each one taken straight from the pen or keyboard of a real person.

While we attempted to organize the material by category, you will soon discover just how difficult that was. For example, does "Is using my debit card with no money in my account the same as writing a bad check?" belong with "Plastic" or "Banking?" Does a question about credit-card insurance belong with "Insurance" or "Credit Cards?" Should we put questions about student debt with "Education" or "Debt?" I even toyed with just one king-size category: Miscellaneous. So how did we end up arranging hundreds of questions and answers? You're about to find out.

So, grab some coffee, sit back and enjoy. And who knows? You just might learn something you've wanted to know but were too embarrassed to ask.

And, should your question not come up—or what you read creates new ones—meet me at the end and I'll tell you how to reach me.

Mary Hunt
California, 2009

Banking

Banks vs. credit unions

Q: What is the difference between a bank and a credit union?

A: A bank is a for-profit financial business run by paid board members whose primary purpose is to make profits for the shareholders.

A credit union is a non-profit financial business that's owned by its members and is run by un-paid, volunteer board members. In a credit union the profits go back to the members in the form of better rates and lower fees.

To find a credit union you can join, go to *CreditUnion.coop* and click on "Locate a Credit Union."

Overdraft protection softens the blow

Q: When a person, who shall remain nameless, overdraws her bank account quite by accident, is there anything she can do to stop the chain of events and horrendous fees?

A: Don't worry. Your secret is safe with me. Banks hope you won't fight back by requesting a courtesy credit, but you should. The minute you realize you have a problem, call the bank or go into your branch in person.

Many banks will credit back the fee or some of it, if it's your first offense.

You need to move into prevention mode by setting up an overdraft protection account that attaches to your checking account. Then, to make sure you never have to use it (you have to pay it back so it's not some kind of gift), get into the habit of checking your balance frequently and never let it drop below, say $100. Ever.

A good checking account

Q: I'm going to open a new checking account at a new bank. I'm tired of getting nickeled and dimed to death with fees where I am now. What should I be looking for in a good checking account?

A: Great question. Here's the minimum you should expect:

- No monthly fee
- A low required balance to maintain free checking
- Free checks and check writing
- Online access to your account statements for no fee
- Free online bill pay for at least 15 transactions per month
- FDIC insurance on deposits (or NCUA if it's a credit union)

To find a bank that offers fee-free checking accounts go online to *Bankrate.com*, click on the "Checking and Savings" tab. You can even compare rates and offers to find the best bank deal.

Best savings accounts for kids

Q: As a big fan of your book, *Debt-Proof Your Kids*, I'm ready to open the kids' savings accounts. Our credit union offers these choices of accounts:

1) a college saver Certificate of Deposit that pays around 5 percent, with $200 minimum deposit requirement.

2) a regular savings account that pays hardly any interest at all but requires only $5 to start.

Which one would be the best option for the kids?

A: Savings accounts are teaching tools for kids, not investment vehicles to create lifetime wealth. The interest they will earn is secondary to the act of saving itself.

What is important is that your kids can walk into a physical bank each "payday," see a teller (or ATM), and fill out a deposit slip. Opening a CD account with your $200 to meet a minimum deposit requirement is over a kid's head. That defeats the purpose because it keeps mom and dad in control.

If the kids start their accounts with $5, they should be able to open their little passbooks and see an entry for $5 with a current balance of $5.

Just keep those accounts growing and you'll have adult kids who are able to make wise financial decisions. Thanks for being a fan.

A great mystery of life

Q: I am university-educated and have an advanced degree in the arts. This is really embarrassing: What is interest? I just don't get it.

A: Don't worry. Your secret is safe with me. There are lots of things in the arts that I don't understand, so we're even.

Okay, let's say you're a photographer. You have a big job offer, which will require you to borrow a camera. You'll have to pay a rental fee, figured by the hour or the day. The longer you keep the camera, the more rent you will pay.

Interest is "rent" you pay on money you borrow. And each month you keep it, you have to pay more rent to the owner of that money.

When you are the owner of the money (say you have a savings account or other kind of investment), you become the lender and others pay you "rent" to use your money. In that case you are earning interest.

In search of Christmas Clubs

Q: Whatever happened to bank-sponsored Christmas Clubs?

A: They all but disappeared when credit cards became so popular. The new attitude was, "Why worry about it? I'll just use my credit cards and pay for it later." Bad idea.

Good news: Christmas Clubs are making a comeback as we see consumer credit tightening.

With a Christmas Club you sign up to have a small amount automatically deposited from your paycheck into your Christmas account each payday. It's a smart, painless way to save for Christmas shopping.

Check around to see if Christmas Clubs are making a comeback in your area.

Not all holiday saver plans pay interest, by the way. Even if yours doesn't, that's still better than paying credit-card interest and creating a new pile of debt because you failed to save cash for holiday spending.

The heartbreak of double-processing

Q: Checks I sent through the mail to pay my bills were processed as ACH payments. I didn't authorized this and ex-pected my checks to be handled normally, as checks.

Now I'm worried that when the checks do clear my bank, the money will be paid from my account again.

Can companies just do this without customer authorization?

A: Welcome to the future. ACH refers to Automated Clearing House, a service that processes paper checks as electronic payments (think: debit card) the minute you hand that check to the clerk.

You really have no say in the matter. When you write a check the money is no longer yours. The merchant can process your check in the most expeditious way possible. You should assume that all checks you write will be turned into electronic payments the moment you hand them over.

You are wise to be concerned about double-processing. That's why you should always watch your account carefully to make sure no checks are deducted twice. Should that happen, make sure you contact your bank immediately.

Private information compromised

Q: Recently I mailed documents to the company that manages my IRA. The envelope came back as "undeliverable," and clearly it had been opened.

Now someone has access to sensitive personal information including my account number, Social Security number, signatures, even a copy of my marriage license with my husband's and my birth dates, mothers' maiden names and so on.

I'm worried.

I immediately signed up for Lifelock. Is there anything else that we should do to protect ourselves?

A: As I was reading your letter, I was shouting "Lifelock!" under my breath (an identity theft protection service). Boy, was I was relieved to get to the end of your note to learn that you have done that already.

I believe you are well protected now, thankfully. In the future never send sensitive documents via regular mail. Send them by FedEx or USPS Express Mail. These provide for guaranteed delivery, proper handling and a signed receipt. That's a small price to pay for peace of mind.

Caught in the overdraft trap

Q: I have a bank account and a credit card that just keeps accumulating late and over-limit fees. I tried to get the bank to close the account to stop the accumulation.

Now I owe $900 for overdrawing my bank account by only a dollar and change.

Is there any way to avoid having to pay a bank that didn't even help me close the account, or waive even part of those fees? I tried to contact them but all they want is payment. They don't want to negotiate.

A: Something doesn't add up here. You don't go from overdrawing your bank account by a couple of bucks to $900 just like that. Sure, I can see how bouncing one check or debit-transaction can set off a chain reaction, but choosing to ignore the situation until it reaches $900 is unconscionable. Blaming the bank is creative but terribly inappropriate.

This is not going to just go away on its own. It's time for you to take responsibility.

Your mention of a credit card leads me to believe you have a pre-established credit line to cover overdrafts. If so, set up a repayment plan immediately.

However, in the off chance you are only assuming you have such an account when in truth you have become the beneficiary of the bank's "courtesy overdraft" policy, you need to move quickly to stop the bleeding. It's possible they are adding a daily penalty every day you are in the red.

Find out exactly what you owe and tell them you will do whatever you must to repay the balance in full. Period. Then get busy selling assets and working extra jobs to see that you do.

In the future make sure you know exactly how the bank handles overdrafts. Do they draw money from your pre-established credit line to cover the amount plus fees and penalties, or do they cover your indiscretion with the bank's funds plus fees and penalties for every day you let it go (much more expensive)? Another option would be that the bank simply returns checks as unpaid and hits you up with a one-time penalty.

These days you have to assume that in the absence of clear instructions from a customer, a bank is going to choose the option that creates the most income for the bank.

Overdrafting fiancée risks relationship

Q: I have "ready reserve overdraft protection" on my checking account. Occasionally I dip into it. I typically repay the entire balance within a week or two, but every few years I may pay it off over a couple months because I've used a larger amount.

My fiancé is threatening to close our shared account because of this. He claims that every time I use the ready reserve, the bank reports it to the credit agencies and it is a ding against his score, even if I repay it before the billing cycle is complete. Is this true? Is this different from other lines of credit?

A: It all depends on how your bank handles its business. Some banks do report to the credit reporting agencies (CRAs), while others do not. If your fiance says this bank does, why are you doubting him?

OK, can we talk just the two of us? Listen to me: An overdraft account is not a savings account. It is not your money. It's not even a credit card. It is emergency protection—very expensive insurance I might add—like fire insurance, something you have but hope you will never have to use. Using it on purpose with intention is unconscionable.

Every time you write a check or use your debit card for more money than you have on account, you get socked with overdraft fees even if they are less than what they would be if you did not have this protection in place.

But worse, every time you overdraft, your fiancé loses faith and trust in you. That's huge and something I hope you will think about.

When a bank goes bust

Q: If my bank is FDIC insured, what happens if the bank goes broke?

A: Most likely another bank will buy up the assets of your bank and nothing will change except possibly, the name of the bank.

Or, the FDIC make take the role of conservator and things will go on pretty much as they have been, with the FDIC making sure all of the insured deposits are safe and secure.

A third possibility, while remote, is that the FDIC just writes you a check for the full amount of your insured account.

If your deposits at one FDIC-insured institution are $100,000 or less (that was increased to $250,000 in 2008 to remain in effect through 2009 and possibly longer) your deposits are fully insured. You can relax.

Want to learn more? Use FDIC's Electronic Deposit Insurance Estimator (EDIE) at *FDIC.gov/edie* to get a printable report of the insurance coverage you have for each of your accounts.

Not all mortgage companies report

Q: We just built a new home and got our loan through a local bank that does not report loan activity to the credit bureaus (Experian, Equifax and TransUnion). Is there anything bad about that?

A: This is not unusual. Lenders are not required by any law to report. The only reason this might be of concern to you is if you will be relying on your payment history with this company to improve your credit score.

Since you got this loan I am going to assume that is not a concern, so you don't need to worry that they will not be reporting your activity in the future.

Timing to get full advantage

Q: My mom always pays her bills on time, but just barely. She waits until the last minute to allow her money to earn interest in her bank account as long as possible. Is this reasonable?

A: Yes, very reasonable for a person who is highly organized and quite fastidious. Your mom is one smart lady.

Over time, even a small amount of interest can add up to something significant. That's a basic principle of finance. But, this method can present problems for the undisciplined person. The most obvious is that missing the deadline will incur expensive penalties. It takes a lot of interest to recoup a single $39 late fee. Another hazard is that having the money available can lead to temptation to spend it for some other purpose.

The 411 on compound interest

Q: I'm embarrassed to say I don't know what compounding interest is. How is that different from simple interest? Do I have to sign up for a special compounding interest account or do all regular savings accounts offer this option?

A: Compounding is a natural phenomenon that happens automatically in any savings account when the simple interest earned stays in the account to become part of the principal balance. In essence the interest then starts to earn interest, too. Think: snowball.

Since interest is added to a savings account automatically (as opposed to being sent to the account holder in the mail every month), the only way to stop interest from compounding in a savings account is to withdraw the interest as you earn it. Don't do that.

Perhaps this is one of the only times in life that being lazy and doing nothing is a good thing. As long as you don't make withdrawals, you'll be the beneficiary of both interest and interest on the interest, which is one definition of compounding interest.

Earning interest in your sleep

Q: You suggest that I save up and keep at least three months' worth of my expenses in a savings account for an emergency.

My problem is that I will have to pay income taxes on the interest I earn on that money. Do you have any other suggestions that may

serve the same purpose without having to pay taxes to cover an emergency?

A: What are you thinking? Not wanting to earn interest is like saying you don't want to earn a paycheck because you'll have to pay taxes on it. Look, the only difference is that you have to work for the paycheck, but you can earn interest in your sleep.

Let's say your emergency fund holds $10,000. These days you'd be lucky to earn 3 percent interest in a savings account, but let's say you can. In one year you will earn about $300 interest. If you are in the 28 percent tax bracket, you will pay $84 of the $300 in taxes. But so what? The reason for the account in the first place is to keep you afloat during a time of financial stress. Besides, you get to keep $216 of the interest. I don't know about you, but I'll pay $84 to make $216 any day. So should you.

Money market funds, accounts ... ?

Q: Is there a significant difference between money market accounts and money market fund accounts?

I need to find a place to park my emergency fund of about $10,000. What should I look for?

A: There are two types of money market opportunities:

A money market account is an interest-earning savings account offered by a federally-insured bank or credit union, with a minimum balance requirement, and limited check-writing privileges. Also called a "money market deposit account," federal regulations limit you to six transfers or withdrawals per month with this type of account.

A money market mutual fund (sometimes referred to as a "money fund") with a brokerage firm carries no FDIC insurance and is simply a collection of short-term debt investments held by a mutual fund company. The value of a share of a money fund should always be $1— it's the interest rate that fluctuates, not the share price.

Think of a money fund as putting money into a savings account that earns interest, but you never know how much interest, if any, it will be until you've earned it. And the money is not insured in the event the brokerage firm goes belly up.

Note: In late 2008 when Wall Street experienced a meltdown, the federal government stepped in and offered brokerage firms insurance similar to FDIC that would insure money accounts up to $250,000. Additionally, this insurance is temporary and set to expire at the end of 2009. Stand by for further developments.

Typically, a money market mutual fund comes with check-writing privileges, similar transaction limitations, and minimum balance requirements as money market accounts.

APR vs. APY

Q: What do the terms "APR" and "APY" stand for and what do they mean. I'm guessing they have to do with how interest is calculated.

A: You're right, it refers to interest— either earned or paid. And terms like APY and APR can be confusing. So let's try to clear it up.

Annual percentage rate, or APR, is a measure of how much interest will be on an annual basis without taking into account compound interest.

Annual percentage yield, or APY is APR plus compound interest—a better measure of how much interest you will actually pay or earn.

Banks often express credit-card interest rates in APR, to better hide just how much you're really going to pay in interest if you allow your balances to roll over into credit-card debt.

When the bank goes up for sale

Q: Our bank is up for sale and I'm trying to decide what to do with our savings account. What bank would you recommend? Thanks for your help.

A: More than likely you will have the option to leave your account exactly where it is under the same terms and conditions. The only thing that will change with the sale is the name of the bank. And that might not even change. You'll just have to wait and see. But if it's FDIC-insured you can relax. You have nothing to worry about.

If you want to earn a better interest rate, consider opening an online savings account (OSA). Online savings banks like *INGDirect.com*, *GMAC Bank.com*, and *HSBCDirect.com* are fully FDIC-insured and typically beat the interest rates of brick and mortar institutions.

Not only will you get higher interest in an OSA, there are typically no fees or minimum deposit requirements as there are with traditional banks.

You can also arrange for an automatic deposit, which is a painless way to save. It's funny how quickly you'll stop missing money you don't see.

Banks rarely decline big fee transactions

Q: Why does my bank allow me to keep using my debit card and withdraw money from an ATM even when my account drops below $0?

A: Banks say they do this as a courtesy so you won't be embarrassed when you swipe your card for a burger and fries, or try to make a withdrawal from an ATM and 27 people are impatiently waiting in line behind you.

Apparently they assume you'd rather pay $40 or more in "courtesy bounce fees" than have your purchase or ATM withdrawal declined.

These days banks derive a great portion of their profits from penalty fees so they are not interested in stopping you from overdrawing your account. I've even heard from readers who ran up penalty fees of $350 or more before the bank notified them that they had a problem.

That should be all the incentive you need to start managing your account very carefully.

Depending on what kind of arrangements you've made with your bank, they dip into your overdraft account to cover the charges (and fees) or they put some of the bank's money into your account to cover the problem.

If you agree to the bank's courtesy bounce protection, it's going to cost a bundle if you ever use it. There will be the penalty fee for doing the deed ($35 per bounce or more), and then many banks will follow with a daily charge of $5 or more until you restore your account.

Banks derive a huge portion of their profits from penalty fees. So don't expect them to stop you from overdrawing your account any time soon.

You must be the one who cares enough to take charge of the situation by making certain you never come close to $0 balance. Ever.

Socked with ATM fees

Q: What's the deal with ATM fees? I'm getting slammed and I can't figure it out.

A: Your own bank should not charge you a nickel to use its ATMs. That needs to be free. Your bank should have multiple machines, so find out exactly which ones they are and where they are located.

When you use an ATM from another bank, expect to pay two fees per transaction: one by your bank for having to deal with the other bank, and a fee charged by the outside bank. Add it up and you're probably paying $3 or more each time you use another bank's ATM.

I'm guessing that you've been using a lot of outside ATMs. That can run up a big tab fast.

Debt-free and ready to save

Q: I'm 23 and have just fought my way out of credit-card debt. Being debt-free is such a great feeling.

Now, I'm ready to really start saving. I asked my bank about the interest rates on different types of accounts and was I shocked!

My bank is paying only 2 percent interest on a certificate of de-

posit (CD), even less on a regular savings account. I'm getting more than that on my apartment security deposit!

When I was paying them interest on my credit-card debt, my rate was 18 percent. How can they get away with that?

A: You rock! Wow, I am so proud of you. It is fantastic that you are debt-free and, I presume, bent on staying that way.

As for the difference between interest rates earned and those paid, welcome to the real world. Banks always make sure the rates they earn (and customers pay on their credit-card accounts) are many times greater than what they pay on savings, CDs and money market accounts.

When the Federal Reserve Board lowers interest rates, it affects fixed instruments like savings accounts and CDs almost immediately. Conversely, the rates customers are paying on variable credit-card accounts don't offer any correlation.

These days credit-card interest rates are skyrocketing! That's just one more reason to never, ever carry a balance on a credit-card account.

I wouldn't be too worried about the rates you are getting on your savings account at this time. What's important is that you are growing your Contingency Fund to at least three months (six is better) of your regular living expenses. If you earn interest, great, but the important thing is that your funds are safe and secure in a federally-insured bank or credit union.

Once you are set with that stash of cash, you'll want to start investing in the stock market where the risk is great, but the rewards can be even greater. At your age, you should be jumping for joy that the market is at historically low levels.

Certificate of Deposit, aka CD

Q: I'm sure I'm the only one who doesn't know, but what is a certificate of deposit?

A: You may be the only one willing to ask, but I doubt if you're the only one who doesn't know.

A certificate of deposit (CD) is a time deposit, offered by banks, thrift institutions and credit unions. Similar to a savings account that is federally insured, a CD is money in the bank with certain conditions and restrictions.

In exchange for you agreeing to leave the money in the bank for a specified period of time (like a month, three months, six months, a year, five years or longer), the bank promises a higher rate of interest than on accounts from which you can withdraw your money at will.

CDs typically require a minimum deposit and may offer higher rates for larger deposits. When you open a CD

you might receive a passbook or paper certificate, but it is common for a CD to show up as an item on your periodic bank statement.

Upon maturity, the face amount of the CD plus guaranteed interest is paid back to the depositor, or it can roll over for another run.

Early withdrawal penalty

Q: What if I put my money in a CD for say one year, but have an emergency and need the money before that? Can I get my hands on it?

A: Yes, absolutely. It would be considered an early withdrawal and for that you would be penalized pretty heavily.

Depending on how far you are from the maturity date, they will reduce the guaranteed interest you would have received. It's called an early withdrawal penalty, and it applies only to the interest, never to your principal or initial deposited amount.

Build a CD ladder

Q: What does it mean to "ladder" certificates of deposit (CDs)? I caught the tail end of this on TV but didn't understand at all what they were talking about.

A: "Laddering" is a method of buying time deposits with varying maturity dates.

CDs and bonds are both examples of "time deposits." When you make the purchase or investment you know exactly when that instrument will "mature" and will have earned the guaranteed amount of interest promised. Here's why "laddering" is a very good idea:

Let's say you have $10,000 to invest in CDs (or bonds) and you want to generate the most interest (income) possible. Shop around for the best rates (*Bankrate.com* is an excellent place to get daily updates on going rates). Now, instead of buying one $10,000 CD, break it up to buy several: One that matures in 90 days, another in six months and so on, divvying up your $10,000 in such a way that one CD is coming due to you every three months for the next year.

If interest rates go up, you will simply replace the maturing CD with a new CD at the higher rate. If interest rates remain the same, you can roll it over for another period of time on the same terms. And if interest rates go down, you will still have some of your money invested for the rest of the year at the higher rate.

Investors routinely ladder their purchase of bonds, which like CDs have specific maturity dates with many having guaranteed rates of interest.

In search of best interest rates

Q: Where can I earn the best interest on my savings?

A: These days online-only banks like *GMACBank.com*, *FNBODirect.com* and *OnBank.com*, are paying the highest rates of interest on traditional savings accounts, money market accounts and Certificates of Deposit (CDs).

In this current economy, you can expect to earn 2 to 3 percent better online than at a standard bank. And even those rates are likely to change before I finish this sentence.

Who needs balance?

Q: What does it mean to "balance" my checkbook? How do I do that? Why should I?

A: To balance or reconcile your account means that the amount of money the bank says you have in your account at any given time is exactly the same amount to the penny that your records say you have. Get it? Balance.

There are four reasons you need to reconcile your account at least once a month:

- To catch the bank's mistakes (they make 'em!)

- To catch your mistakes (ditto)

- To avoid really expensive bounce fees

- To feel like a genius

When you go for long periods of time (well, in your case like forever) without settling up to make sure the bank and you agree on how much you have in your account, you're handing over your power to whatever the bank says you have. They're not perfect. Banks are run by humans, and humans make errors.

You make errors, too. Not only with math, but things like forgetting to write down an ATM withdrawal or other transaction.

Sure, it's great to check your balance online every few days, but that may not reveal any *faux pas* the bank makes.

Okay, enough with the lecture. The next time you get your statement, allow that to be your new starting point. Accept the balance the bank says you have and then reconcile your account every month.

You'll find simple fill-in-the-blank instructions with a form on the back of your statement, or you can find something similar online. You'll feel so in control of your money every time you can you'll balance your account to the penny.

Saving vs. investing

Q: What's the difference between saving and investing?

A: It's all about risk and reward. Money in savings is very safe, there is no risk provided your money is in an FDIC-insured bank, (most banks are these days). You can never lose a single nickel of the money you put into that savings bank account, up to the current limit of $250,000 (through 2009 and perhaps longer).

Investing means that you choose to put your money at risk in a place where you could lose some or all of it. So why would anyone do that? To get a bigger reward.

While your money is safe in a bank account, there isn't much reward. You're lucky these days to earn 3 percent in a traditional savings account. But the stock market is a place where money can grow like crazy! And you must be willing to accept the risk that you could lose, too.

So where should you put your money? I'm conservative enough to recommend you need both savings and investments. Start with saving. You need a nice healthy "foundation" of money that is safe and earning some amount of interest—at least enough to pay all of your bills for three months (six is better) without a paycheck. Once you have this set, you can afford to put some money at risk to improve your chances of a greater reward.

The need for protection

Q: What is overdraft protection and how does it work?

A: First, let's define: An overdraft occurs when withdrawals from a bank account exceed the available balance, which gives the account a negative balance. A person can be said to have "overdrawn" or an account to be "overdrafted."

It used to be that if you wrote a check for more than you had in your bank account, the bank would return the check as unpaid, because of insufficient funds (NSF is the term which stands for "not sufficient funds") available to pay the check. Ditto for trying to withdraw cash from an ATM or attempting to use one's debit card for a purchase amount in excess of the account balance. However, even if the transaction was rejected or the paper check returned NSF, the bank would slap a penalty fee for the infraction.

Banks have long offered protection against the unfortunate occurrence of overdrafting one's account, called overdraft protection. A customer could elect to have his or her savings account as a backup source of money to cover or agree to open a line of credit at the bank (similar to a credit-card account), from which the bank would grab money to cover the problem. That line of credit would require repayment under similar terms to a credit card.

Overdraft protection is not cheap, but makes sure your mortgage payment is not rejected for lack of funds (thus triggering a gigantic late fee), for example. There's always a penalty fee of some kind, even when funds are available from a secondary source (like a savings account) to cover the check.

Things have changed in banking in the recent past. These days, most banks have given themselves another option for customers who have not signed up for overdraft protection. They call it "courtesy bounce protection," and it's quite stunning.

When an unprotected customer overdrafts his or her account, the bank takes some of the bank's money, drops it into the account to cover the overage and slaps on a big penalty fee—even if that customer would not have accepted the offer had he or she been notified of the problem. Then the clock starts ticking as the bank charges a daily fee against the account until the account owner deposits sufficient funds to cover the courtesy loan, penalty fees and daily fees as well.

This means that a $4 burger could easily end up costing $40 to $50 or more, depending on how long it takes the account holder to figure out there's a problem. We're talking 700 to 1,000 percent APR on these kinds of short term loans.

Remarkably, the courtesy overdraft schemes that banks have going for themselves do not fall under truth in lending laws that require lenders to fully disclose the terms and conditions of a loan.

It is worth noting that the Federal Reserve Bank has supposedly been considering some kind of action to stop this outrageous practice, but so far nothing has been done. Banks continue to count heavily on these kinds of penalty fees to boost their profit margins.

Banks love it when you overdraft your account—especially when they get to float the loan by showing their customers this kind of "courtesy."

Bank online? How could that be safe?

Q: What is "online banking?" Call me paranoid, but it sounds so dangerous.

A: Let's have a short history lesson, shall we?

In the "olden days" when you wanted to make a bank deposit or withdrawal, you had to go to the bank—a building made of bricks and mortar—to make a deposit, cash a check, or dig through your safe deposit box. And you had to speak to a teller to do any of the above.

Once a month the bank would send a statement in the mail showing all your checks and deposits together with your current balance. Let's call that "walk-in banking."

It was a big leap into the future when banks automated in a way to allow customers to call on the phone, punch in their account and Social Security numbers to hear which checks and deposits had cleared, and that account's current balance.

Wow. So modern. But also terribly worrisome for many who thought it was quite unsafe to access their bank accounts over the phone.

Then, along came the amazing—albeit considered very unsafe by many—automated teller machine (ATM), where even after the bank closed you could make a deposit or withdraw cash by simply punching in your account number and personal identification number (PIN). ATMs eventually found acceptance as more reliable (and occasionally even better looking) than human tellers.

With the advent of the Internet and personal computers, banks made it possible for customers to check their accounts online, through the bank's website, using the customer's unique passcodes. Once connected, customers had real time access to their checking accounts, savings accounts and credit-card accounts, too—anytime day or night.

So is online banking safe? It is at least as safe as any other access you have to your accounts, provided you are careful to never access your account from a public computer or open network (like free WiFi in a coffee shop, airport, or other public place).

No method is guaranteed to be perfect, however banks use very sophisticated encryption to keep customers' information safe and sound. You have the same protection from fraud as if someone stole your paper checkbook and tried to forge your name.

To sign up, go to your bank's website and follow the instructions. Easy.

Automated bill paying

Q: What is "bill pay?" I know it has something to do with paying your bills online and somehow I just can't see how this is safe.

A: You're right. Bill pay refers to paying your bills electronically via the Internet (or in some cases by telephone) rather than by writing paper checks and sending them through the U.S. Mail.

Most banks now offer online banking for their account holders, which often includes a "bill pay" feature. While some charge a nominal fee for the service (usually a flat monthly rate or fifty-cents or so per transaction) many, including Bank of America and Citibank, offer this service completely free.

Most online bill paying connects to your checking account. Paying with a credit card is also an option—not a very good one perhaps, but an option nonetheless.

There are also non-bank bill paying websites, like *PayTrust.com*, where for a fee you can get complete bill management. With this service you receive, review, pay and organize your bills online. Check it out. It just might be right for you.

Another option for online bill paying are websites including Mvelopes, MSN and Quicken that act as "web portals" for online bill payments to hundreds of entities.

Here is an example: Quicken partners with hundreds of merchants and companies for its online Bill Pay service and charges consumers $9.95 a month for up to 20 payments, and $.50 per transaction for each additional payment.

Each of these entities handles bill paying a little differently, so you need to check out each one to learn all of your options.

Online banking helps you become more of a banker, running your accounts like a small business that you control every day. You are always in control, deciding who to pay, how much to pay and when to pay.

Caution: It's easy to get hooked on online banking. You'll understand when you find yourself checking your bank account as often as your email.

Automatic online bill paying

Q: What is the difference between online "bill pay" and "auto bill pay?"

A: The same difference between writing a paper check to your insurance company every month, or authorizing them to deduct your payment directly from your bank account. One is manual, the other automatic.

When you pay bills online you have the choice to pay them manually, one at a time or you can set up an automatic schedule.

With auto bill pay, you select the payee, the amount and the exact day of each month you want to pay that bill. Now it goes on auto-pilot, paying your bills for you, before they're due.

Take your mortgage payment, credit-card payments and other recurring payments that will cause you a big fat headache if you ever pay late. You know when these payments are due, so you can set them up to be paid, say five days early.

Now you'll never be late, and you won't have to remember.

Since you're in charge, you can go back to manual pay or change the payment amount or date any time. You're the boss.

Auto bill pay is a lot like a slow cooker. You can set it and then forget it.

Rewards checking accounts

Q: I'm looking for a place to earn the best rate of interest on m   y Contingency Fund, which is

(drumroll, please) about $18,000 and growing.

Recently I came across a "rewards checking account." It looks like a checking account that pays about 6 percent, when savings accounts in the same bank are at less than 1 percent interest. Is this some kind of scam?

A: Rewards checking accounts are the latest in creative products from banks, and whether they're scams or not depends on how disciplined and clever the account holders are. And you are right, as I write rewards accounts are paying rates as high as 6.1 percent, if you meet the monthly requirements—with "if" being the operative word.

Before you get too excited about all the interest you can earn, know that there are very strict rules you must follow to earn interest.

A rewards checking account is strategically connected to a debit card. To earn the interest you have to use the account a minimum number of times a month, using a debit card to make purchases. If you fail to do this, you forfeit the rate. And you must agree to receive your statements electronically.

There may be other requirements as well, which you will find when you read the terms and conditions.

For me the sticking point is that a rewards checking account must be used and used often to qualify for that great interest rate. That's fine if you keep a large sum in your checking

account anyway, and are not opposed to using a debit-card.

Technically, a rewards checking
account might be an option for your
Contingency Fund, but I am hesitant
to recommend it. You'll have to do
quite a dance each month to qualify
for the reward interest while exposing
the funds to mindless spending.

However, if you are extremely stal-
wart and have a propensity for finding
ways to make offers like this work in
your favor, you can find a bank in
your area that is offering a rewards
checking account along with the
terms and conditions at *Money-
Rates.com*.

Consumer Plastic

Debit card bounce fees

Q: Is using my debit card with no money in my account the same as writing a bad check?

A: Yes, and maybe worse because of the stunning way your bank deducts electronic (debit card and ATM) and paper check transactions from your bank account. Trust me, it's not what you think.

If your balance drops below $0, each check, debit transaction and ATM withdrawal that comes through will bounce and immediately trigger a $34 penalty fee. The problem is the way the bank handles your account that makes small transgressions more expensive.

Your bank doesn't honor transactions as they arrive; they pay them at the close of the day according to size— from large to small.

Here's an example: You have $532 in your account and your checks and debit-card transactions arrive at the bank in this order on the same day: $62, $88, $18, $2 and $402.

If the bank honored them in the order that I listed them, you would incur one bounce fee of $34. You'd have enough to pay all but the $402 check.

However, since the bank pays your transactions from large to small, they will pay the $402 first then $88, $62, $18 and $2. You will get slammed with more than $100 in fees because the last three items will bounce at a cost of $34 each.

Since paper checks are usually written for larger amounts they are more likely to be honored first, leaving your typically smaller debit-card and ATM transactions to go boing-boing!

Banks pull this sneaky stunt for a reason. They count on penalty fees to boost their profit margins.

Tiny but deadly

Q: My bank just sent me a new debit card with a mini-version for my key chain to swipe through debit readers.

The whole concept sounds unsafe even though it would be convenient. I'm not sure if I should keep it. What's your advice?

A: I'd shy away from using the mini-card. A debit card is less safe than a credit card to start with because it doesn't carry the same federal protection if the number is stolen.

Having that plastic dangling from your key chain increases the chance that something will go wrong.

Think of all the times you've lost or misplaced your keys or left them sitting unattended on a counter for a few minutes. You don't want to add the worry of having your account wiped out if it falls into the wrong hands. I'd cut up the mini-version and stick to the regular debit card, if you just can't face life without the darned thing.

We loved you, now go away

Q: I have two credit cards I keep at $0, and never use. They have $5,000 and $7,500 credit limits, respectively.

In the same week I received letters informing me that these accounts have been closed. I have excellent credit, so I don't understand what's going on.

A: Shocking, isn't it—especially when you think that not long ago banks were tripping all over themselves telling us how much they loved us in an effort to get us to accept more and more credit.

The global economy is going through a serious "credit crunch," resulting in most banks lowering credit lines and closing accounts that have had little or no recent activity. Having experienced the horrific sub-prime housing debacle, banks are doing everything they can think of to reduce their exposure to risk and restore their profit margins.

These closure actions will hurt your credit score if it changes your debt-to-credit-limit ratio. If you have another account or two in good standing with little or no outstanding balance, this probably won't impact your score much, if at all.

However, if you do have other balances that represent more than 30 percent of the credit limit (both individually and when you add together the debt and compare that to the combined credit limits) plus the loss of these two accounts with their hefty credit limits, the closures could seriously impact your score.

Not a chance it's both debit and credit

Q: My debit card is also a credit card as long as it has a Master-Card logo, right? Please settle this argument I'm having with my husband.

A: Oh, this is so easy: No, it is not.

There is absolutely no way in all the universe that you could possibly have a piece of plastic that is both a debit card (money is extracted from your bank account at the time of purchase) and also a credit card (that when used, you get a temporary loan with the opportunity to pay the money back with no interest if you do that within the grace period).

Debit cards and credit cards are regulated by two very different federal laws. They do not function the same, and are not issued the same—even though they may have the Master-Card or Visa logo, and appear to be identical to the point that even a sales clerk cannot tell the difference. Does anything about all of this look like an effort to confuse consumers?

So, again the answer to your question is: No way is your debit card also a credit card—no matter what card you have and even though the clerk asks, "Debit or Credit?"

Argument settled.

Why do they ask, "Debit or Credit?"

Q: Why do store clerks sometimes ask, "Credit or Debit?" when I pay with plastic? How should I respond?

A: This is probably one of the most confusing things in the world of consumer plastic, so grab some coffee. This is going to be long.

First, understand that nowadays credit cards and debit cards look alike. They have the same Master-Card or Visa logos. A retail clerk doesn't know what you are using. So even if you swipe a credit card (which absolutely cannot be used as a debit card), she may still ask "Debit or Credit." (Respond "Credit" or she may ask you to input your PIN which would be all wrong with a credit card.)

The reason they ask this question is so they will know how you wish your debit-card transaction to be *processed.*

There are two methods by which debit cards are processed to extract money from your bank account to cover a debit-card transaction.

Not all retailers are set up to process both ways, however. So, not every retailer asks you that horribly confusing question, "debit or credit?"

There are two ways that debit-card transactions are processed:

Direct debit-card transaction: This requires you to input your PIN to complete the transaction. This PIN-based debit-card transaction removes the purchase price from your checking account almost immediately.

When asked "Debit or Credit?" you should respond "Debit" if you elect for this to be a PIN-based debit-card transaction.

Deferred debit-card transaction: This requires you to sign your name on the sales slip to complete the purchase. This signature-based debit-card transaction is called "deferred" because it can take up to two or three days for the purchase price to be removed from your checking account.

When asked "Debit or Credit?" you should respond "Credit" if you want a signature-based debit-card transaction.

Think of a PIN reader (that little machine where you type in your PIN) as a direct connection to your bank account. Once you punch in your number and hit "Enter" the money's zapped out of your account—even if you don't have enough to cover the purchase price.

Don't assume that if the purchase was approved, you have sufficient funds to cover it. In the unlikely event you don't have enough money in the bank, you will overdraft or bounce your account and the transaction will be completed. The bank will cover your little indiscretion and then slap you hard with punitive fees for having gone over.

Think of a signature-based transaction as taking the long way home. A signature-based debit-card transaction gets put into the pile of credit-card transactions for the day and is processed with them. This may be the reason someone made the rather curious decision to call this a debit-card "credit" transaction. It has to do with the way the item is processed—not that it becomes a credit-card transaction.

One more thing: Merchants hate signature-based transactions because they have to pay a fee, as if you'd used a credit card. Some retailers will not offer you the signature-based option if it has a PIN reader.

On a PIN-based transaction, you, the customer, will pay the fee if there is one. And you can be sure that if your bank is not currently charging you a fee every time you swipe your debit card, it will soon. Count on it.

One last thing. If you do not know if what you have is a debit card or a credit card, there are a couple of ways to discover the truth.

If you receive a statement each month that lists all of your transactions for the month and shows a payment due (with the option to pay the full balance or a smaller minimum payment), you have a credit card.

If you receive a bank statement that shows the checks, online transactions, ATM withdrawals and deposits you have made during the month—but there is no minimum payment due—you have a debit card.

Still confused? Call your bank (the number will be on the back of the card) and ask. Don't be embarrassed. They have no idea who you are. And truth be told, they don't even care.

Blowing the wad with a debit card

Q: I hardly ever carry cash and rarely use credit. I use only a debit card. But still there are times I feel out of control. How can I get some control over my spending?

A: Merchant research groups have proven it over and again: Customers who shop with plastic spend about 30 percent more than those paying with cash.

I believe that's because credit and debit cards (even checks) are stand-ins for our money. They're not the real thing, but more like "play money."

I know for myself that swiping a card or writing a check for say a $50 purchase doesn't require the same kind of mental consideration as paying with cash.

I suggest you put yourself on a cash-only diet for the next 30 days. Don't even carry a checkbook or plastic. Except for payments you must send through the mail, force yourself to pay with cash.

It is not convenient and you have to plan ahead for how much cash you'll need for the day.

Keep a written record of how you spend the cash, too.

While making the switch to cash will be quite an adjustment in the beginning, I predict your mindless spending will disappear.

Tip: If you are concerned about being caught short in case of an emergency, keep a large denomination ($50 or $100) Traveler's Check or two tucked into the back of your wallet. I'll bet you'll have a tough time cashing them, but you'll know you are prepared if you get stuck.

Credit-card interest rates to the moon!

Q: I'm hearing from friends that their credit-card companies are increasing their interest rates even though they've never been late or gone over limit. I have good credit, but now I'm worried. Should I be?

A: Banks today are trying to reduce their risk by taking a very hard look at customers who do not have good to excellent credit. And they're scrambling to recoup losses they've suffered through the whole sub-prime home mortgage mess. They're boosting interest rates like crazy, now, while they can.

Come July 2010, new rules will prevent banks from making these interest rate increases on existing balances for cardholders who follow the rules.

To keep this from happening you need to pay all of your bills on time, pay more than the minimum payment on any revolving balances and keep a low balance on your accounts. Even then you may not be able to prevent an increase. But, you can keep your balance at $0, in which case the interest rate becomes a moot issue.

Credit-card limits in the tank!

Q: Banks are lowering my credit limits. What can I do to protect myself?

A: If the issuer is really concerned about the risk you pose, lowering your limit close to your current balance will reduce their exposure to loss.

Typically, they will not drop the limit below your current balance.

Here's the danger you need to consider: Any charges you make or fees you incur could easily push you over that newly-lowered limit, so you have to be careful.

That being said, you should always fight back when your credit-card company makes an arbitrary decision like this that could damage your credit standing. Call the company and request they reverse their decision. Point out that you've been a great customers for lo, these many years. Mention that other credit grantors are anxious to accept your business (don't, however, close your account; simply dialogue).

It's always possible your account was bundled in with several million others, so don't take this personally.

And the ideal number would be ...

Q: How many credit cards should I have?

A: There is no magic number, but fewer is better. The more cards you have the more accounts you need to manage. And these days, the more cards you keep, the more you need to use frequently to keep them active.

For many of us the temptation to overspend is too great. All you really need to maintain a good credit score is one good all-purpose credit card.

Keep it paid down to $0 every month, make your payment well before the due date and never use more than 30 percent of your available

credit, and you'll have nothing to worry about.

Should we have closure?

Q: Should I close all the accounts I have but don't use that often?

A: No. Once you opened them, the damage was done. Closing them will only make things worse. For now just make sure you keep them at $0 and locked up in a safe place.

It's likely the issuers will close them for you if they become inactive. Just make sure the total available credit you do maintain is well above the amount of credit you use and that you keep those targeted accounts active.

First the bait, then the switch

Q: The ad promised a great interest rate, but when I got approved for the card my rate was much higher. Did I get scammed?

A: I don't know if I'd call it getting scammed, but you've definitely experienced the old bait and switch.

They drew you in with promises of a low interest rate (it was a tease), got you to apply, and when they decided you didn't qualify for the better deal, they made the switch.

These days only people with good to excellent credit scores—above 740—will get those advertised rates. If you have a lower score, your application will be rejected or you'll be offered a card with a higher interest rate. It's in the fine print.

What is the grace period?

Q: Is there a law that says how long the grace period must be? (And if you don't mind, what is a grace period, exactly?)

A: The grace period is the number of days between the credit-card purchase and when you will be charged interest. Here's how it works:

When you pay your balance in full during that time you get an interest-free loan. If you don't pay the entire balance—opting to pay either the minimum payment required or more—you forfeit the grace period. You'll get it back once you get back to $0.

A credit-card issuer is not required by law to grant a grace period, however most do.

Some card issuers give 30 days to pay, but a grace period of 20 or 25 days is more common. Some cards have no grace period at all.

The grace period, as part of the terms and conditions of a particular credit card, can be changed by the issuer with only 15-days written notice to the cardholder.

Always check the due date when your statement arrives. In some cases, you may need to pay that bill as soon as you get it in order to avoid a late fee.

Your card company is required to mail your monthly statement 14 days before the payment is due. When the new rules kick in July 2010, banks will be required to give you 21 days from the day your statement is mailed to pay your bill.

The perils of cosigning

Q: I need your help. Recently a lender turned down my brother for credit. It's my fault. He generously agreed to cosign with us on a pet-care credit card because we could not qualify. He was helping us pay for our dog's surgery.

Now because of my late payments (sometimes 90 days), his credit has been damaged severely. What can I do to clear this up? It's not his fault. It's mine.

A: I don't have good news. The lender required a cosigner because it did not have confidence in you. By cosigning, your brother took a leap of faith the credit-card company wouldn't.

I am surprised they haven't come knocking on his door for the payments. But, given those nice big juicy late fees and high punitive interest rates piling up, I'm sure they're enjoying the ride knowing that eventually he'll make good when you default.

Your brother would have been better off to make the payments each month and for you to reimburse him. That way he could have ponied up to protect his credit rating even during the months that you were late reimbursing him.

He has few choices and none of them are good. The best of the bad would be for him to pay off the balance in full. At least that will stop the bleeding, so to speak.

Even though the late payment history will remain for seven years, he might be able to explain his way around this in the future provided the late-payment pattern had a definite ending.

Unfortunately, his credit score is going to be trashed for a full seven years after that last transaction on that account. That will really hurt if he wants to qualify for a mortgage or some other major purchase.

My advice to him, to you and to everyone is to never cosign on a loan. If the lender has no confidence in the borrower, why should you? You'd be better off to give that person the amount of money he or she is trying to borrow because that's probably what you're going to do in the end, anyway. That way you won't be paying a big load of interest and late fees on top of the gift.

If you can't make it a gift, just say no. Tell these dear friends and relatives you're doing them a big favor by not helping them to get in over their heads with an obligation they cannot handle.

Credit is a privilege, not a human right

Q: I've just discovered that my parents are being discriminated against because they don't have a credit card.

It's a huge injustice if you discriminate due to color, race, or religion and this is totally unacceptable in our society.

If you don't own a credit card you are not allowed to get a rental car, you cannot fly on an airplane and I'm sure there are more issues of this nature that I just haven't uncovered yet. Cash is not an option with these services. Isn't this unacceptable?

A: I understand your frustration. It does seem unfair that some companies these days are adverse to cash. However, I don't think this is a matter of civil rights.

Credit, like driving a car or owning a home, is a privilege, not an entitlement. The same goes for air travel and car rental. Those are not rights guaranteed to us under the laws of the land, but opportunities and privileges.

Businesses, in my opinion, should have the right to offer their services under any lawful terms and conditions they choose. I'm such a capitalist and fan of free enterprise, I cannot imagine enacting laws requiring companies to accept cash or to force banks to extend credit as a matter of civil rights.

Living with cash only is possible, even for your parents. It's just a little more difficult sometimes.

Take your examples of renting a car or buying an airline ticket. You cannot do either on the spur of the moment without a credit card. You have to plan ahead.

I just called randomly, five travel agencies. All five will accept cash for airline tickets. And most car rental companies will accept cash as well. You must be prepared to put up a cash deposit of $400 to $500, refundable upon return of the car. That seems fair to me.

I recommend that every family needs one good all-purpose credit card for the reasons you cite, as well as to establish a good credit score.

For those who have trouble qualifying, there's the option of a secured credit card. To get the card you must deposit cash into a savings account (usually about $300), which is held on deposit to guarantee payment in the event the cardholder defaults.

A secured credit card is a good way to establish credit because after a couple of years with a good track record it can be converted to a regular card account. To find a list of companies offering secured credit cards including terms, look at *IndexCredit Cards.com*.

Leave 'em alone, they'll go home

Q: Should I cancel old credit cards that I no longer use?

A: No. It seems like the logical thing to do, but if you close old accounts you may lower your credit score. Two of the factors used to calculate that score are history (how long you've had credit) and debt-to-limit ratio (how much of your available credit is being used).

Closing an old account can shorten your credit history and increase your debt-to-limit ratio. Both will hurt your credit score.

Leave them alone unless there is a compelling reason, like an annual fee, or a child who is a cosigner and might go on a spending spree.

Here's an important tip: For accounts you want to keep active, use them three or four times a year to keep the accounts open. Then pay the balance in full immediately. Banks don't want inactive accounts and they are aggressively closing them.

Sounds like a book title

Q: Can I pay my credit-card bill with a credit card?

A: Technically, yes you can. Some online bill paying programs give you the option to pay all of your bills with a credit card.

You could take a cash advance on one card, deposit that money into your bank account, then write a check to make the payment on another card. So yes, sadly, you can pay your credit-card bill with a credit card.

But may you do it? Not if you're asking me, which I believe you are. No, you may not!

That would be so dumb because while it might keep you out of hot water for a precious few weeks or months, eventually it's going to come back to bite you. If you can't keep up with the first card, what makes you think you'll be able to handle balances on two card accounts?

Instead of that nutty idea, you need to go on a spending freeze, sell assets, get another job or do whatever you must to keep your payments current and that balance paid in full and I mean sooner rather than later.

The credit-card signing myth

Q: Do I need to sign my credit card? I've heard that I can avoid credit-card fraud if I leave it unsigned.

A: Yes, you must sign it. Forget what you've heard. That card is not valid unless and until it is signed.

Visa and MasterCard require a clerk who is handed an unsigned card

to ask for picture ID and have the customer sign the card on the spot. Otherwise, the transaction should be refused.

A lot of people think they can reduce the risk of fraud by writing "See ID" or "Ask for ID" on the back of the card rather than signing it. This does not negate your responsibility to sign the card and it does not obligate the clerk to request ID.

The risks of rewards

Q: Friends tell us that we should be using a credit card that rewards us in some way, instead of our plain old Visa card that does nothing for us.

What type of credit card should we be using that is accepted at nearly all gas stations, and most hotels and restaurants?

A: You left out a very important morsel of information. Are you carrying credit-card debt from one month to the next? If you are, you have, in my opinion forfeited the privilege to play the reward game. You need to stop using your credit cards until that glorious day that you are not carrying a balance.

Let's go ahead and assume you have no credit-card debt. Even then, reward cards can be tricky. Most of them charge an annual fee. You have to do a lot of charging over a year's time to earn enough rewards to offset that annual fee. And there are other limitations and conditions one should always consider before jumping onto the rewards wagon.

Credit-card offers change like the wind. I could list a couple of reward cards you might want to consider right here, and they could be obsolete by the time you read it.

So instead, I will direct you to *IndexCreditCards.com*, one of several sites that keep tabs on current credit-card offers with their terms and conditions. You will find credit cards organized by what they offer. Look for one with no annual fee.

One word of caution: You could easily shoot yourself in the foot if you got hooked on earning rewards. Running up big balances every month to earn the maximum reward can be quite risky.

Or, in some way figuring the reward offsets the purchase price can turn into crazy thinking. Just one late fee or a couple of months paying interest on a big balance will wipe out your rewards in a big hurry.

Never forget that credit-card companies exist to get as much of your money as they can. They are not outreach ministries in search of ways to make your life better. They do not care about you, nor are they anxious for you to come out the winner when they come up with these marketing campaigns that give cash back or some other reward.

You have to get up pretty early in the morning to win at that game.

Partial payments not good enough

Q: Are credit-card companies allowed to send you to collection even though you've been making monthly payments, just not meeting the payment required?

A: They sure can. If you do not abide by the terms and conditions of your contract with the company, you are in default.

While a credit-card company is required by law to accept any amount of money at any time and apply it to the customer's account, if the amount received by the due date is less than required by the terms of the agreement, they'll slap you with a late fee. And, if that late fee pushes your outstanding balance over the credit limit, they'll slap on an over-limit fee, too.

If the account remains in default, they can and probably will send it to collection.

Something else to consider: As long as you are in default they will continue to report you to the credit bureaus as late. Continual "past-due" entries will wreak havoc on your credit score.

Do we owe if they go bankrupt?

Q: With all the economic turmoil, many national brand stores are closing and people have credit cards from these stores. What happens to your credit rating if one of these stores goes under and you have a credit card with them? What happens with the cards that still have balances?

Do people have to pay the total balance before the store closes? I'm sure there are many people like myself who would like to know.

A: In credit scoring terms, it doesn't matter who closes the account, you or the issuer. Some people incorrectly think it's a bigger black mark if the lender shuts it down, but that isn't true. The leading FICO scoring formula doesn't differentiate. Closing a credit-card account reduces your available credit, and that's a negative for your credit score. How big a negative depends on a variety of factors, but if you have other cards and lots of available credit, it shouldn't be a big concern.

As for carrying a balance on a credit card from a store that files for bankruptcy, your account will be managed by a court-appointed receiver. While the specifics will vary from one case to another, there is no chance in the whole world that the debt will be forgotten. You still owe.

Adding authorized users

Q: I was watching a financial program advising to add your

child to your credit-card account, but not give them a card. If your credit is good, then your children will benefit with a history of good credit.

Also, the program advised to do this for family members who do not have good credit to restore their good credit. What do you think?

A: Adding a spouse or child to your credit card as an "authorized user" has long been a good way to improve that person's credit score, because your good history with the account could be imported to a spouse or other relative's account.

In 2007 things went sideways. Credit repair companies began abusing this feature by "renting" authorized-user slots from people with good credit ratings and selling them to strangers who wanted to boost their scores.

It got crazy because strangers would buy slots on dozens of different cards, boosting their scores by tens or even hundreds of points.

Lenders pressured Fair Isaac (creators of the FICO scoring model) to drop authorized-user information from its calculations.

They did, followed by loud protests from consumer advocates who argued the change could punish millions of innocent parties, including spouses whose entire credit history depended on authorized-user information.

Legal experts also warned that ignoring information regarding spouses on authorized credit lines could be a violation of the Equal Credit Opportunity Act.

Fair Isaac says the most recent FICO 08 formula will factor in authorized-user accounts. Just be aware this is not always a good thing for the authorized user should things change in the future.

Authorized user gets burned

Q: My husband was an authorized user on his mother's credit-card account. When she died, she had an outstanding balance of nearly $16,000 and zero assets.

The credit-card company wrote off the balance, but reported the charge-off to both my husband's credit report and mine, too. I wouldn't have thought that they could do either.

Do you have any suggestions as to what we can do? Our resulting low credit scores are affecting our ability to obtain a home loan.

A: You have discovered the downside of a tactic many people have used over the years to build a great credit history.

The way it works is that an authorized user gets to use the account, but is not lawfully required to pay on it.

The authorized user benefits (or in your case suffers) from the fact that all activity on that account is reported to both the cardholder's and the authorized user's credit file.

I do not know why this is being reported to your credit file, however. Is it possible that she added both of your names as authorized users? Perhaps the laws in your state consider his debts your community property.

Regardless, you should move immediately to dispute this on your credit reports so it can be removed if indeed it has been reported, in error.

Highest rate or smallest debt?

Q: If you had high credit-card balances, would you target one card at a time to pay off or would you spread the payments around?

Situation: I owe $10,000 on one card, $4,000 on another and $3,000 on the third. If you got a bonus of $600—would you divide it equally or send the whole amount to the $10,000?

A: I did have very high credit-card balances, so I have an opinion based on experience. But first let me say there are several schools of thought.

Some experts would tell you to target your debt with the highest interest rate. That's a good thought, but if that debt is also your largest debt, $600 will hardly make a dent and you can see how discouraging that might be.

My preferred method (preferred because it gives a big emotional pay off and that's what all of us need to keep going) is to line up your debts in the order they will be paid off.

This generally puts the smallest one at the head of the line. Keep making all your minimum payments as required, but as you get additional funds like this $600, apply them to the debt at the top. And when it is paid, take its payment and add it to the payment of the next debt in line.

When two are paid take both of those payments and add to the payment of debt third in line, and so on until you are debt-free.

Think of a growing snowball to understand how my Rapid Debt-Repayment Plan works. To see a really cool demonstration, go to *DebtProofLiving.com* and click on "RDRP Calculator Demo" under Quick Links. My Rapid Debt-Repayment Plan has helped thousands of people to get out of debt quickly. I am confident it will work for you, too.

Getting that first credit card

Q: I am a sophomore in college and want to establish credit by getting a credit card. I have a part-time job, but it is not steady, and I am unsure as to what companies offer credit to students with low income. How can I find a good credit card?

A: You are every credit-card company's dream client. You are enrolled in college and have never had a credit card. Statistically, you will keep your first credit card for at least 15 years, paying the credit-card company a lot of money.

Head for your college bookstore and pick up a credit-card application. They'll be sitting on the counter, or if not, ask the store manager. Read the fine print closely. You want a card that has no annual fee, at least 25-days grace period and low interest. You will have no problem qualifying as typically the credit cards offered in college and university bookstores cater to students.

Or go to *IndexCreditCards.com*. Click on "Student Credit Cards" to see a list of the current offerings, together with the terms and conditions on each. Read all of them, then apply for only one.

One last thing: Promise me that if you are ever unable to pay your balance in full during the grace period, you'll turn that card over to someone you trust for safekeeping until you can. Credit-card ownership should never assume credit-card debt.

Hopping from one card to another

Q: I have many open lines of credit from playing the balance transfer game, most of which I can't even tell you what company or how much. I've moved several times and have completely lost track.

How can I find out which accounts are still open, and how do I contact the companies?

A: Start by ordering your free credit reports, one from each of the big three credit bureaus, at *AnnualCred itReport.com*.

Your open lines of credit will be listed on each of your credit reports along with the name and address of each creditor.

If the information is incomplete (for example, Experian does not display the last four digits of credit account numbers), use the credit bureau's free dispute service. You can do this by mail or use that bureau's online dispute service.

Within 30 days you will receive more detailed information on the items you've disputed.

Having many open lines of credit can damage your credit score. However, once open the damage has been done. Closing them may only make things worse. It's important that you pay all of your account balances to $0 every month you use them. Then watch your credit reports like a hawk.

The more lines of credit you have, the more vulnerable you are to identity theft. You should consider the services of an identity theft protection company.

Credit "insurance" a bad deal

Q: I signed up for a Cardholder Security Plan on my largest credit-card debt. It will pay up to 12 monthly benefit amounts to my credit-card company in the event of total disability, involuntary unemployment or unpaid family leave of absence. Or, if I die it will pay the outstanding balance.

This insurance costs 75 cents per $100 of my current outstanding balance. I have a large balance and I am paying more for this plan than I pay in interest each month.

How do you feel about this kind of plan?

Is it worth it for me to continue with the plan or would it be better to cancel it and hope and pray that nothing happens that I will need this service?

Thanks for your advice. I think you are wonderful and a godsend.

A: Cancel it. The kind of credit insurance you describe (every company has its own version with a different name) is just about the most expensive insurance on the face of the earth. Even if you could afford it, it's lousy insurance. There are typically all kinds of provisions in the fine print that make it difficult to collect.

If you can't afford to pay your balance in full every month, for sure you cannot afford this pricey add-on.

The very best thing you can do for yourself and your future is to pay that large credit-card balance off quickly.

Instead of paying $75 every month to the company to insure say a $10,000 balance add that amount to your regular payment each month. Now that money will do you some good instead of lining the pockets of your credit-card company.

With the credit insurance cancelled, the amount you were throwing away on insurance can go to reduce the principal balance. And provided you do not add any new purchases (please don't do that!), you will be amazed how quickly the balance will go down. What you were paying in this bogus "security plan" will go to securing your future, not pad the card company's profit margins.

Thanks for your kind comments. I think you're pretty terrific, too.

Auto pay to save? You bet!

Q: I received an offer from my credit-card company to reduce my interest rate from a whopping 28 percent to 5 percent if I authorize them to deduct automatic payments from my checking account.

I signed up. Did I do the right thing? Should I contact my other credit cards to see if they offer the same?

A: Yes, yes and yes! The only pitfall I see is the possibility that you'll get complacent making only the minimum monthly payment as deducted from your bank account.

The company would be very happy if that's all you ever paid. I wouldn't be surprised if that's their motive in this deal. They don't want you to pay off your balance because that means their interest income dries up.

If you can use this tactic to get the interest rate down and then supplement the automatic payments with an additional payment during the month—and absolutely stop adding any new purchases—you'll be out of debt in record time.

Skip-a-payment? Not a chance

Q: I got a note from my credit-card company offering to let me skip my December payment. This would give me a little more shopping money. But I'm suspicious. Why would they do this?

A: Oh, the infamous skip-a-payment notice. These used so show up around the Christmas holidays, but now we're seeing them in the spring, just in time for summer vacations and fall time, too. The pitch goes like this:

You're such a valued customer, as our way of saying 'Thanks' you can skip your payment this month! Go ahead. Do a little extra Christmas shopping on us since you'll have one less payment.

If you fall for this little scam here's what will happen: The interest you owe this month is added to the balance. It's like you made a new purchase.

Next month you'll owe interest on the interest you didn't pay this month. Anything here sound familiar? It's called compounding interest.

You will be increasing the time and the total interest required to completely pay off that debt. And the company knows that if they can get you to increase the balance, chances of you ever paying it off in full are greatly reduced. Here's a much better idea. Tell them "No Thanks," by sending in a double payment, this month.

Get rid of credit-card offers

Q: I am looking for the phone number to call so that I can get off the credit-card application junk mail list.

I absolutely love your daily, "Everyday Cheapskate." Thank you for such great advice.

A: And I absolutely love hearing from you! You want to call Opt-Out at Prescreening at 888 567-8688, or go to *OptOutPrescreen.com*.

Now, before you pick up the phone to dial, let me tell you what this is all about and what you can expect.

Federal law allows the credit reporting agencies like Experian, Trans-Union, Equifax and Innovis to sell data about you to banks and credit unions for marketing purposes. Apparently you (like millions of others) have been hearing from these companies with offers for preapproved credit cards.

You'll be happy to know that the law also states that these credit bureaus must give you the opportunity to "opt out" from having your information available on the open market. Providing the phone number above is the result of the credit bureaus complying with that law. One call will get your request to all four bureaus.

The phone call will be completely automated and you will respond using your phone's keypad. It takes less than four minutes.

You will be required to give your personal information via this automated call, including your telephone number, name, address and Social Security number. Don't worry about this. The credit bureaus already have all of your information. You won't be giving them anything new, only helping them identify you.

You will have the opportunity to opt out for a two-year period, or permanently. And if for some reason you ever want to "opt in" in the future, you can do that too by using this phone number.

In about a week you will receive a follow-up letter in the mail confirming your request to opt out with a request that you sign and return it.

It will take a few months for the effect of opting out to make a difference in the mail you receive. Be diligent and patient. Eventually the offers will go away.

Credit cards for kids

Q: Recently, I received a credit-card solicitation from Capital One for my 16-year-old son. It said this is a chance for parents to help their children 16 years or older to build good credit.

He doesn't even have a job so how can he build credit? If he has the money to buy what he wants he doesn't need credit. So, if he doesn't have the money to pay the bill he wouldn't be building credit—he would be building debt.

I am sending a letter instructing them to remove my son from their mailing list as long as he is a minor in my household.

A: Thanks for sending me a copy of the offer. Wow, I thought I'd seen everything, but I was wrong. For Capital One to spin this into a matter of responsible parenting is in my opinion, an example of desperate marketing.

Capital One is not the only company that sees our children as the future debtors of America. Just remember that your best defense is to educate your son to be a financially responsible young man.

How can this be legal?

Q: I am slowly paying off my debts, but I got a shock today. One of my credit-card companies (Company A) decided to sell my account to Company B. When I called they said Company A no longer carries accounts in my state.

I accepted that. But Company B's interest rate is 26.4 percent. Company A was 16 percent. They've changed my rate to 26.4 and not on just new purchases, but on my entire balance as well. Is that legal?

A: If you go back and reread the application you signed, in the fine print you will find something like "... *terms of which may be changed at any time and for any reason.*"

While your chances of getting that interest rate reduced are slim, I suggest you exercise your only option: Beg for mercy.

Call and in your most assertive-yet-courteous manner suggest that you may take your business elsewhere unless they would like to lower the rate.

Don't hold your breath, but if your payment history is exemplary, they might do it to keep you as a customer. If that doesn't work, consider switching the entire balance to a low-rate, no-fee card. You can find a current list at *IndexCreditCards.com*.

In late 2008, the Federal Reserve Board announced new rules for credit-card companies that would preclude them from raising interest rates retroactively. Of course, we do not know exactly how this will work, or what they will not be able to do, or what will be allowed.

Unfortunately, you'll have to wait until July 2010 to find out. The Fed gave credit-card companies an 18-month grace period before they must comply.

The infamous activation sticker

Q: Why does my renewed credit card come with a sticker saying I have to call from my home phone to activate it?

A: That card goes through many hands before it reaches you. But until it is activated (by you) it's worthless to anyone who might want to steal it.

Only the legitimate credit-card owner can activate it with a call from the cardholder's home number—the

number that matches the one given on the application. It's a security issue. Which brings me to this huge warning:

A new website allows credit-card thieves to place phone calls and make the call appear as if it came from any phone number. So, credit-card thieves can steal new cards from the mail and then find out what the card owner's home phone number is.

Using the website, they place a call to activate the card and make the call look as if it came from the card owner's home number. The card is activated, and the card can be used fraudulently.

The best way to avoid becoming a victim of this scam is to watch your mail and keep track of incoming credit cards.

As your cards expire (or if you apply for a new card) you should expect to receive a freshly-issued card in the mail. If you don't, find out why. I'd suggest calling the card issuer just to get an idea on when you should expect your new card.

Balance transfers require juggling act

Q: I have eight credit cards and I play the balance transfer game on a regular basis to keep the interest rates at the lowest they can be.

I plugged in all of my balances and current rates into your RDRP

Calculator using the shortest pay-off method and making the same payments every month as you suggest.

My rates change every few months when a promotion expires. What is the best way to handle this with my Rapid Debt-Repayment Plan? Should I just make a new plan each time I do a balance transfer? Thanks for all your help.

A: Yes, when an interest rate changes re-input your data and print out a new Rapid Debt-Repayment Plan (just one of the cool Debt-Proof Living Online member benefits).

By the way, you didn't ask, but I must warn you that opening and closing credit accounts, or playing the "balance transfer game" as you call it, has every possibility of trashing your credit score.

While getting out of debt as quickly as possible is laudable, I suggest you stick with the cards and accounts you have now and focus on finishing your Rapid Debt-Repayment Plan.

Wife should become a joint-owner

Q: My husband and I have one credit card in his name only. We never carry a balance. At age 68 I have no outside employment, nor have I ever.

My husband wants me to get a credit card in my own name to build a credit history in the event he passes before me.

Could you recommend any resources that would tell me how to take the necessary steps to obtain a credit card? How and where can I learn about the different credit cards to determine which is the best choice for me?

A: Your husband is right. It is important that all women—career women, full-time homemakers, single mothers and divorcees—establish credit in their own names.

Have you ordered your credit report at *AnnualCreditReport.com*? If indeed there is no such file in your name and Social Security number, it will come back blank. But there's a chance you have a credit rating if you've been listed on a mortgage or auto loan.

Rather than you gettting a new credit card your husband can call his credit-card company and request an application to add you as a joint owner on his account. Adding your name to this credit-card account should be sufficient for credit-building purposes. And, in the event of his death, the account would remain yours.

That dreaded credit-card mentality

Q: Do you think it's a good idea to put all of your purchases during the year on a credit card that gives a year-end rebate? I heard of a man who does this and by charging and being disciplined he actually makes money.

A: You've left out a few significant details. Like who is this guy? Warren Buffett or Bill Gates? And how do you characterize "making money"?

On an account that earns 2 percent, you'd have to charge $25,000 in a year to make $500—and that's assuming no annual fee, no slip ups, no finance charges and no overspending just to get some cash back. And that also assumes that you know for sure you will have a job and the cash on hand to pay that big credit-card bill every month.

I suppose that for a very disciplined, highly organized person who is not living from paycheck to paycheck, it might work out OK. But generally speaking, I think it's a lousy idea if for no other reason than it encourages a kind of credit-card mentality.

Volunteer for reduced credit limit?

Q: I recently paid off a credit card that has a high credit limit. Is it appropriate to ask the company to lower my credit limit? If so, would this be reported negatively on my credit report?

A: I'm assuming you want to reduce your credit limit as a kind of safety measure against ever getting into a big debt mess again in the future.

The problem with such a move, while certainly commendable, is that it could severely impact your credit score.

You want to maintain a credit limit that is significantly larger than the balance you would ever carry on the card—even for a few days.

To achieve and maintain a good credit score of 740 or higher you need to have a lot of credit you don't use. A larger credit limit will provide that for you, provided you never use more than 30 percent of your available credit.

A high score will qualify you for the lowest insurance premiums and interest rates on mortgages and auto loans, should you be looking at that in the future.

Don't let go of 20-year history

Q: I have had the same Citibank Visa account since 1988. I pay on time, and have often paid it down to $0. If I cannot get them to give me a better interest rate, should I let that card go even though I have an excellent credit history with this company?

I have other cards, like department store credit cards, but this is my only major card in my name alone.

A: No, do not close this account under any circumstances. A credit-card account with more than 20 years of history is a precious commodity. Credit scores love longevity.

My best advice is to pay off the account one last time, then keep it paid down to $0 each month. Now the interest rate becomes a moot point.

It's not that great that you have all those department store credit cards, but the damage has been done. Closing them now could make things even worse, as far as your credit score is concerned.

Two-cycle billing method

Q: What is meant by the "two-cycle billing method" on a credit-card account. What kind of cycle do I want to see?

A: By law the card company must disclose, among other things, the interest rate on the account and the method by which the creditor will figure how much interest you owe on your balance if you allow it to roll over from one month to the next. Two-cycle billing is one method of calculating interest.

Let's start with the simplest method, known as the average daily balance single-cycle billing method.

The company records the balance on your account for the 30 days in the billing cycle, adds them together then divides by 30 to get your average daily balance. Then they multiply by your annual percentage rate (APR) and divide that product by 12 to determine the amount of interest you owe for one month. That's the finance charge.

With two-cycle billing, they determine your average daily balance using the 30 days in the billing cycle plus the prior 30 days (60 days total) and divide by 60 to determine the average daily balance.

For the person who usually pays his or her balance in full and only occasionally uses the account for either convenience or to pay for a large item over a two or three month period, the two-cycle billing method can be a killer.

Note: In late 2008 the Federal Reserve Board announced new rules that will ban credit-card companies from using the two-cycle billing as a method to calculate finance charges. However, those rules do not become effective until July 2010. That in itself is amazing. The Fed gave credit-card companies an 18-month grace period before they must comply with the new rules.

Life without a credit card

Q: I am fearful of owning a credit card because of my history of credit-card abuse.

How can I buy airline tickets and maybe other things that seem to require a credit card to operate now that I've chosen to have no credit cards?

A: It's less convenient to do some of these things without a credit card, but possible nonetheless.

For plane tickets, you can go online or call an airline directly to book a flight. Most, if not all, will hold your reservation for 24 hours.

Now, go to a travel agent or even one of the airline's ticket offices (not the airport) to make your payment.

Call ahead to learn what forms of payment that office accepts. In addition to credit cards, it will likely be cash, money order, debit card or a Traveler's Check. A personal check is probably not an option unless your mother owns a travel agency. Even then, don't count on it.

If you are a member of the Automobile Club of America (AAA) you can pay for airline reservations at any of their offices because they also offer travel services.

Renting a car is trickier. Well before you will need it (weeks if possible), call around to find out which companies will cooperate with a cash rental. Some require a credit report, a substantial cash deposit ($300 to $500), plus corporate approval.

Local independent car rental companies in the city where you will be renting are often more willing to accept a cash deposit at the time of rental in lieu of a credit card.

Some companies will accept a debit card for car rental, but will put a hold on a big chunk of money in your bank account, which will act as a security deposit on your faithful return of the vehicle.

Mail order and online shopping is particularly troublesome without a credit card. Don't do it. If you pay online with a check, debit card or money order and then have a problem—like it never shows up or the company files for bankruptcy—you'll be on your own and out the money.

Buxx up for teens

Q: I would love your opinion on a credit card for teens called Visa Buxx (*VisaBuxx.com*). Thanks and keep up the great work. You have been a lifesaver for our family!

A: The Visa Buxx card is not a credit card, although it looks just like one because it has the Visa logo and hologram. It's not a debit card either.

It is a reloadable payment card, very much like a prepaid phone card or a gift card. Visa Buxx card is marketed to teens ages 13 to 18, and their parents.

Here's how it works: Parents "load" the card with any amount of money they choose. The teen now has a plastic device that looks exactly like a credit card and spends like cash in 18 million places.

When the preset amount is spent, the card no longer works until Mom and Dad fill it by transferring funds from their bank or credit-card account to the child's Visa Buxx.

Visa insists this is a wonderful way to teach teens how to budget and handle money.

I insist Visa is after our kids and will stop at nothing to make them dependent on plastic at the youngest age possible.

First they came after our college students then they targeted high schoolers. Now they have our young teens in the cross hairs.

The Visa Buxx card is a sneaky way to get plastic dependence started early and with the full approval and cooperation of parents.

To me, plastic is an adult privilege that should not be granted to children, period.

If you want to trust your kids with money (you should, by the way), see my book *Debt-Proof Your Kids* for how to do that starting as young as when they are toddlers. Trust them with CASH!

Saved by credit counseling

Q: We've been in credit counseling for five years with Consumer Credit Counseling Services. CCCS has been a very good experience for us.

Even through several layoffs, job changes and the birth of our second child, we persevered and will make our last payment this month on what started out as $45,000 of unsecured debt. Hooray!

Here is our dilemma: My husband thinks that with all of our debt paid off we are "cured" and now he can buy some of the things he's been wanting.

I'm afraid we won't be able to resist temptation after all of these years of doing without.

We are working together to build our Contingency Fund and Freedom Account so we're on board there.

But how can we face the world of credit without getting sucked back in the black hole? Yikes!

A: Well, first off let me toss a little confetti your way, do a couple of cartwheels, and say Congratulations! This is huge. I am so proud of you.

The most important thing I can tell you is that you are not about to cross the finish line, even though it might feel like it. So get that kind of "having arrived" attitude out of your minds. In truth, you are about to make it to the starting line.

Everything you have been through is bringing you out of the darkness of debt and back to point zero. That is a sobering thought and one that should confirm in both of you that you do not care to go back, ever!

I don't know what you mean by "face the world of credit," but I sure hope you do not mean using a credit card to buy things because you don't have the money to pay for them. No way! That should NEVER be the reason to own a credit card.

Together you have to decide your life values. What have you learned? What do you truly believe about money and consumer debt? Unsecured debt should be banned from your life forever. Anything short of that would be like an alcoholic believing he'll be able to take just one drink.

You need to adopt a zero-tolerance rule when it comes to unsecured debt. Unless you do, you will get all wishy-washy. You'll start making allowances and exceptions and before you know it you'll be back in trouble where you owe more on a credit card(s) than you can reasonably repay in a single month.

You will need one good all purpose credit card between you (no annual fee, 25 days grace period and accepted in many places), but do not carry it with you.

Lock it up with a rule that you only use it when both of you agree and then only for securing a rental car or hotel room or paying for something you must buy through the mail. Then, make a commitment to each other that if the day ever comes that you cannot pay the balance, if any, in full during any one 25-day grace period, that card is gone. Ship it off to a trusted friend or counselor.

As for all those things your husband wants, that's what your Free-dom Account is for. Create a subaccount in your Freedom Account with his name on it, titled: Things I've Been Wanting. Make a page for yourself, too.

Provided you have your Contingency Fund in place, the money you are not sending to CCCS each month that has been managed through their Debt Management Program can go straight into your Freedom Account. The balances will build quickly. You're going to be amazed.

Parents who bail out their kids

Q: My daughter who is in college got a credit card. She got in over her head and is now unable to pay.

My daughter works part-time and makes a very small salary. With the high interest and late fees, the balance is now over $2,500. I have decided to step in and handle the account.

How can I negotiate with the card company to settle for less than she owes? I don't know how she got this card on her salary but she kept quiet about not being able to make the payments until we started getting collection calls for her. I appreciate your thoughts and expertise.

A: Call customer service and pose your question to them. Tell them you are the mom, you're quite upset with your daughter and you want to bail her out. *"What can you do to help me out here? If we can come to terms I'll send you a check today."* The worst they can say is that they will do nothing. But they might consider a compromise particularly if they've had a lot of trouble working with her. Just keep in mind that she will owe federal and state income taxes on any amount forgiven if it's more than $600.

Why do these companies give kids such outlandish lines of credit? Because they know parents will rescue their over-extended kids and not just one time, either. The statistics show that in most instances parents will save the day at least twice.

Now that I've told you how to approach the company to negotiate with them, can I jump in with a little unsolicited advice? Don't do it. Don't bail her out. If you do, I believe you will live to regret it.

Unless your daughter has to suffer the consequences of her actions she will not learn from her mistakes.

If you bail her out now, I predict that within two years she will be in twice the amount of debt that she is now, and very likely with the same company. These companies aren't dumb. They know if you did it once, you'll do it again so what do they have to lose?

You don't want to see a bankruptcy and a divorce or two in her future, but that's exactly where she's headed if this problem isn't addressed now.

As painful as it will be for you to refuse to pay her debt, it will be a valuable maturing process for her. I don't underestimate how painful it will be for you. She may have to drop out of school for a semester and go to work full time. If she's really interested in getting an education, she'll be back.

I know that may sound harsh, but she has to understand how unacceptable this is.

Bank error means big headache

Q: Help! We transferred our credit-card balance from a bank card we've had for several years to a new one for the lower interest. Now we are receiving bills with balances from both banks.

We've had three-way conversations to try to straighten this out. The new bank with the new account says they sent a check to the old account and that it has cleared. The old bank says they have received nothing. Meanwhile, we're getting hit with finance charges, too. This is outrageous. What do we do?

A: Wow. And I thought I'd heard every balance transfer nightmare out there, but this is a new one for me.

You are in a tough position because if you don't make the required payment on time to your new account, you'll lose your introductory interest rate.

If you don't make payments to the old account and you become delinquent, you're looking at a seven-year blemish on your credit report.

I suggest you become a very noisy customer. Call both companies daily. Insist that the bank with the new account send you written proof of payment. And let both companies know that you have filed a complaint with the Federal Reserve Board.

You can do that at *FederalReserveConsumerHelp.gov*, or call 888 851-1920.

Banks do what's best for them

Q: My husband and I are self-employed. About a year ago we relied on a credit card with a $10,000 limit at 9 percent interest to keep the business afloat. We took a $2,000 cash advance to cover payroll, but just one time.

We have been making payments each month by separate checks on both the purchase balance and the cash advance, which is at 22 percent. Imagine our horror recently when we discovered none of the payments have been credited to the cash advance, and that not one penny can or will be, until the full amount at 9 percent interest is paid in full.

Can they do this and if so what can we do to get around it?

A: First the bad news: I am sorry to tell you that yes, they can because you agreed to those terms when you signed away your life to get that card.

The fine print carried standard language like, "Payments and credits will be allocated to pay off low rate balances before higher rate balances." That probably didn't mean much to you at the time if you even read it, but now you know why that language was tucked in ever so sneakily.

Here's a very important truth: Credit-card companies do not exist to help you or your business. You'd be better off to think of them as loan sharks. They invested $10,000 in your business with the sole intent to get the greatest return on their money possible (wouldn't we all love to find a way to earn 22 percent interest?).

You might consider transferring the entire balance to a new card, but be very cautious. The fine print regarding the transfer of a cash advance balance could turn out to be worse than what you have now. My best advice is to make paying this debt your highest priority and then consider it a very expensive lesson.

Somewhat good news: New rules go into effect in July 2010 that will allow the account holders (you) to make additional payments on an account, and to stipulate the portion of the outstanding balance to which that money will apply. Until then brace yourselves.

All credit-card companies are raising interest rates like crazy as they gear up to face these new rules that will cost them a lot in lost revenues. I have no doubt they'll find other ways to restore the massive profits they will lose due to the new rules—at the expense of their debt-ridden customers.

I doubt if I need to stress the obvious: You need to get out of debt as quickly as possible, then stay out!

The default rate is late pay punishment

Q: I called Citibank about getting a lower interest rate on my account. Currently it is at 24.24 percent, because I was one day late for one payment.

The customer service rep told me that my rate has already come down for future purchases, however it will remain at 24.24 percent until my balance is paid in full. Is this right?

I am paying $100 a month right now; the minimum payment is $90, of which $84 is interest. This is one expensive lesson. I am doing your Rapid Debt-Repayment Plan and am real frustrated with what I just learned.

A: I'm afraid they have the right to do just about anything they want. And you agreed to that when you signed up to get that card. It was in the fine print.

Believe me, they couldn't wait for you to be five minutes late so they could stick you with the highest interest rate possible (often referred to as the "default rate"). But I wouldn't give up. Call once a week without fail and ask them to lower your rate. Once you have 12-months of on-time payments you should find success.

I'm wondering how strong you've become in your resolve to add no more new debt?

While I don't often recommend "card hopping" (it can wreak havoc on an already tenuous situation if you are not highly disciplined), perhaps you should look for a new low- or no-interest card to transfer the entire balance. Go to *Index CreditCards.com* under "Low-Rate" and "Low Intro/Promotional Rate."

Have you considered setting up auto bill pay for your credit-card accounts? That will help ensure you are never late again.

Who are these people?

Q: Who's in charge of Visa and MasterCard? Who founded these companies? Is there actually a building where these businesses operate? Who are the CEOs of each? Who makes the rules?

I asked the people at my local bank if there's an address or headquarters somewhere. To my amazement no one, including the manager, could tell me.

I called my credit-card company, Chase Bank. They couldn't tell me. I even wrote to my newspaper. No answer there either.

Who's accountable or regulates these companies? Who watches over them?

A: MasterCard and Visa are trade associations. They are not banks and they do not issue credit cards or debit cards. They offer memberships to banks and credit unions who are then allowed to slap the Visa or Master-Card logos on their plastic products.

Member banks of these trade associations pay a lot of money for the privilege of using the MasterCard or Visa logo on their cards.

In exchange, MasterCard and Visa operate massive marketing and advertising campaigns. And they work very hard to get merchants signed up to accept MasterCard and Visa cards from their customers.

MasterCard Worldwide Inc., was founded in 1966, and currently is headquartered in Purchase, New York. Robert W. Selander is President and CEO. At last count it had 5,000 employees. Officially, MasterCard offers financial services and payment systems.

Visa International was founded in 1970, is headquartered in San Francisco, Calif., and has 6,000 employees. Joseph Saunders is Chairman and President. Officially, Visa is a financial services company offering payment systems.

So I'm the only person who knows this? Well, and now you!

Caught in a shell game

Q: We moved and I failed to notify Shell Oil Company of our new address. A $17 balance went 60-days overdue.

My Equifax FICO score fell from 731 to 628 because of that one event. I have mailed the payment and a pleading letter to erase the mark. We've never missed a payment or been overdue before.

I called Shell and the lady on the phone was ugly. I'm devastated by what this has done and now fear that all my other credit cards will raise their interest rates, and with our large credit-card balances this will have a major financial impact.

How long will the late payment show on our credit report? What more can we do to restore our good credit rating quickly and stop other credit companies from raising our interest rates?

This was simply an accident and a one-time occurrence. Why did my score drop over 100 points?

A: FICO scoring is done by computers with no human decency factored in. FICO is not fond of late payments, especially when they go to 60-days.

However, FICO will take into consideration that this is rare for you. Your score should rebound after six months to a year of good behavior even though this mark will remain on your credit report for seven years.

Your more serious problem, as you point out, is that all of your creditors may jump at the chance to increase your interest rates because of this infraction—a practice that is referred to as the "universal default," a provision which some banks have voluntarily abandoned.

I am hopeful that will not happen and that your credit score will not suffer long-term from this one lapse.

Death to the cash advance

Q: I made a huge mistake by taking out big cash advances on my credit cards. I used the money to gamble. I have over $30,000 in credit-card debt on eight cards. Because I've gotten behind on some of them, the interest rates are high—20 to 30 percent.

My husband does not know about this and I keep trying to pay them down, but I'm not going anywhere but down.

Together my husband and I gross about $90,000 annually. What can I do to get this debt down where it is somewhat manageable? Please help.

A: When I received your message I thought it was a hoax (I get those now and then). But verification proved it to be true, sadly.

First, let's look at the numbers. This is just a rough estimate, but at 28 percent interest, if you pay only the minimum each month on $30,000, it will take you 2,706 months (225 years) to be rid of your debt and will cost $415,089 in interest. OK, so that's not going to work.

If you commit to paying a flat $1,200 each month it will take about 38 months to be rid of the debt including $15,548 in interest. Mathematically speaking, this is doable assuming the card issuers do not increase your interest rates.

Now, let's get real. What are the chances of you sneaking $1,200 every month out of your joint funds to pay a gambling debt you believe you can keep secret from your husband? I'd say those odds are about as good as the ones you faced at the poker table.

Sadly, you have put yourself into the greatest losing position of all. I predict that without intervention you will lose your job, your home, and your marriage. You can pretty much kiss your future good-bye.

There is a way out for you, one that requires a lot of courage:

First, you must tell your husband, seek his forgiveness and his help. Come clean and do it now. Next, you need to find and join the closest chapter of Gamblers Anonymous. Find a GA meeting directory at *Gam blersAnonymous.org*.

Hand over all of the credit cards to your husband and then do whatever you must to pay this debt quickly. I'm talking a second (possibly third) job, selling assets, moving into a cheaper area—basically stripping your life to the bare essentials.

The way I see things you have an opportunity with a lot of very hard work to become a winner. I pray you'll take it.

Capital One scores with no foreign fees

Q: I read your newspaper column every day and consider myself a responsible, credit-card balance-paying consumer. Still, I believe I got ripped off. Here's how:

I traveled overseas for business. My employer instructed me to use my credit card to get the most favorable exchange rate. I did. When I received my bill there was a $164 "foreign transaction" charge. I was irate, called and was told that Citibank imposes a 3 percent charge on every purchase made in a foreign currency, which is billed as a finance charge.

I will get reimbursed under the terms of my business travel. But non-business travelers won't have this option. Is this a scam?

A: Almost every bank charges some kind of a fee on credit-card purchases made in a foreign currency (yep, it's in the fine print). And on top of that, Visa and MasterCard charge a 1 percent processing fee on international transactions.

Had you written prior to your trip, I would have told you that Capital One does not impose a foreign currency fee, and it also eats the 1 percent fee that Visa or MasterCard impose. That's a pretty good deal.

Early payment is great

Q: I have a credit card through my credit union. When I charge something I pay it off in person the next time I'm there, usually before I get my statement.

I have learned that I need to use credit to keep my good credit rating. Is it okay to pay even before I get my statement?

A: It's great that you pay your balance during the grace period, even before you receive your statement. You do not need to carry a balance on your credit cards or pay interest to generate an excellent credit score. Your method is keeping that account active. Good job.

Slapped for being late

Q: Chase has raised our interest rate to 29.99 percent because we were late one time. They really know how to stick it to their customers. How can we fight to get my rate lowered?

A: Customers who carry credit-card balances are at the mercy of the card issuer, and Chase seems to be one of the most difficult.

You can call and ask them to reverse their decision, but I wouldn't hold my breath with Chase.

In the past I've been in touch with Paul Hartwick, Communications and Public Affairs at Chase. He says that if a customer signs up for automatic payments and makes on-time payments for 12 consecutive months, Chase will reset that customer's rate to the lower, original rate.

That might be your solution, as painful as 12 months will be.

Use it or lose it

Q: I received a letter from one of my oldest credit-card issuers stating that since I had not used my card in such a long time, they cancelled it. I don't have a balance on the card and kept it only for emergencies.

I have other card accounts, so this isn't a problem, but will this cancelation affect my credit rating?

A: Your FICO score will undoubtedly take a hit because 1) FICO gives points for longevity and 2) your total available credit will drop when this account is no longer taken into consideration in determining your score.

Credit card for student on a budget

Q: My son is a college student and wants to begin establishing credit. He is interested in finding a credit card that would be right for him—a college student on a budget.

He did apply for a card and they turned him down for lack of credit. Could you suggest a card or a way to get his credit started?

A: I understand your son's desire to begin building good credit and I do applaud that. I just hope that he understands that a credit card is like a power tool.

If you don't know what you're doing, it can do more damage than good. That being said, I suggest he head on over to the bookstore on his college campus. There he will find applications for any number of credit cards that are targeted for unemployed college students with no credit history. Credit-card companies are foaming at the mouth to be a student's first card.

They know that statistically the student will one day have a well-paying job and that he will keep (and use) that card for at least 15 years.

Customer service off base

Q: I made a credit-card payment on time using online bill pay but later received a late payment fee and a finance charge for having not paid within the grace period. I complained and they reversed the charges.

The customer service rep instructed me to make my payments five days in advance of the due date in the future. I asked why, and she said they don't "process" the payments necessarily on the day they receive them, even electronically.

Where in the fine print are we instructed to make the payment at least five days ahead to avoid fees?

A: If this is your credit-card company's policy, it is, in my opinion, in clear violation of The Fair Credit Billing Act of 1974 (FCBA), the federal law which regulates credit cards.

Section 164 of the FCBA requires businesses that offer open-end credit (consumer credit cards) to credit all payments to your account on the date they are received. It goes on to say that they may post the payment on a later date if doing so would not cause you to incur any late fees.

Creditors are permitted to make rules for their particular credit-card products such as setting a reasonable deadline (date and time of day) for payment to be received to be credited on the same date. You can read the full text of the FCBA online at *FTC.gov*.

If your credit card is issued by a national bank, you can file a complaint with the Comptroller of the Currency, the federal office that regulates national banks.

National banks can usually be identified because they have the words "national" or "national association" in their titles or the letters "NA" or "NT&SA" following their titles. See "Filing a Formal Complaint" at *OCC.treas.gov/customer. htm* for instructions.

If your card is not through a national bank, contact the Federal Reserve Board *FederalReserve.gov* to make your complaint.

Rental car insurance abroad

Q: Is there a credit card that covers insurance when you rent a car in a foreign country? I plan to rent a car on an upcoming European vacation.

A: Many credit cards purport to cover car rental insurance anywhere, Visa Gold for example, but I would not rely on this if I were you.

As you know, credit-card companies can change their terms and conditions at will. At best, the way I read the fine print is that even if you are covered, you have to pay for all of the costs associated with the accident. Then they reimburse you once you get home and file the claim.

If you are involved in some kind of incident, you will have to come up with the money to pay the car rental company at the time you return the car. Imagine yourself in a foreign country—most likely not fluent in the language—shaken up from an accident.

Once you get home you'll discover what the credit-card company requires from you to make a claim for reimbursement (copies of police reports, damage estimates—the list is remarkably long).

My advice is that it is more than worth it to pay for the local car rental insurance and chalk it up to part of the expense for your trip.

Difficult to pay the balance to the penny

Q: This is petty perhaps, but how does one ever completely pay off a credit card?

We paid off a credit card recently (hallelujah!) by sending a check for the exact amount of the balance due taken from the monthly statement.

The next month we received a bill for $1.91—all of it was a finance charge! Sure, it's not much,

but that was discouraging. Any suggestions?

A: Well, you've just discovered another of the credit-card companies' tricks. Because companies use the average daily balance method to compute interest, it is nearly impossible to pay a credit-card balance off to the penny if you've been carrying a balance of any amount.

You could spend a lot of time and trouble calling and haranguing customer service to time your payment with their billing cycles. Or bite back:

When you're ready to make that final payment in full, add $5 to the amount you owe. When your next statement arrives with a credit balance, call customer service and request that they send you a check for the credit balance.

They probably won't do it unless you close the account, but how nice for them to owe you for a change.

Cleaned up my act, can't get credit card

Q: I ruined my credit ten years ago in the usual foolish way people do with non-payment and slow payments.

Even though I am much more careful and responsible now, I cannot shake the bad credit history.

My bank does not offer secured cards. Do you have any suggestions to help me get a credit card?

A: Negative credit items will automatically come off your report after seven years; a bankruptcy will stop being reported to the credit bureaus after ten years. Your report should be cleaning itself if your missteps took place that long ago.

As for getting a secured card, go to *IndexCreditCards.com*, and look for "Secured Credit Cards" under "Bad Credit Credit Cards."

You will get a list of cards available including each one's terms. Read them very carefully.

Secured cards are for people with bad credit that require some sort of deposit for approval. Most cards listed report to credit reporting agencies, potentially helping you reestablish credit.

Just make sure that you are not shooting yourself in the wallet by opting for a card that has excessive fees.

Blank checks in the mail

Q: We have a number of credit cards that keep sending us blank checks. I routinely shred them as soon as they arrive. How can we stop the credit-card companies from sending them to us?

A: You can request that your company stop sending these so-called "convenience checks" (which if cashed turn into very expensive loans) and I hope you do. But don't expect much. I have heard from several readers who found success, but most report that no matter what they do, the checks keep coming.

Keep your shredder in good operating condition because I have a feeling it's going to get a good workout for the foreseeable future.

Balance transfers leave a bad taste

Q: About six years ago I decided to work toward becoming debt-free. Not wanting to help the credit-card companies get rich by paying lots of high interest, I worked up a plan.

Every six months or so, I would find a credit-card company that was offering a credit card with a special six months of zero percent APR on balance transfers (making sure that there was no balance transfer fee) and I would transfer my balance.

In this way I was able to pay off all my credit-card debt while paying little to no interest.

The problem? My husband and I now have 15 credit-card accounts, with a total credit limit of approximately three times our annual income.

Currently, I have been trying to close one account about every six months or so to protect my credit score.

Do you suggest that I keep this up for the next seven years, or should I just bite the bullet, close them all, and let my credit rating take a hit? My score is 750.

A: Given the delicate nature of credit scores and credit limits these days, identify the two accounts that you've had the longest and target them as the one's you want to keep active. Then just sit back and do nothing with the others.

More than likely the companies will cancel the other accounts for lack of activity. Since you have so much open credit, losing some of that might well improve your already very good credit score.

While I want to commend you for being so tenacious and clever in getting out of debt, I also want to caution other readers.

Your method for paying down debt is a very risky proposition. Zero-percent teaser rates are becoming scarce.

And even if you can find and qualify for one, it's not easy to hang onto it. If you are ever late with a payment—by even five minutes— you'll get socked with a big default rate.

This tactic is like playing with fire. It's easy to get burned.

What happens to Mom's debts?

Q: My mother passed away leaving a credit-card balance of $3,500. I had been paying her bills while she was in a nursing home and had no income. As her son, am I now responsible for this credit-card debt since she has passed away?

A: No, you are not, unless you are a joint owner on any of her accounts. If your mother was the only person on the account, the credit-card company, upon notification of her death, will look to her estate for payment.

Generally (laws vary from one state to another), that will be handled by the executor of her estate. If she left assets (a home or anything of value), those assets must be liquidated to pay her creditors before assets can be distributed to her heirs. If there are no assets, the credit-card company will eat the loss.

Check out Nolo Press (*Nolo Press.com*) for excellent self-help books to help you settle her estate without spending a lot of money on attorney fees.

I am sorry for your loss and wish you well during this difficult time.

One account, multiple balances

Q: We have one credit-card account with three separate balances, each subject to a different interest rate.

Each month our entire payment is being applied only to the lowest interest balance while the balance with the highest interest rate continues to grow by accruing greater interest for that account. Our total balance isn't budging at all. We're spinning our wheels because of all the interest being added every month.

I've figured out that in the 28 months it would take to pay down the low-interest balance for this account, we will have accrued an additional $1,700 on the high-interest balance. Is this legal? What can we do?

A: It just kills me to have to tell you that yes, it is perfectly legal. You agreed to this when you accepted the credit card.

If you dig into the fine print of the agreement you signed, you will see the company reserves the right to apply your payments in any way they want. And they want to charge you all the interest they can for as long as they can.

I assume that you started with a low-interest balance transfer, and then you added some new purchases at a much higher interest rate plus cash advances at the highest rate of all. There is nothing you can do to change the way the company is allocating your payments.

Weigh carefully the idea of transferring the entire balance to a new card with a much lower rate of interest. Then do not add one single purchase or cash advance (death to cash advances, by the way) in the future.

Which debt to target first?

Q: I have five credit cards with a total balance due of $1,900.

Is it better to pay the card with the smallest balance first, the highest balance first, or the one with the highest APR first? Thanks!

A: While there is no wrong or right answer to your question, I have a very strong opinion (which of course I believe is the right answer!).

Concentrate on the smallest balance first, while keeping current with your payments on the others. Why? Because paying off debt is hard work.

Reaching that first $0 offers such a huge emotional payoff, it will give you the incentive to keep going until you can reach another $0 balance, and then another, until you are debt-free.

If you concentrate on the largest balances, or even the one with the highest interest rate, it could be a very long time until you get to that first $0.

The chances of you giving up are much greater the longer you go without reaching the coveted $0 balance. And I want you to the best chance of becoming debt-free as soon as possible.

By the way, check out my Rapid Debt-Repayment Calculator demonstration at *DebtProofLiving.com*. This is a remarkable tool that creates your debt repayment plan for you based on the method I just eluded to. While you can view the demonstration, only members of *DebtProofLiving.com* have access to all of its wonder and usefulness.

Department store card dilemma

Q: My husband and I want to cancel various department store credit cards that we do not need or use. Is there any harm in doing this?

A: I used to tell people to close accounts they weren't using. But things have changed. Closing accounts can never help your score, and often it can hurt.

Shutting down credit accounts lowers the total credit available to you and makes any balances you have appear larger in credit score calculations.

Of course, if you have no outstanding unsecured debt, having too much available credit can also have a damaging effect on your score.

If you don't use your cards much and your credit score is already high (750 or higher), the damage caused by shutting down department store cards will be minimal and may be worth the peace of mind. I would do that gradually, over a period of time—like no more than two or three accounts spread evenly over a year.

Go to *IndexCreditCards.com* for a comprehensive list of all credit-card offers currently available. And read the fine print.

A few new credit-card rules go into effect in July 2010, and will halt this crazy practice by the card companies. As of that time, if you pay more than required on your card account, it must be applied to the balance with the highest interest rate, or spread proportionally if you have several rates on the same account.

Is that a debit or a "death" card?

Q: Why are you opposed to debit cards?

A: Oh, let me count the reasons.

1. Debit cards don't offer the kind of protection against fraud that credit cards offer. Debit cards come under a much weaker law (The Electronic Funds Transfer Act) that says your liability is capped at $50, but only if you notify the bank within two days of losing your debit card.

If you wait longer than two days, you could lose as much as $500. And if you don't report a problem within 60 days (at first you may not realize that someone has snatched the cash from your account), forget it. You are stuck paying for the thief's spending spree. You could lose everything in your checking and every account attached to it, too.

Individual banks can increase protection for their customers but they are not required to.

2. It can take months for a bank to complete a fraud investigation. You'll have to get a police report and do all the leg work. Even if you prevail and the bank shows you uncommon mercy, you will not have your money during the time it takes to resolve the issue.

3. If you have a dispute with a merchant where you purchased something with your debit card, good luck. The merchant already has your money; this is not the case with a credit card. Your bank is not required to help you dispute your debit-card purchases the way a credit-card company must, by law.

4. Using a debit card to secure a rental car or hotel room is often allowed but not very smart. When it is, the vendor is likely to freeze a portion of the money in your account without even telling you. It can take up to a week to return this money to your account after you've checked out or returned the rental car.

Think about it: You believe you have a certain amount in your account and you go ahead and write checks or make payments. Then, only to find out too late when they all bounce, the money in your account has been frozen because you used a debit card to secure a transaction.

The problem is this can happen radomly and catch you way off guard.

Can you say massive overdraft fee and penalty fees?

5. Debit-card use is not reported to the credit bureaus, even if your debit card carries the MasterCard or VISA logo. Surprised?

Those are the main reasons I am not a fan of debit cards. The biggest reason is item #1 above. Debit cards don't protect you, they don't help you build a killer credit score, and they can sneakily tie up the money you have in your bank account.

Hint: You can turn any credit card into a "debit card." When you make a purchase with your credit card, immediately deduct the purchase amount from your checkbook as you would if you paid by check. Just make that a habit. And even go ahead and write the check and make it payable to your credit-card company.

When your statement arrives, pop all of the checks into the return envelope (or void them and re-write one check for the full amount) and send it off immediately.

Now, you have the best of both worlds: The money came straight out of your bank account as you made the purchases and with no fees assessed. You have all the protection and benefits of a credit card, but none of the debt. And your activity is reported to the credit bureaus every month to make sure you are building a great credit score.

Debt

How much debt is OK?

Q: Is it ever OK to have debt? How much debt can I afford?

A: Sure it is. Not many of us could be homeowners or purchase a car without a mortgage or loan of some kind. These days it's difficult to finish a college education without incurring some amount of student debt. But there needs to be self-imposed limits.

Mortgage debt: Your monthly mortgage payment—including principal, interest, real estate taxes and homeowners insurance—should not be more than 28 percent of your gross monthly income (before taxes). This is your housing expense ratio.

Your total monthly debt obligation should not be more than 36 percent of your gross income. Total debt includes the mortgage payment plus other obligations such as car loans, child support and alimony, credit-card bills, student loans, condominium association fees. (Note: Certain lenders may be more lenient.) This is your debt-to-income ratio.

Student debt: A good rule to follow is that your total student debt should not exceed the first year's income in your chosen field of study. There's a great calculator, the Debt Wizard, at *MappingYourFuture.biz*, that will help you determine just how much you can afford to borrow for college.

Auto debt: Your loan should be for no more than 36 months. With this kind of aggressive pay-back structure you can be pretty sure your car won't go upside-down where it's suddenly worth less than your outstanding debt. And you won't get caught in the trap where you are still making payments and big repair bills at the same time. Stick to this rule and you'll have time to save up for the next car.

Credit-card debt: It is never okay to have credit-card debt. It's just too expensive. If you are charging more than you can reasonably repay in that same month, you are overspending. It is going to come back to bite you.

Can I send less than a payment?

Q: Will my credit-card company take less than the payment required and not charge me a late fee as long as I call ahead and tell them?

A: By law credit-card issuers must accept any amount you send them at any time during the billing cycle, and apply it to your account as received.

So yes, you can send less but that will not preclude a late fee if the amount is less than the minimum amount required. And calling to in-form them you will be late will not stop a late fee and negative reporting to the credit bureaus.

Ripped off, left with a judgment

Q: Two years ago I dated a guy who cash-advanced thousands of dollars on two of my credit cards by using ATMs. I couldn't prove to the bank I didn't withdraw the money, so I sued him and won a $7,000 judgment.

He lives in another city and I don't know how to collect the judgment. I'm in a horrible situation because my debt payments and living expenses exceed my income.

Do you have any suggestions for how I can get this debt taken care of? I will not consider bankruptcy.

A: Yes, call Consumer Credit Counseling Services to see if you can qualify for credit counseling.

You will be able to get a free session with them and they will assess your situation and make a recommendation. Hopefully you will qualify to enroll in their excellent program.

A book, *Collect Your Court Judgment*, by Gini Scott (Nolo Press), will tell you how to collect that judgment yourself without hiring an attorney or collection agency.

Unfortunately, I don't have a recommendation for helping you learn to make better choices in men. Hopefully you've learned enough to write that book yourself.

The best of the bad

Q: We need a new furnace before next winter. We saved some money but not enough to pay for it in full.

Heating contractors offer financing at outrageous interest rates of 17.99 percent and up.

We could borrow from our credit union, borrow against my 401(k) at 1 percent over prime, or put it on a credit card (11.99 percent).

We don't have enough equity to take out a home equity loan. Can you give some direction?

A: Oh great. So you're expecting me to make the decision about whether or not you and your family freeze to death next winter?

Seriously, you didn't give not replacing that furnace as one of the options, but it's one you need to consider.

Be honest. Is replacing the furnace this year a life and death situation? Can't you find some way to make it through at least one more winter? I hope so, because that's my recommendation.

The "some money" you have saved is a good start. So buckle down and keep going. Soon you'll have enough to pay cash.

If you cannot wait, for sure you do not want to borrow from your 401(k). That is just too risky in these times when job security is in the tank. And new credit-card debt? You cannot afford that double-digit interest.

Have you checked to see if your utility company or local governmental agencies have any special assistance programs to encourage homeowners to install more energy-efficient systems?

I hate to see you go into debt for this, although to borrow for a home improvement is better than say borrowing to pay for a wedding or vacation.

By putting the money into your home you are protecting the value of an appreciating asset.

If you absolutely must borrow to get this furnace I suggest a short-term loan from the credit union at the lowest rate possible is the best choice of those you've presented.

Tired of working and paying bills

Q: I am thinking about filing for bankruptcy. Actually, I have already retained a bankruptcy attorney.

I have recently divorced and resigned from my $60,000 a year job to become a hairstylist. My problem is that I have $67,000 of unsecured debt. I do not want to go to an 8 to 5 job every day, because I am just plain tired.

I am 40 years old and want a stay-at-home life. I will receive $40,000 from my job, but want to keep it for retirement. I also want to go to school for computer programming. What shall I do?

I cannot possibly get on a debt-payment plan because I don't have enough income to repay my creditors. Is my only choice bankruptcy?

A: Let's see here: You borrowed $67,000, spent it all, and now you're too tired to pay it back; you want the rest of us to pay your debts so you can walk away from a $60,000-a-year job to stay home, do hair, stash $40,000 for your retirement and go back to school in your spare time.

You don't need a bankruptcy attorney, you need an integrity transplant.

Life is tough and the people who overcome adversity are those who are willing to take responsibility and do what's right.

Get some industrial-strength vitamins and beg for your old job back.

Grab a financial tourniquet

Q: I am deeply in debt. I am borrowing and borrowing just to keep up with the minimum monthly payments. I am a bookkeeper at heart so tracking my spending is not the problem. However, I'm wondering what you might say to encourage me on what to do or what step to take next.

A: Sounds like you are bleeding to death, financially speaking. You cannot continue to pay your credit-card bills with a credit card! It's time for drastic measures.

That might mean moving in with family members for a while, selling assets to pay down your debts so you can afford to make the payments without borrowing, take on an additional job or work more overtime.

Perhaps you will have to do all of those things for a time.

I don't know your specific situation but I can tell you this: Drastic measures are the tourniquet you need now!

It occurs to me that you may be an excellent candidate for credit counseling.

A reputable and trustworthy organization can go to your creditors on your behalf and set up a payment schedule you can handle by reducing interest rates.

Your situation is not hopeless. There is a way out, I am confident of that!

I'm praying that you will find the courage to do what may be very difficult right now, but will eventually come back to bless you many times over. Go to *NFCC.org* to find the closest credit counseling office to you.

No interest, no payments, no sense

Q: How terrible is it to take advantage of those 12-month interest free, no-payments deals to finance my new computer?

I have the cash, but it seems silly to turn down no payments for a year, if I can keep drawing interest on the balance and have the computer, too.

A: How terrible? Oh, about as terrible as a root canal without anesthetic.

Statistics say that about 72 percent of those consumers who fall for these slick deals do not pay the balance within the time period the way they planned. Why do you think retailers love these deals so much? They pull in all kinds of very lucrative business!

What happens is that during those 12 payment-free months other needs arise that appear more urgent than paying off the item—in your case the computer.

Face it: you don't know what's going to happen in the coming year.

With $1,200 sitting in the bank, you will have many opportunities and temptations to use it for something else more urgent. Stuff happens and as long as the $1,200 remains in your control, chances are great that something more will come up that will cause you to reconsider paying off the computer.

Also, keep in mind that if you are late by even five minutes in making full and complete payment as required by the credit agreement, some huge interest rate will kick in *retroactively* to the purchase date.

Why take that chance? Why go through the credit-application process which puts an inquiry on your credit report?

Why sign a deal that has a 28.99 percent default rate right there in black and white (or higher ... I just picked a typical rate)? So you can earn twenty bucks on a thousand bucks in your savings account (that's what we're talking about here, if you're earning 2 percent)? I suggest it's just not worth the risk.

If you're going to acquire the computer, make sure you also own it.

Pay for it now.

Oh woe is ... you!

Q: I don't know where to begin. I don't know why I'm even writing other than I feel like I'm at the end of my rope.

I'm struggling with feelings of guilt, loneliness and unhappiness. No one I know understands.

I'm in debt about $7,000, not including a new van we bought for $24,000 and our mortgage of $68,000.

I'm reading your book *Debt-Proof Living* and I subscribe to *Debt-Proof Living* newsletter. I think they both have great information, but I just can't do it.

My husband doesn't understand and is really not interested in the bills and debt. Together we make about $65,000, have three kids under age three and pay $870 a month in day care.

I've known debt all my life. It's like I play this game: Pay something off and charge something more. I cannot tell you how many times I've paid off one charge to open another again and again.

I just get sick every time I think of all the money I've blown and how far ahead I could be. I want the immediate gratification to get out of this mess now and can't stand to look at the big picture of at least three years to pay everything off but the mortgage.

I just can't see it happening because my old habits will kick in and something will get charged. I will always be in debt.

A: You're right. You are a hopeless case. With your bad habits, feelings, uninterested husband, three toddlers and a job outside the home you have every right to just give up.

You'll never get out of debt anyway, so just stop trying.

You should also give up everything else in your life that does not bring immediate gratification, like paying your mortgage, exercising, working on your marriage, building character in your children and paying your taxes.

You should probably forget about being a stay-at-home mom, too. You have only 15 years left with them anyway, so what's the point?

Keep knocking yourself out to bring home $10,000 a year—if you're lucky—so that by the time the kids are ready for college in 2024 you can add a big pile of regret to the guilt, loneliness and unhappiness you feel already.

Okay, do I have your attention? Did I startle you when I just held up a mirror so you could take a look at yourself? That's exactly what I intended to do.

And now I want you to look me straight in the eyes so I can assure you that you are wrong. Dead wrong!

Your situation is no more hopeless than you want it to be. And someone does understand—I do! You have so much to be thankful for—health, a steady income, three beautiful children, a husband who comes home every night. Sure, you have some challenges but you also have choices. You can see yourself as a hopeless addict who cannot stop debting or acknowledge that you do have control over your attitude and your actions.

You didn't get into this mess overnight and you aren't going to get out that quickly, either. First, you must turn around so you're headed in the right direction (you do that by making a specific commitment followed by an equally specific plan) and then take one step at a time. Here are steps you can start taking right now:

1. Stop debting. No one can force you one more dollar into debt with-out your permission. Ask your husband to hold you accountable to this commitment.

2. Keep a daily written record of every dime you spend. Even if you do this exercise alone, it will be very enlightening.

3. Finish reading *Debt-Proof Living*. It you will open your heart and mind to what I've written for you in these books—and allow God to empower you as a woman, a wife and mother—you will have the tools you need to take control of your life and move to financial freedom, joy and peace of mind.

You can do this, I know you can! There are few things more powerful than a woman committed to a mission.

I am excited for you because I know what can happen when you make a decision to debt-proof your life.

What's up with NGC?

Q: Do you know anything about the National Grants Conference seminars? I attended one and basically it boils down to paying a $800 fee for their services in acquiring grants for six months, then only $25 a month after that. What do you know, good or bad, about this or any cheaper alternatives?

A: Thank goodness you checked first. The Better Business Bureau of Chicago reports that the company's file contains complaints alleging misleading advertising on an infomercial and misinformation as to grant acquisition. Pretty serious allegations. You need to conduct your own independent search to see what others are saying.

As you know, NGC charges a huge fee to become a member, which entitles the individual to all company research on various government grants, two days of classroom training and two reference manuals. National Grants Conference does not obtain nor fill out grant applications for members.

The federal government publishes information and instructions on all its loan and grant programs including the American Recovery and Reinvestment Plan of 2009—and provides it to consumers free of charge.

The Catalog of Federal Domestic Assistance contains an index of all federal financial opportunities and is available at most public libraries and on the Internet at *CFDA.gov*.

Only cash is same as cash

Q: What do you think about buying our much needed furniture on a 12-months-same-as-cash plan?

I am so tempted to go ahead and get new furniture and pay it off next year, but am hesitant to incur more debt.

A: If you don't have the cash to pay for the furniture today, what makes you think you'll have it a year from today? Even if you believe you will, the store is betting that you won't.

Guess what? The odds are decidedly in their favor.

Here's the way those deals work: You have to fill out a credit application. If after checking your credit score they approve you, they will defer payment of interest for 12 months provided you pay the amount in full on the due date and not one second later.

If you are late or cannot pay in full for any reason on day 366 you lose your deferment, and the interest rate kicks in retroactively to day one. And you better believe the interest rate will be outrageously high (I've seen 29.99 percent, but have heard of higher rates in other states).

These stores know from experience that something like 72 percent of those who fall for these ploys do not have the money to pay in full and end up making payments for many, many years.

The furniture will be worn out and trucked to the dump long before it is paid for. I cannot think of a situation so desperate that would warrant this kind of debt.

There's a huge secondary market of great used furniture out there, no matter where you live. Look in the classified ads, at garage sales, consignment shops and flea markets. Let friends and family know of your need. Make do and in the meantime start making those hefty payments to yourself—not the furniture store.

People who actually have it know the truth: only cash is the same as cash!

Consumer rip-off: credit insurance

Q: We took out a consumer loan for $15,000 eight months ago at our local credit union. They told us that disability and life insurance were required for them to give us the loan.

They struck the phrase "insurance is not required" in the loan documents and made us agree to a premium of $1,134.

Is there any way we can cancel the policy and save that money?

A: Attorney Robin Leonard, author of *Money Troubles: Legal Strategies to Cope With Your Debts* (Nolo Press), tells us that credit insurance is required by many lenders to protect themselves in case you die or become disabled before you repay the loan.

As a condition of the loan, you must buy a life and or disability policy that names the lender as the beneficiary. In most states the lender cannot require insurance in excess of the amount of the loan. In a few states,

such as Alaska and Maryland, lenders cannot require credit insurance except for loans for real property. In California, the amount of the insurance must be approved by the state insurance commissioner.

Credit insurance, for the most part, is a consumer rip-off. Insurance companies collect over $2 billion a year in premiums, yet pay out only $900 million. However, if you have agreed to the terms that require you to carry credit life and disability insurance, you dare not let those policies slide or your lender may cancel your loan, or make the payments and charge you for them.

Your best bet is to talk to your lender about letting you drop the insurance. If they refuse, offer to add them as a beneficiary to an existing life insurance policy you may have already. Leonard advises that many lenders will drop the requirement if you've repaid more than 50 percent of the loan.

Restitution is its own reward

Q: Now that I am getting on track with managing my money, I am coming into contact with a bit of extra cash.

After much pondering, I decided to contact a past creditor who had "charged off as bad debt" my account.

When I called I asked if they would consider a settlement. They said yes and offered to consider it paid in full if I sent them 75 percent of the outstanding balance. I jumped at the chance. Hooray!

One more debt down the drain and out of my life!

Wait... what's this? Instead of "Paid in Full" my credit report now states "Settled Less Than Full Balance." I couldn't be happier regardless of how it was done, but does this have a more negative impact than if I would have paid the balance in full?

A: By settling this debt you have made a positive move because a charge-off is really horrible. What you have now is less than horrible, although still a negative.

It would have been better if as part of your negotiation you could have included that they would also report this "Paid as Agreed" without a mention of the settlement. That would have been perfectly legal and a choice they could have made. It's probably too late now, but it wouldn't hurt to ask them to amend their reporting. Regardless, doing the right thing is its own reward. You did right and your credit report now reflects

Trash credit report or lose home?

Q: We are considering a home equity line of credit (HELOC) now that interest rates are so attractive.

We want to eliminate high interest credit-card debt and also have funds available for home improvements.

I understand that a HELOC uses our property as collateral. Under what circumstances would this be a good decision?

A: High interest credit-card debt is a huge problem and I understand your reasoning. But transferring unsecured debts to your home is a bad idea. That move could put you in an even worse situation down the road. You have to look at the big picture and then weigh the dangers.

Let's say something happens to seriously reduce your income like a medical emergency or sudden job loss so that you cannot keep up with all of your payments, if for only a season. If we're talking about credit-card payments you'll get socked with late fees and a blemished credit report, but that's about all. Of course that is terrible, but not devastating.

On the other hand, if you transfer those debts to a HELOC and you cannot keep up, the lender will foreclose and take your home.

Spending your precious equity to "eliminate high interest credit-card debt" feels like you've done something righteous. But that kind of thinking is so wrong-headed. You've only moved your debts around.

Credit-card companies know that customers who pay off big balances have a high likelihood of running those balances back up to the max and possibly higher than before the next time around. The average time it takes to do that is just two years. But you'll still have that new HELOC payment. To me this second hazard is more likely than the first, although both should be taken very seriously

Borrowing against home equity to finance improvements that will increase market value is sometimes advisable, but only if the loan to value ratio does not exceed 80 percent and to the extent that you have sufficient income to handle the new payment.

Suffering with a single income

Q: I have read your book *Debt-Proof Living* and I love your plans, but you only address families with two incomes.

I quit a high-paying job to be a stay-at-home mother, so we had to turn to credit cards to furnish our home and buy all the things we needed.

When the first baby came along I was a crazed mommy who bought all kinds of stuff. The debt snowballed.

We have $43,000 in credit-card debt including a home equity loan, plus we have a car payment. We are living paycheck to paycheck and having a tremendous amount of trouble.

Can you please address single income families? I am desperate and I will do just about whatever you say—short of exotic dancing. Ha!

A: I don't know what you've been reading but it's nothing I've written.

Everything I write and teach is based on the 10-10-80 formula which applies to all situations and all demographics from a single mother living on welfare to a couple with a seven-figure income:

Give away 10 percent, save 10 percent and live on 80 percent of your income.

These days being a stay-at-home mother is for many families a real luxury that requires a lot of sacrifice. I can only assume that when you came home you felt entitled to continue living as if you had two big incomes.

You can live that way for a while, but not for long as you are learning. You cannot pick your favorite lifestyle without regard for your income and then snap your fingers to make it happen.

The choices you made to get so deeply in debt may require you to forfeit many of the luxuries you now enjoy. If things are as desperate as your letter indicates, you may need to sell the house and downscale to a smaller place you can afford. You may have to go back to work, which may not be best for your kids or what you want to hear, but something you may have to do anyway.

Believe me, I know what you're going through. I've been where you are, and worse. I know the fear and panic that comes with an out-of-control financial situation. And I know how tough it is on a marriage.

I also know that you can turn around your desperate situation if you are willing to take responsibility for what you've done and the choices you've made.

Dealing with debt collectors

Q: I was out of work for six months. During that time I lived off my savings and 401(k) and put my MasterCard on the bottom of the pile of bills.

They called me several months ago and said I had to pay a certain amount to keep my account from being turned over to a collection agency, which I did.

The following month, I got a call from a collection agency telling me they now have my account. They are putting a lot of pressure on me.

I'm paying them $300 a month as requested, but with my new job I am really struggling. How do I handle this? How can I relieve the pressure?

A: You are protected by the Federal Debt Collection Practices Act (FDCPA). Among other things it allows for your creditor, the bank that issued your MasterCard, to turn your account over to a "third-party collec-

tor." The law states the conditions under which that collector can contact you, and also gives you the right to refuse to deal with that collector.

The law also says you can stop a debt collector from contacting you by writing a letter to the collector telling them to stop.

Once the collector receives your letter, he may not contact you again except to say there will be no further contact or to notify you that the debt collector or the creditor intends to take some specific action.

It's important that you understand that sending such a letter to a collector does not make the debt go away if you actually owe it. You could still be sued by the debt collector or your original creditor.

Under the circumstances, I suggest you tell the collector to stop. Then go back to your original creditor (the bank who issued your MasterCard) and without getting upset, tell them how they breached their agreement with you. You kept to the terms of the agreement but they did not. Let them know that you have been paying down the debt and that you are not running out on your obligation.

Ask them to agree to accept a payment plan you can handle. If you are unsuccessful, I would suggest you consider credit counseling.

Learn more by visiting the National Foundation of Credit Counselors at NFCC.org. From that site you will be connected with the Consumer Credit Counseling Services office closest to you.

You can read the FDCPA by logging on to *FTC.gov* and clicking on "Debt Collection" under Quick Finder.

Refuse to live in fear

Q: I am just beginning to develop my Spending Plan and Rapid Debt-Repayment Plan, having just read *Debt-Proof Living*. I am so excited about getting out of debt.

What I fear the most is when I complete my Spending Plan I will have no money left over other than my small "allowance." What will I do if I've forgotten some serious expense and have no money to cover it?

A: Your fear of running out of money is something you've experienced before. Fear is the reason you got your credit cards in the first place—you were afraid you might run out of money, right?

And sure enough you did run out because you knew you had that credit-card "safety net" and you got used to spending all of your income.

Then you discovered your safety net had a big hole in it. You landed up in debt.

Now you've made a decision to debt-proof your life. You're creating your plan and that is fantastic.

Call this a season of adjustment or even sacrifice, but refuse to live in fear. Look fear in the face and say, "I am not going to let you control my life!" Then direct all of your energy to looking for every possible opportunity to not spend money so you can build your safety net even more quickly.

You will be amazed how fast things will come together for you. Just keep going, live the plan every day and don't ever give up!

There's a reason it's called HEL

Q: We'd like to do some major home repairs and improvements that will run in the tens of thousands of dollars. We've been thinking about a HEL (home equity loan) or HELOC (home equity line of credit). However, I am very nervous about borrowing against the equity in our home. What do you think?

A: There was a time I would have reluctantly said that as long as you are plowing the money back into your home in improvements, it might be an okay thing to use your home's equity to do that.

But, given the events of the past year or so as the housing market has tumbled drastically in this country, we're seeing things from a different perspective. Many of those who now find themselves "underwater" where they owe more on their homes than they are worth, owe the fix they're in to having stripped their home's equity to do just as you suggest.

I am not fond of the idea of the home equity loan. Your goal is to pay your mortgage in full before you retire. You will never achieve that if you get into the habit of pulling out the equity.

As for your home improvements, get a plan together. Set your priorities. Then tackle one item at a time with money you have saved. That's called "paying as you go."

With this plan you avoid a new big monthly payment on the HEL, you protect your investment by keeping your home well-maintained, and you get to enjoy the satisfaction of having done that without going into debt.

Back to work, bigger salary

Q: I will be returning to work with a big promotion after taking a year off to have a baby. My salary was $34,000 when I left; I will resume working with a $65,000 annual income.

During my time off we ran up more than $10,000 in credit-card debt. We have been living paycheck to paycheck. Things have been really tight financially.

My next paycheck will be almost double what it was when I left for maternity leave. I want to set up something now, a plan, to keep from falling into a trap of "Wow, look at all my money!"

I have all your books, should I re-read one of them? Which one? We are both 37 years old so I want to try and set us up well.

A: Congratulations on the new baby and the promotion. You are fortunate indeed in these times when people are getting more pink slips than promotions.

I am happy to hear that you are concerned about this increased income leaking through your fingers. It will for sure—unless you protest to the contrary.

Haul out your copy of *Debt-Proof Living* and start reading. The plan is the same whether you're making $34,000, are living on a single income, or making $65,000. It's the same for every income and every situation, whether a person is single, married, retired, rich or financially challenged: 10-10-80.

You give away 10 percent, save 10 percent and then arrange your living expenses to fit within 80 percent of your income.

The 10 percent savings goes into your Contingency Fund. From the 80 percent you fund your Freedom Account, your Rapid Debt-Repayment Plan (RDRP), and the rest of your living expenses. This is The Plan.

Now for a few words of caution. As "rich" as you may feel, you have a huge new expense to consider: day care for your child. Plus, this salary increase will more than likely push you into a higher tax bracket. Both are going to nibble away at your newly-improved income to the point that you may feel as though you have made little financial progress, if any.

Please be very careful to not see yourselves as having a lot more disposable income. Managed well, you will do well. Just be very careful, stay focused, and make sure that no matter what, every day you live the plan!

Big debt, no savings

Q: In a nutshell: We are both in our 50s, have $23,000 in credit-card debt, no savings, and a big mortgage payment. My husband works full time and I work part-time (I'm looking for a second job). We contribute $400 each month to my husband's 401(k). I have been thinking of taking this $400 contribution and redirecting it to debt-reduction for one year only. I am feeling desperate, as I recognize we probably only have about ten years of full-time work left in us.

Should we do this?

A: My answer is a qualified "Yes." But let me warn you, that move alone is not going to fix your situation and allow you to retire in ten years.

First off, that $400 in pretax dollars will be more like $325 when you see it in his paycheck. $325 x 12 =

$3,900. If you pay every penny of that amount to pay down your credit-card debt, you'll still be in the $20,000 range depending on the interest you are paying.

What you need is a complete plan that addresses your lack of savings (what will you do if you face an emergency?), your unsecured debt, and paying off your mortgage before you retire.

The good news: This is not an impossible situation. You'll be amazed by what a difference ten years can make. Or 15. With the current state of the economy, I think early retirement will be a thing of the past.

Building emergency fund trumps car debt

Q: My husband and I have finally paid all of our unsecured debts ($22,000 worth), but we still have one debt to deal with—we owe $15,000 on our car.

Unfortunately, we made the mistake of buying new about a month before a friend gave me your book, *Debt-Proof Living*. Anyway, we definitely want to pay this obligation as soon as possible, but I quit my job and my husband will be downsized from his current position sometime soon.

At this point our Freedom Account is only partially funded and we have about $4,000 in our Contingency Fund.

Should we continue paying more than our required payment on the car or make the minimum payments each month and use those additional funds to build our Contingency Fund?

We have not been able to come to a decision and would very much appreciate your insight on this matter. Thanks!

A: You paid off $22,000 of credit-card debt? That is remarkable! And you're doing so well on the other parts of your plan as well.

While your desire to rapidly pay off your car is noble, I believe it's the wrong decision as long as your Contingency Fund is not up to the level you need, particularly as you prepare to go through the potentially deep waters of underemployment.

I recommend that you pull back to making the required payments on your car each month and concentrate on building your Contingency Fund to at least $10,000 (six month's expenses would be better), and as quickly as possible.

While having a car payment isn't ideal, it's not as risky as a credit-card balance. In the worst case scenario you could sell the car to get rid of its loan. But if you hit a snag in the future and don't have enough in your Contingency Fund to keep you afloat, you'll feel compelled to run back to the credit cards for a bail out.

A paid-down car loan will do you absolutely no good if your husband

gets sick or for some other reason his income is further diminished.

Above all you need a well-funded emergency fund to handle any unexpected financial emergencies.

Need legal advise, can't afford a lawyer

Q: I've been enjoying my subscription to Debt-Proof Living newsletter for many years.

Three years ago and after 27 years of marriage my husband traded me in for a younger model. Through the divorce and difficult adjustment period I relied on your website, *DebtProofLiving.com* to keep me going. I did all I could to pay off a tremendous amount of debt. In exchange for keeping the house, I also inherited half of our debts through our divorce settlement.

At age 50 I went to work. With my meager paychecks, child support for our three kids and your website that encouraged me every day, I made good progress. I scrimped and saved and didn't buy things for myself. I was desperate to get the debt down so that I could start saving.

My ex-husband recently passed away very suddenly. Now I am left with no support payments and a salary that does not even meet the mortgage payment. His new wife has stopped all payments on the credit cards that remained in both of our names.

Can you offer me any advice? I have no money for a lawyer, and am lost in trying to get advice.

Time and again you have encouraged and motivated me and I'm hoping you can help me now.

A: Well, this is not good news at all. I am so sorry for all of the pain and agony you've been through. But now more than ever you need to be strong and courageous.

You must become an advocate for your minor children. You do not say if their father had a will or living trust. Perhaps you do not know. There are laws to protect children and I cannot help but believe that even if the children are not specifically named in his will, they have a legal claim to their father's estate.

You absolutely need to speak with an attorney who specializes in family law and or wills—and soon. A good law firm will give you the first session at no cost so you can discover your options. Take a look at *AVVO.com*, a site where you can ask a lawyer a question without charge.

Spend some time at *Nolo.com* a self-help legal site. Click on Family Law and Wills and Estates. You will find excellent articles that will help you to formulate the right questions.

As their custodial parent, you must learn what legal positions and options your children have. Be unwavering in your commitment to protect their legal interest in their father's estate.

Even if he specifically wrote them out of his will (doubtful), there are circumstances under which a will can be contested.

I cannot stress enough how important it is that you move quickly on this. And for others reading this, let this situation underscore the need for life insurance whenever there are children and others dependent on another's income. Even in a situation like yours where there is a divorce and ex-spouse, someone should have put a life insurance policy in place to cover you and his dependent children in the unlikely event of his early demise.

Hang in there. You know how to be strong and courageous, so just keep doing what you've been doing. Things will get better if you refuse to give in! And never, ever give up.

Let it go or try to sell it?

Q: I cosigned a loan for my grandson for an expensive truck. He had a job at the time and I thought he would hold up his end of the bargain to make the payments. I have ended up borrowing money to make the payments when he couldn't.

I really need advice from someone who has nothing to gain from this situation. As far as I can tell, the truck is worth at least $10,000 less than the outstanding balance on the loan. Should I let it be re-possessed or will it help my credit rating to try to make some more payments?

I have struggled with this for over a year. I will never again cosign with anyone, but this has been done and now I must deal with it. I am almost at retirement age and need to be saving money instead of paying on a truck for a young man who has not proven to be responsible.

A: Oh, my. I am just so sorry to hear this. Unfortunately, you have just learned a very difficult lesson. For the benefit of your fellow readers, let me explain why you should never cosign a loan. The reason a person needs a cosigner is because he presents a risk so great not even an experienced, professional lender is willing to take. There's your clue. It's a risk you cannot afford to take, either.

If you really want to help that borrower, make sure the money you lend is money you can afford to be a gift. Then, if you happen to get any repayment, consider it a bonus. If you cannot afford to make it a gift, you really cannot afford to cosign.

Okay, back to your deadbeat grandson. It's time to put a stop to this nonsense. Get the keys to the truck, clean it up and put a For Sale sign on it. Call the bank and tell them what you are doing. If the amount you can sell it for is not enough to pay off the loan, you will need to come up with the balance in cash. While an expensive lesson, this will be less damaging to your credit than a voluntary repossession.

As for your grandson, the most loving thing you can do is turn this into a lesson he will not soon forget. Require him to sign a promissory note for the full amount he owes you including past payments and interest. If he doesn't have the cash to start making payments, let him know he will be working for you to pay off the debt. Don't let him walk on this.

Which debt to target first

Q: I have two credit-card balances that I am trying to pay off. You suggest targeting the smallest debt first and then combining that payment with the minimum payment on the other one, thus paying the larger one off faster.

My smaller credit-card debt has an interest rate of 1.99 percent which I negotiated for the entire balance as long as it takes to pay off. The larger credit card has several layers of interest rates which average about 10 percent. Wouldn't it be better to pay off the larger debt at the higher interest rate first, and then pay off the smaller one?

A: By targeting the shortest debt first the Rapid Debt-Repayment Plan addresses the mathematical aspects of rapidly repaying debt and also fulfills the need many of us have for frequent emotional payoffs when tackling something difficult. Of course this is more dramatic when a person has a greater number of debts than you.

I suggest you use the RDRP Calculator (an online member benefit) at *DebtProofLiving.com* and figure your payoff plan both ways—allowing the calculator to determine the pay off order and then a second time using the manual override to put your largest debt in the first position.

Compare the two scenarios then choose the method that's right for you. What really matters here is that you kick your repayment efforts into high gear.

By the way, that 1.99 percent interest? Don't get too used to it. Regardless what they "promised," the fine print in your contract is the ruling authority. They can (and they will, trust me) change the terms any time for any reason. Get ready for them to jack that rate to 15.99 or more.

I know I must sound like a broken record, but I will say it again: You need to do whatever it takes to pay these credit-card debts as quickly as possible. You cannot afford what's coming if you delay.

Mom and the DMP

Q: I just learned my 80-year-old mother is enrolled in a debt management program with a credit counseling organization. She has

credit-card debt in excess of $15,000.

She has agreed to pay $533 plus a $50 fee each month to this group. This is more than half of her monthly income.

I don't know how she ever got that much credit since her annual income is $15,500. What can we do to help? Do you think her credit-card companies would work with me directly to save that $50 monthly fee?

A: It's likely that your mom's monthly payment exceeded $533 a month before she entered the program. A $50 monthly fee for debt management services may be excessive, but not by much. Perhaps you need to consider this is a good thing for your mother.

She likely had to relinquish her credit cards which will keep her from adding to her debt. It is admirable that she realized she needed help and went through the steps to get into counseling.

Her creditors will not speak with you about this unless you are an authorized signer on her accounts. Credit-counseling contracts are not typically binding. She can quit anytime. And her creditors are not bound to continue with the terms they granted her while she was in counseling.

It is not at all surprising that your mother was able to get credit on her meager income. In the past, if you could sign your name that's about all it took to get credit. Age and income had little to do with it. She would not likely be able to get that kind of credit now.

Self-employed and struggling

Q: I am very embarrassed to be writing you about this matter, but I feel like I'm drowning and I don't know where else to turn for help. I am a 29-year-old, college-educated woman and I always felt like I was smart enough to keep this from happening to me.

I have been enrolled in credit counseling for about six months and I make a single payment for my credit-card debt through their debt management program. They worked out a plan with my creditors that reduced the interest rates on some of my credit-card accounts, and waived some of the penalties.

I am self-employed and business has been slow. As a result I have fallen further behind on my mortgage. As of this writing, I'm 90 days past due on my first mortgage and well on my way to being 120 days late. I'm current on my unsecured debts because of CCCS.

What do I do? I am not sure it's possible to avoid foreclosure and bankruptcy, however I am willing to do anything.

A: You need to make two very important phone calls now. The first is to your mortgage holder. When you call you may be connected to Customer Service, but that person is not the one you want to speak with. Ask to be transferred to someone who can help you avoid foreclosure.

Instead of foreclosure, your mortgage lender might agree to restructure or modify your loan.

The second call should be to the credit counseling firm that is handling your debt management program. They need to know that you are about to lose your home. They may be able to help. You cannot continue to keep current on your unsecured debt payments while your home mortgage payments are in arrears.

Here's a basic rule of thumb for which bills to pay when you cannot pay all of them: Do not make payments on nonessential debts when you have not paid essential ones even if your nonessential creditors are breathing down your neck.

An essential debt represents a serious obligation that if not paid could produce severe, even life-threatening consequences like losing your home.

Once you've determined which debts are essential, prioritize them according to the severity of the consequences you will suffer for nonpayment. Always assume that your landlord or mortgage lender will immediately proceed to evict or foreclose if you are late with a payment. This makes your mortgage payment essential.

Finally, if your business is unable to support you with a paycheck large enough to cover your basic financial needs (all of your bills and expenses), you need to recognize that it is not a viable business. You need to find a job that pays you a reliable income.

I hope you will make these two phone calls right away. While things look bleak now, I have confidence that you will find a way through this difficult time.

Can I buy a car with a credit card?

Q: My husband thinks we should transfer our $21,229 automobile loan at 8.49 percent interest to a credit card. We have credit-card offers of 2.99 percent interest for the life of the transfer.

I can see why he likes the idea, but it just does not feel right to me. I argue that if we are late on a couple of payments the rate could shoot up. He said we are never late but we have been a day late on one recently, and we totally lost another bill and did not know about it until the late fee was charged the next month.

Please advise. I don't think I can hold him off much longer.

A: Tell him for me that this is a lousy idea! Buried in the fine print of every credit-card agreement is language that says the credit-card company can

change the terms and conditions of the agreement at any time and for any reason. The company could honor "for the life of the transfer," or not. Credit cards are considered "open end" contracts. An auto loan is "closed end," and that makes all the difference.

From now until July 2010 when new rules go into effect that will reign in some of the outrageous things credit-card companies do, you can be sure they're going to jack up interest rates all they can in anticipation. For now the sky is the limit on interest rates.

Even if they promise a fixed rate, don't assume that's like a fixed-rate mortgage. They can change the terms, including a fixed rate, at any time and for any reason, by giving you 15-days written notice.

I hope you can persuade him to stick with the loan you have or refinancing that auto loan at a lower rate. Take a look at *CapitalOne.com/autoloans*. At this writing the rate to refinance starts at 6.95 percent.

Paying rent and a mortgage, too

Q: My husband and I recently moved to the Midwest. Unfortunately our home in New Hampshire hasn't sold and it's been on the market for months. We can no longer make the mortgage payments and pay rent, too.

We have attempted to work with the mortgage company, requesting either a loan modification or a short sale [the house would be sold at a loss and the mortgage company would take the loss]. In both cases the mortgage company has denied our request, but has not explained why.

We do not know what to do next and unfortunately we might have to foreclose on our home or go bankrupt.

Do you have any suggestions on what we could do next? Is it better to foreclose or claim bankruptcy?

A: That's like asking if it's better to have a stroke or a heart attack. I would prefer you have neither.

You need to know that your mortgage is a secured debt. The lender is fully protected against bankruptcy proceedings because you have already pledged the house and land as a guarantee on your full and faithful repayment of the mortgage. That means you could file for bankruptcy and still lose this home because the mortgage lender won't be bound by your bankruptcy protection.

You made a colossal mistake when you moved before selling your New Hampshire home. Stop seeing yourselves as the victims of an unreasonable lender.

Instead, take full responsibility for the situation and make a commitment that you will do whatever it takes to turn this situation around. Taking on second and third jobs, moving in with relatives until the house sells and liquidating a second vehicle are some ideas that come to mind.

I don't know what drew you to the Midwest, but perhaps it's time to pack it up and move back. Otherwise you could end up with the equivalent of both a stroke and a heart attack.

Overwhelmed by hefty auto loan

Q: I have a credit card with a large balance of $12,722 at an interest rate of 7.75 percent, plus an auto loan of $18,562 at 6.49 percent interest.

I have the funds to pay one of these debts in full. Which one should I pay first and why?

I seem to be more overwhelmed with the car payment of $446, but obviously the interest is higher on the credit card. Please help me with your advice.

A: There are more things to consider here than the interest rate spread on these two debts.

Under normal circumstances I'd suggest you concentrate on the credit-card debt first because it is an unsecured debt and most dangerous to your credit history and resulting credit score.

However, you said something very telling. You are overwhelmed by that big car payment. These days most car loans are upside-down (you owe more on the loan than the car's market value), and this makes it unsecured for all practical purposes.

All that to say, if paying off your car will give you an emotional boost to keep going until you are debt-free, do it. Then, before you get too used to having additional cash each month, add as much of that car payment as you can to the credit-card payment.

How to spend a windfall

Q: Every year, my husband gets a bonus (about $3,000) from his work. We have credit-card debt of about $5,000 and no savings at all. Should we use the bonus to pay down the debt, use it to start our Contingency Fund, or split it in half?

A: Nothing trumps having a Contingency Fund (CF)—that pool of money that you keep in a safe place earning interest from which you could pay all of your bills for at least three months (six is better) without a paycheck. Call it an emergency fund.

You need a CF more than you need to repay your credit-card debt quickly. Here's the reason: Let's say you were to pay that $3,000 toward your credit-card debt, and in a few months your husband is laid off, or you have some other financial crisis. How will you pay for that?

If you have no money set aside for emergencies, you will feel forced to run to your credit cards for a bailout. You'll be in worse shape than ever. That's the reason so many people find it next to impossible to break free from credit-card debt.

Putting that bonus money into your new CF is going to really give you a new outlook on your financial situation. Finally, you'll know that you're making progress. You'll be re-energized and more determined than ever to pay down your debt quickly and to stop using those credit cards to make any new purchases.

You'll find yourself willing to be more frugal and to forego buying things you really don't need right now. That's because money in the bank changes everything.

Investing borrowed money backfires

Q: Do you think credit-card companies would grant partial or total forgiveness of debt for a couple in their 70s with ten or more accounts and a total balance of $90,000?

We have never been late or missed a payment and have always paid the minimum. How can a couple of this age keep this up? One of us is still employed full time. Whom should we contact to see if this is possible?

These accounts are not a result of extravagant spending or mismanagement, but of two large, high-risk investments of over $40,000 each. One was for investing in a young man and his startup company, and the other was to help a son keep up with mortgage payments. Otherwise, we are extremely frugal and able to live on very little.

A: You need to understand this basic truth: Credit-card companies are in business to make money. They are not humanitarian organizations on a mission to improve the lives of people in need. They do not care personally about their customers at all. Period. End of story.

I am very sorry that you have found yourself in this horrible situation at a time when you should be enjoying a carefree retirement.

As to your question about "forgiveness," there is nothing preventing you from calling these companies to negotiate with them. Look for the Customer Service number on the back of the credit cards. Let's say they would consider a lesser amount because that's a way for them to generate cash now. Could you more easily come up with say $70,000 rather than the $90,000 you owe? $50,000 or even $30,000? Also, be aware that the IRS will be notified of any settlement arrangements and the forgiven amount may be considered taxable income.

The bottom line is that you made extremely poor decisions to "invest" money that wasn't yours to lend. Now

you have to deal with the consequences.

The way I see this you have three choices and two of them are not what I would consider to be moral or ethical, but they are choices nonetheless.

First, you could go after these two young men to whom you loaned the money and ask that they repay you.

You don't give a lot of detail, but it appears that you did loan them the money. If these were outright gifts or "investments" you now consider lost, forget this option.

The second choice would be to refuse to pay your creditors and hope that, upon learning that you have no significant assets, they would simply write off your debts. In that case they might opt to sue you hoping to secure legal judgments that they would collect from your estate.

Or three, you could attempt to file for bankruptcy. You would need to speak with a bankruptcy attorney to see if you qualify. Just let me warn you that it's not cheap these days to go bankrupt. It will cost you a significant amount in fees, at least $2,500.

I wish I had a better solution for you. I can't imagine how difficult it must be to be facing this situation at this time in your life.

Intercepting wages may be legal

Q: My nephew is having his wages garnished by a credit company for a past-due account. Are they allowed to really do this?

A: Generally, if your nephew has a job and the creditor has sued, won in court and received a judgment, they may be able to grab up to 25 percent of your nephew's wages until that judgment is satisfied.

The process, permitted in nearly every state, is called a "wage garnishment." To garnish his wages, your nephew's pay must be above the poverty line, no other garnishments must be in effect (unless the garnishment is for child or spousal support) and he must not have filed for bankruptcy.

Financially immature

Q: My co-worker's parents signed over their home to her and she has just sold it. She knows she will be responsible for the capital gains at the end of the year. One thing she is going to do is pay off her credit-card debt.

She called the company and asked if they would negotiate a discount if she paid it off in full. She was told that she could talk with someone about that, but her credit score would drop substantially.

Should she negotiate the discount or just pay it off to preserve her credit score? She is 52 years old, recently purchased a new vehicle and doesn't have any plans to move from her current home.

I suggested that she continue to use it and pay it off monthly, which

would build back her credit score. Am I correct here?

A: Settling an account will trash her credit score for a long time to come. I have no idea how long it would take her to restore it as you suggest.

One thing she may not have heard about is that the portion that is "forgiven" immediately becomes taxable income.

Something about this really bothers me. I am assuming that the balance on her credit card is the result of years of buying stuff she could not afford. So why on earth would she expect any merchant, retailer or card issuer to give her a discount now that she is able to pay the balance in full? She spent the money, she owes the money. Period.

She needs to write a check for the full amount as soon as possible to stop the horrible accrual of interest.

I would also give her this unsolicited advice: Spend the money to meet with a financial planner. The last thing she wants to do is pay more taxes than necessary or to use this newly found wealth to dig herself into a financial nightmare.

I could be wrong, but she seems to lack financial maturity.

Speeding up mortgage repayment

Q: In a recent column, you told a reader how she could pay off her home mortgage more quickly by applying an additional amount to the principal each month. Would this principle apply to a car loan or a student loan?

I owe $23,000 on the car and $5,200 on a student loan. My monthly car payment is $440 at 7.9 percent and my student loan is $281 at 8.5 percent.

A: Generally speaking, yes. However, you need to research all of the terms and conditions of the loan(s) you want to prepay ahead of schedule.

Some loans are structured in a way that the borrower has to pay the total amount of interest, regardless if the loan is paid early or over the term.

Some are subject to a "prepayment penalty." The logic is that if you pay the loan early you will deprive the lender of some of the interest you promised to pay, so you will be penalized a percentage or a specific amount if you pay it off early.

Most unsecured debts, such as credit cards, can be paid early, thus saving a great deal of interest. And even if there is not much financial incentive to paying debts early, the emotional payoff should not be underestimated because it is huge!

Drowning in auto debt

Q: We are upside-down in a car loan we cannot afford. We bought the car and then had a baby. We cannot afford both.

We have a second car that is paid in full, and we can easily live with just one vehicle. But I can't seem to find a way to get rid of the other one. We are drowning.

A: While this is the pits, it is also an opportunity to learn a very important lesson regarding wants and needs.

While it pains me to even bring up the words "new loan," this is a way you can get out of this mess.

Go to your credit union or a family member willing to help you, and work out terms for a signature loan that will cover the difference or the "gap" amount between what you owe and the price you can get for the car. Once you have a buyer, execute the gap loan to pay the lender so you can complete a title transfer to the buyer.

Now you have an unsecured debt which isn't ideal, but with payments considerably smaller than what you are paying now.

Once the loan is paid, keep making those payments to yourself so you will have options when it comes time to buy another car.

His good credit not good enough

Q: My wife and I could be a poster couple for credit discipline. We borrowed money 45 years ago to build the house we still live in.

We paid it off in just seven years. Everything else has been pay-as-you-go. We've had the same Visa account for 22 years with no late payments or interest charges.

Recently, Progressive Direct included a "Notice of Adverse Action" with my insurance renewal. It stated: "We did not give you our lowest possible premium due to the following information that we evaluated from your credit history: 1) Earliest reported account or loan opened after age 45. 2) No history of car loans or leases was provided. 3) One loan or account with a satisfactory current payment status."

Your column advocates the very things we have been doing, yet an insurance company apparently deems such people to be irresponsible and suspicious. I think their underwriters are overrated. What do you think?

A: You are victims of technological times when computers—not people—evaluate risk factors and determine the creditworthiness of individuals. Your best credit history (paying off that mortgage in just seven years) occurred before the advent of credit history files and credit scoring. Having only one source of credit is considered a "thin" credit file.

Personally, I'm thrilled you've had no car loans or leases and they should be, too. But alas, computers only follow instructions. If I were you, I'd go back to your insurance company and insist that a human re-evaluate your situation and that you be granted the lowest possible premium

based on what you have told me. And if they refuse, I'd start shopping.

While many insurance companies now use a scoring system similar to a FICO score to predict an insured's likelihood of paying premiums on time, not all will be so rigid that they won't consider your specific situation.

Debt charged off, still owed

Q: If a creditor has recently moved a debt to the "charge-off" status does that mean they are no longer expecting us to pay? Should we go ahead and send payments? What do we do?

We are working with a financial counselor and implementing our Rapid Debt-Repayment Plan to get out of debt.

A: A charge-off means the creditor has given up attempting to collect what you owe and most likely has turned over the debt to a third-party collector.

Absolutely you still owe the money, and you may still be able to work directly with the creditor—preferable to dealing with a debt collector.

I suggest that you contact the creditor immediately, explain your commitment to pay what you owe in an effort to work out a payment plan. I am confident they will be willing to work with you.

I am so happy to learn you are facing your debt mess and doing something about it.

When I read you are implementing my Rapid Debt-Repayment Plan (DebtProofLiving.com), I was tempted to do a cartwheel right here in front of my desk. But I took pity on my staff, choosing instead to say I am so proud of you and to send you my best wishes across the miles.

Getting out on your own

Q: How can I get out of credit-card debt? CCCS told me I do not qualify to let them help me with repayment, saying my debt is too high. I'm at a loss on what to do now.

A: Most credit counselors have guidelines that determine who qualifies for their services. Typically they want to see a plan that will get you out of debt in three to five years. If they do not see that as possible, they will suggest a person consider bankruptcy.

I could've never qualified for credit counseling when I was so deeply in debt. I guess it's a good thing that I didn't know bankruptcy was my only alternative. I might have considered that. But, I didn't.

It took 13 years, but we got out of debt—paid back every dime, plus interest and penalties. That just feels

good to be able to say that. I guess you could say I became my own credit counselor, and so can you.

In a nutshell, here are my Rapid Debt-Repayment Plan rules:

1. Stop. If you carry a balance stop using that card. You have to stop adding to the debt or you'll never get out.

2. Pay the same. Adopt your current minimum payments as your fixed monthly obligation from now on, even if the creditor would accept less.

3. Create order. Line up your credit-card debts with the smallest at the top.

4. Gang up. Once you pay off that first debt, take its payment and add it to the fixed payment of the next debt in line (debt #2). Repeat until you are debt-free.

I am signing you up for a one-year subscription to *Debt-Proof Living Online*—a gift from me.

As a member you have full use of my Rapid Debt-Repayment Plan Calculator, access to online support groups and daily motivation to stay on track.

Once you log in, go to Member Tools and find the RDRP Calculator. Input your debt information and it will create your payment plan. Follow it closely and you'll be out of debt sooner than you can even imagine!

A demonstration of how the RDRP Calculator works is in the open-to-the-public area of the website and will show all of my readers just how this works. It is slick!

Home equity to pay off credit cards

Q: I am wondering if it is a good idea to refinance my home and pay off all my credit-card debt, which is about $20,000. My lender says this is a good idea.

I currently owe $156,000 on my mortgage, my home's market value is $200,000 and the interest rate would be 8.1 percent. My FICO score is 642. What do you think?

A: Lenders love to push the idea of stripping your home's equity as the solution for credit-card debt. I think it's a lousy idea.

The interest rate you suggest is not particularly attractive because your credit score is below average.

As bad as your situation is now, if you are unable to stay current on your credit-card payments, they'll trash your credit score. That's bad, but not devastating.

If, however, you move that debt to your home and then you miss a payment, you will lose your home through foreclosure.

Buckle down; get serious about paying off your credit cards now. Stop looking for shortcuts and phony fixes.

Start paying and stop charging and I think you'll be excited to see how fast you can get out of debt—not just move your debt around so it feels like you're doing something good.

Start with a good foundation

Q: I'm a single mom with a 12-year-old son. I make a fairly good living as a paralegal at a top law firm.

I've been smart about planning with a retirement fund and a college savings plan for my son. But as far as saving money goes, I've got nothing. Despite my good salary, I still find myself living paycheck to paycheck. If I were laid-off today, I wouldn't know what to do.

A co-worker suggested that I see a financial planner. How can a pro help me?

A: A financial planner helps individuals determine their short-and long-term financial goals and devises a plan for how to reach them.

You're doing well with some of your long-term goals, but I'm concerned that you've overlooked the basic foundation of every good financial plan: You need an emergency fund equal to at least three months' expenses (six is better).

You don't need to pay a professional to tell you that life is uncertain—you could face a season of unemployment or other income-zapping emergency. You need to get prepared now.

I suggest you take the money you might have paid for this advice and start building your fund. As it grows so will your confidence and peace of mind.

Once you reach this goal you'll be ready to meet with a financial planner who will help you create a plan for investing and building wealth.

Time to face the music

Q: I am in a similar debt situation to yours when you started your journey to becoming debt-free.

I have been ignoring my creditors because they scare me. But, I'm ready to face them now. How do I get started? Thank you so much for your life-saving tools.

A: What helped me was to focus on something for which I was grateful, then to visualize the person on the other end of the phone as someone with life problems even worse than mine.

Make the calls. What's the worst that can happen? They won't hang up on you or call the police. Anything short of that you can handle.

State the facts and be truthful without groveling. Acknowledge that you are behind but also that you have a plan to make full repayment. (Your creditors will be impressed when you can articulate that.)

Say that you do not want to file for bankruptcy, but you need some help. Then ask for a reduction in your interest rate or a payment plan you can handle. Be specific.

I think you will find most creditors willing to at least listen. In fact, some credit-card companies have programs to help overextended customers get back on track. And for those who are not cooperative, don't give up. Be pleasant, say thank you and hang up. But persist.

Call again in a week. And again, and again. And in the meantime, do whatever you must to make your minimum payments on time every month.

Regretting the timeshare

Q: On a recent family vacation we purchased a timeshare on a whim. The salesman kept saying it was a good investment and that it would pay for itself.

We put the $7,000 down payment on a credit card and the remaining balance is $20,000. We really don't want this timeshare, the guy just kept insisting.

Since then we've had some unexpected things happen that resulted in us buying a new car. We really cannot afford the timeshare now. I am willing to forget the $7,000, but don't want this to affect my credit. What should we do?

A: Unfortunately there are thousands and thousands of regretful timeshare owners who fell into a slick salesman's trap while on an emotional high of a family vacation.

I don't know the terms and conditions of your contract, but I have to assume it is legally binding. If you default by not paying the remaining $20,000, the company is likely to sue you for it. Likewise, if you do not keep up with the maintenance fees and taxes. You need to sell it.

Before you do anything, have an attorney review your contract. If you can prove you were tricked through deceitful sales tactics, you may have grounds to cancel the whole deal.

Try to find a willing buyer. Here are the things I would do:

Go back to the facility and perch yourself outside the room where these high-pressure sales presentations are occurring. Approach attendees who are in the mood to buy with an offer of a great deal on your resale.

That's the closest you'll ever get to a targeted audience for your specific property.

You can also list your timeshare with a resale broker (Google "timeshare resales"). But, prepare yourself. You'll be one of thousands of people trying to sell.

And next time, do yourself a favor. Skip the sales pitch and go for a swim instead.

Take the sure thing

Q: We live in Nevada and own a second home in Arizona. My husband wants to sell the Arizona property to pay off our credit debt, auto loan, and HEL (home equity loan)—about $65,000 total.

I disagree. I think we should rent the Arizona property to generate income and benefit from its future appreciation.

My husband is concerned that if we are unable to rent it out, we will not be able to handle two mortgage payments plus our other debts, as well.

What should we do?

A: Let's say you sell the Arizona property, pay off your debts and then it turns out you were right. Even though you forgo a return on investment, you are debt-free and you own a home in Nevada.

But, let's say you don't sell and it turns out he was right—you can't rent the house and you can't keep up with both mortgages plus the big load of unsecured debt, too. In that case you could lose everything. You have to see that as a real possibility.

My advice is to see this as an opportunity to show your husband a great deal of respect by trusting his decision.

There's something in this for you, too. This gives him the opportunity to meet your need to be taken care of and to feel financially secure.

This looks like a win-win. However, before you do anything, be sure to check with a tax professional to learn what taxable event, if any, selling the Arizona property will trigger.

Hands off the 401(k)

Q: My wife recently left her job last year due to health problems. We are doing okay on one income. If we cash in her 401(k) retirement account we could pay off about 80 percent of our high-interest $14,000 credit-card debt.

Would it be worth it to pay the penalties and rid ourselves of this debt or should we take the long road, endure the high interest rates on the unsecured debts and pay them off over time?

A: Generally is it not wise to use an appreciating asset (the retirement account) to pay for depreciating goods and services (the credit-card debt). Once you cash it in it's done growing. If you leave it alone, that account—as small as it appears now—will continue to appreciate over time to be there in your retirement years.

The big problem with your idea is what cashing in now will cost. First, you will never see 10 percent because it will be deducted as a penalty for early withdrawal. Then you'll owe federal and state income tax on the full amount. At least 40 percent of her account balance will vanish.

See this account as a valuable asset that is simply out of your reach for now. If you put yourselves into rapid repayment mode, you can wipe out those high-interest credit-card accounts quickly, even if all you can pay are your minimum monthly payments each month.

The secret is to stop adding new purchases, fix your monthly payments at their current amounts and follow the payment schedule. I am confident you can keep your hands off the retirement account and still get out of debt!

Give yourself a clean sweep

Q: I recently received a "Clean Sweep" offer from my credit-card company. It's basically a loan to pay off credit cards in a certain number of months. The only thing is you don't know the interest rate (APR) until you get the loan. Is it worth pursuing or not such a great idea? Thanks.

A: I am trying to figure out why any credit-card company would just out of the blue make you an offer to forego the current lucrative deal they have with you in favor of something that would put you into something that would be better for you. I have a feeling the new deal is even better for them than what you have now.

While I don't know enough about the offer you received to comment on it specifically, I would bet a year's pay this is anything but a clean sweep. And should you accept, you will end up in a worse financial position in the long run.

New debt is not the solution for old debt and you should never agree to a loan before you know all of the terms.

Personally, I would run, not walk, from any offer that refuses to tell me the interest rate before I have signed up to accept it. Somehow I cannot see where such a thing would be legal, but you need to do your own due diligence on that should you decide to proceed.

Straighten up and fly right

Q: I am a pilot for a major airline and have a lot of debt, $70,000 plus a mortgage. I'm not proud to say we have no savings or emergency fund.

Soon I will get a windfall of about $40,000. Should I pay down the unsecured debt?

A: If you do that you'll have $30,000 in debt plus a mortgage. Sounds a lot better, for sure.

But what happens next month when you have an unexpected emergency or next year when you lose your job? You'll feel you have no choice but to run to the credit cards for a bail out and before you know it you'll be back at $70,000, or probably more.

My advice is to use that windfall to fund your "Contingency Fund" which is a pool of money equal to three months' (six is better) living expenses.

Sock it away in a safe place where it can earn some interest. Now, live as frugally as you can and attack that $70,000 nut with all the gusto you can muster.

Put yourself on a strict spending diet. Just knowing you are not sitting on the edge of financial doom will give you the courage to endure short-term sacrifice. If you are a member of *DebtProofLiving.com*, you have the tools you need to turn your financial situation around.

All you need now is persistence and determination.

Lots of smaller payments with caution

Q: At the highest point, our credit-card debt was $7,000. Instead of making the one payment each month as required by our credit-card issuer, I followed a tactic you suggested in *Debt-Proof Living* newsletter.

I made a payment every time we got paid. Sometimes that meant I could make a small payment every week. I would take as much money as was left over from each paycheck and apply it to our debt, even if it was only $25 spread over all of the accounts.

Because I pay our bills online it was easy—no checks to write, envelopes to find or stamps to buy.

We paid the entire amount in about one year. We discovered that when we made only one payment each month—even if it was more than required—extra money during the month that we swore we'd use to boost our payments, mysteriously disappeared.

I highly recommend multiple payments throughout the month as a way to pay-off debt rapidly.

A: Good for you for knocking those debts out and so quickly, too.

Credit-card companies are required to law to accept any amount at any time, unlike mortgage lenders who can reject a partial mortgage payment. Somehow $20 a week is less painful than say $50 a month.

I want to caution readers who wish to follow your example to make sure the company has received at least the minimum monthly payment required before its due date. Getting socked with a big late fee can reverse the best of good intentions.

Penalty to prepay debt

Q: I am currently conscientiously repaying my debts but one of my creditors charges a prepayment penalty of three-months' interest. What should I do?

A: That must be an auto or home-equity loan. Credit-card accounts never contain a prepayment penalty.

No matter, my best advice is to do whatever it takes to get out of debt. Pay it. Then make a personal commitment to never agree to a prepayment penalty again.

And by the way, I am so proud of you. This is terrific news.

HEL vs. HELOC

Q: We have decided to pay off a bunch of bills and do some much-needed repairs on our house.

Can you tell me the difference between a home equity loan and home equity line of credit? Which would be better?

A: With a home equity loan (HEL) you get a loan, pledge your home equity as the collateral and walk away with a check for the full amount of the loan. You will pay a loan fee and closing costs. The average rate on a fixed-rate HEL at this writing is about 8.55 percent, 15-year fixed.

A home equity line of credit (HELOC) is a revolving line of credit, a lot like a credit card, except that like being in HEL, your home is the collateral.

You don't get a check at closing, but rather a checkbook or debit card to access the funds as you need them.

You make payments on the amount you've drawn out, not the total amount you have available. Rates on HELOCs now average about 5.27 percent, variable.

A HELOC has several drawbacks you should know about:

First, the interest rate will be variable. It looks very low now but could go through the roof quickly when the economy rebounds and the Federal Reserve Board increases interest rates. (Raise your hand if you remember the

1980s when interest rates shot to 22 percent. Anyone? I see those hands!)

A HELOC could wreak havoc on your credit score if you draw out the maximum amount available. Because it is a line of credit, it will appear that you are borrowing faster than you can repay in the same way a maxed out Visa or MasterCard account pulls down your credit score. To be prudent you should never be using more than 30 percent of your total HELOC.

Something else to consider: Most lenders charge hefty fees on HELOCs including an annual fee of $50 to $75 just to keep the line open.

Many HELOCs provide for a penalty of $250 to $600 if you repay all that you've taken out during the first three years. And if you get it and then don't draw on it? Expect a "nonusage" penalty of $50 a year.

I know it's only a coincidence, but "HEL" is certainly an appropriate acronym for spending one's home equity. While you didn't ask my advice, I hope you have thought this through.

Treating your home equity like your personal ATM could be a decision you will regret for a long time to come.

Bill Collectors 101

Q: How do bill collection agencies work? Do they start with letters demanding payment and if not resolved come to a person's home? Or would they turn it over to a court of law?

A: Third-party debt collectors (aka bill collectors) are regulated by a federal law, the Fair Debt Collection Practices Act (FDCPA). You should be familiar with this law as it also protects you, the consumer.

The FDCPA says that a collector may contact you in person, by mail, telephone, telegram, or fax. However, a debt collector may not contact you at inconvenient times or places, such as before 8 a.m. or after 9 p.m., unless you agree.

A debt collector may not contact you at work if the collector knows your employer disapproves. The only way the debt collector will know of this is if you or your employer expressly tell them.

Debt collectors may not harass, oppress, or abuse parties they contact.

You can stop a debt collector from contacting you at all by writing a letter telling them to stop.

Please note, however, that sending such a letter to a collector does not make the debt go away if you actually owe it.

You could still be sued by the debt collector or your original creditor, and be totally unaware if you instruct them to not contact you in any way ever again.

You can read all of the provisions of the FDCPA at *FTC.gov* or find it at your local library. Hope that helps.

May this be information you only know but never need in a personal way—if you know what I mean.

Desperately broke

Q: I am out of money and I mean not a dime left after I pay bills. Sometimes I don't even have enough for food.

I have been considering credit counseling to get some breathing room. It would be nice to buy a tube of lipstick now and then for my mental well-being.

My credit is shot and I'm feeling desperate. This way at least the creditors would get regular payments and checks that don't bounce. Am I wrong to consider this kind of help?

A: You're not wrong at all; in fact credit counseling could be the way out of your financial straightjacket. I am a big fan of credit counseling, but it is not for everyone. Nor are all credit counselors trustworthy. There are lots of sleazy groups out there masquerading as charitable "non-profit" counselors.

Make sure you are working with a reputable organization you can trust. Expect an initial interview to determine if you are likely to be successful in their program (typically that means you are unable to meet your current minimum payments, are several months behind, employed, and if

married, your spouse agrees to enter the program).

The counselor will work with your creditors to come up with a payment plan you can handle, which could include lowered interest, fees waived and payments restructured.

The tricky part is that instead of paying your creditors every month, you will write one check to the organization's Debt Management Program and they will make the payments.

The last thing you want is to hand over your money to a company that has not proven itself and you have not checked out. (Oh, the horror stories I've heard.)

Even reputable credit counseling does not come without side effects. Even though your creditors may agree to a scaled down payment plan, they will likely report you as paying less or differently than originally agreed. That could blemish your credit report, the price you may have to pay to get yourself back on a good financial track.

Where to put an extra C-Note

Q: I just got a raise that translates to about $100 a month spendable. I have no savings and am working hard to rapidly repay my credit-card debt. How should I use this money?

A: You are smart to be thinking of this now. Without specific direction and a plan, that $100 could easily evaporate into thin air.

While your debt is very expensive for you, I do not recommend you use these new funds to repay the debt more quickly. Instead you should build a Contingency Fund with your raise. Without money you can get your hands on in an emergency, you will be forever running to credit cards when the car breaks down or you experience a temporary lapse in employment. Just make sure you park it in a safe place where it can earn some interest.

Do not dip into your Contingency Fund unless you are faced with a genuine emergency. You need a minimum of three months' living expenses (six is better) in your Contingency Fund. I suggest that you check out on-line savings banks like GMAC Bank.com or HSBCDirect.com, for the highest interest rates.

There's a hole in our roof

Q: I am a new reader of your column and have just begun trying to follow your advice.

My husband and I work for a Fortune 500 company. Because our "savings" is in stock and stock options, we don't have a lot of cash on hand.

Here's my question: Our house needs a new roof and it is going to cost about $7,000. Should we bite the bullet and cash in some stock options, even though I know in the long run we could get so much more for them (we are a stable company, and our stock will eventually go up).

Should we get a home equity loan? Or, should we pay half in cash and get a loan for the other half? If so, what kind of loan would be best?

A: How bad is this situation? Is your roof leaking so horribly that all of your possessions are getting ruined? Is this situation presenting a safety or health hazard to your family?

If not, I suggest you patch and repair as necessary to get through at least more season.

Next, temporarily discontinue contributing to your company's stock purchase plans. Divert the money you have been contributing to build your roof fund. Crash save—sell stuff you don't need, work extra hours, give up a luxury or two for a short time. Do anything and everything you can to accumulate this money you need.

Once you have paid for the roof, just keep saving. Aggressively. You need at least $10,000 cash in a savings account (or six months' living expenses) at all times so you can start funding your own emergencies. This is what I call a Contingency Fund. It is your best hope for breaking your dependency on credit when faced with unexpected and irregular expenses.

Once you have gone through the steps to build a strong financial foundation you'll be in a good position to resume your investment program.

I am sending you a copy of my book, *Debt-Proof Living*, which is my simple money management plan that makes it possible for anyone to live without debt. It's an easy read and will give you a road map to financial freedom.

By the way, if your roof is in such bad shape that you're sleeping under the stars—and you absolutely cannot live one more day without a new one—I believe I would sell enough stock to cover the bill. I hope you can avoid doing that but if you must, be sure to check with your tax professional first. Cashing in could trigger a tax event and you want to know about that ahead of time.

Thanks for reading. It wouldn't be much fun to write a column no one reads. I am grateful for you and all of my loyal readers.

Guilt-free manicures

Q: Isn't there a way that one can be fiscally responsible and still enjoy having a weekly manicure? A manicure is something I enjoy, so why do I need to give up my manicures?

A: Of course there is. For me the word "cheapskate" is about balance. I know that might sound weird, but you have to understand that for a good portion of my life I was way out of balance. I was a credit-card junkie.

I spent all we had, plus I ran up all the credit anyone would give me. Debt nearly destroyed my marriage, my family—my life!

Since then I've experienced a real change, but it didn't happen without a change of heart, mind and a long journey to financial freedom.

What I learned is that I need to live according to a formula: I need to give to make sure I don't become greedy, I need to save so I don't lie awake at night worrying that we're going to run out of money, and I need to not spend money I don't have. To me, this is balance: Giving, saving and living below my means.

As for your manicures, you be the judge. Is that ten dollars money you should be saving or paying toward debt? Then you probably can't afford it. But if you're giving, saving and able to pay all of your bills without depending on credit and still have money to spend, getting a manicure is one of life's pleasures.

If that's the way you choose to spend your money, then enjoy it to the fullest.

A $20,000 umbrella

Q: I need some advice. My husband is 71; retired and collects a pension. I'm 58, employed, and planning to take my Social Security at 62. I will also get a private pension when I turn 65.

We have debts!—a mortgage of $45,000; credit-card bills of $19,000; and other loans totaling $15,000.

I am expecting $20,000 in the next several months from an estate. Should I save that for a rainy day, pay off what I can with what cash I have, or just say "let's party and who cares?"

We have no problems meeting our bills; have an excellent credit record, but little cash remains at the end of the month. Any advice?

A: While the option to party is tempting, my advice is to take the $20,000 and park it where it is not at risk and earning at least enough interest to stay ahead of inflation.

It may appear that you're set with enough money to enjoy life together for many years to come, but life doesn't always turn out the way we plan. You'll sleep better knowing that you have money in the bank.

The infamous mystery means

Q: My husband has two jobs— he is an artist and a salesman. He earns commissions from both jobs so we never know what our income will be.

I work part-time and am paid hourly. How do I go about setting up a budget?

A: The mistake many who live on "mystery means" make is to spend whatever amount of money they earn as they earn it.

They multiply a good month's income by 12 and figure that's their annual income and they set their lifestyles accordingly.

Then, they starve during the lean months, allowing all the bills to go past due hoping a good month will follow soon.

The secret to living on an uncertain income is to determine the very minimum you need to live each month. Now put yourselves on that "salary." No matter what comes in during any month, pay yourselves only that set amount.

Now you know exactly how much your income will be in any given month so you can budget. Allow any overage to sit in reserve to cover your salary during coming lean months. I am sending you a copy of my book, *Debt-Proof Your Marriage*, with hopes you will read all of it, especially the step-by-step plan in Chapter 22, "How to Stay On Track on a Roller Coaster Income."

Being self-employed (or commission-based, which to me is about the same thing) can be either rewarding or horribly debilitating. It all depends on your willingness to be disciplined and to exercise great restraint when one month it appears that your ship has come in. Don't believe it.

Next month could produce little, if any, income at all. You have to learn to handle both.

Tipping hairdressers

Q: When your hairdresser is also the owner of the salon, should you still tip 15 to 20 percent for good service? I have always heard that the answer to that question is no, but I'm not sure. What is your thinking on this?

I very much enjoy reading your newspaper column. It encourages me every day!

A: Tipping is a custom for which there are no rules, only guidelines based on trends and etiquette that vary from one region to another.

It does seem, however, that what you suggest—not leaving a tip if your hairdresser is also the salon owner—was customary at one time. But that is no longer true in most areas. In fact, of the 87 people I surveyed from all around the country, 79 said it would make no difference—they would leave the same tip whether the owner did the work or not.

So, even if you believe that is wrong, it puts you in an awkward position if everyone else is leaving your owner/operator a tip.

Getting pink-slipped

Q: I learned today that I'm losing my job in a few months. I am in a quandary whether to squirrel away every penny I can or pay off my debts now.

I have $18,000 in my emergency fund and credit-card balances totaling $3,000.

A: If you knew for sure you would be paycheck-less for only a week or two I would advise you to pay off that $3,000 right away. But who knows? One week could turn into months—perhaps many months.

My advice when facing a season of unemployment is to hoard cash. If you get severance pay or other lump sums, don't book a cruise! Sock it away.

If you have been paying more than required on your debts, pull back to the minimums for now.

Also, go on a spending diet. The tactic here is to make sure you can stay current on all of your obligations for that unknown period of time that it will take to find your next job.

When you are once again employed, you will be in good shape to embark on an aggressive plan to repay your debts quickly.

Never underestimate the peace of mind that having money in the bank can bring during times of uncertainty. That can mean the difference between finding a great job and jumping on the first thing that comes along because you are barely hanging on by your fingernails.

Good luck with that job search. I'll be anxious to hear all about it when you land in your new position.

Borrowing from her 401(k)

Q: Recently I took a loan from my 401(k) retirement account. I'm paying it back with interest. However, now I'm wondering if I'm doing the right thing. I have no savings at all.

In essence I'm repaying myself, so should I stop repaying the loan and use that money to begin building an emergency fund instead?

A: If you stop making payments, the balance owing will be considered a withdrawal. The IRS doesn't take kindly to that. So, expect to get socked with a big penalty, plus you'll immediately owe taxes on the amount you did not repay.

Bottom line, you'll owe an amount equal to 40 percent or more of that remaining balance. Ouch! My advice is to repay it as quickly as possible.

However, you should think about reducing or discontinuing your regular 401(k) contributions. No penalties there. You can begin that emergency fund with the additional funds you'll see in your paycheck. You can always resume contributing to your 401(k) in the future.

Credit Reports, Credit Scores

Credit score breakdown

Q: How are credit scores calculated? Is there a formula?

A: There is much about credit scoring that is proprietary to the Fair Isaac Company, which created the credit score in the first place. That means we are not allowed to know exactly how they take the information in our credit files and boil it all down to a three-digit credit score. Nice, huh?

We do know that the FICO model created by Fair Isaac Company, bases 35 percent of your score on your payment history, 30 percent on how much of your available credit you're using at any moment (the lower the better), 15 percent on how long you've had credit, 10 percent on how long it's been since your last application for credit (longer is better) and 10 percent on the mix of credit you have and use.

What "mix" means is not specifically called out but we do know that it's better to have both revolving accounts like credit cards and installment accounts like mortgages and car loans, rather than one or the other.

Who's on whose credit report?

Q: My husband and I do not have, nor ever have had, any joint credit or bank accounts—with the exception of one mortgage.

Since we do have that one joint mortgage with a bank, how does this affect our individual credit reports? Will all of his credit history now show up on my credit report as well, and will my credit history show up on his credit report?

A: Only those accounts that you hold jointly or on which you are an authorized user, will show up on your credit report.

Your state's laws, however, may have a different take on whether or not you can be held liable for one another's debts. Some states have "community property" laws that might hold you responsible for your husband's debts even though you are not on the account. You would need to check with an attorney on that.

Bankruptcy recovery

Q: Almost two years ago we filed for bankruptcy. We are now back on our feet and gaining momentum but wondering how we can go about repairing the damage caused to our credit.

We would appreciate any information or suggestions you might have to offer.

A: Time is a great neutralizer for the effects of bankruptcy. It will be reported to the credit bureaus and show on your credit file for ten years. That doesn't mean you won't be able to get a mortgage or other type of financing for a decade, but since your credit score will be severely damaged, you will likely pay higher insurance premiums. And you will not get preferred interest rates on a mortgage and other loans.

The best thing you can do now is to live a financially responsible life. Make sure you pay your bills on time. Don't take on new debt. Don't open credit accounts haphazardly. If you apply for say a home mortgage in the future the lender will want to see a consistent pattern of change in the way you manage your money.

Credit score of 750 is nothing to sneeze at

Q: My credit score is 750. The report I received says my score would be higher if I didn't have so many open lines of credit (credit cards that I have not cancelled). These are cards for smaller stores that I do not use anymore.

I have heard that you should not cancel credit cards because it will hurt your score. In this case, would it be advisable for me to cancel these small credit cards?

A: Crazy, isn't it? If you have too much open credit, apparently that is a negative. If you close too many accounts at the same time, that can be a negative because you've screwed up that delicate ratio of debt-to-available-credit.

I can only imagine that you have so much available credit, you've tipped the scales in a way that is keeping your score down. But a score of 750 is very good. If I were you I would be satisfied and do nothing. If you do decide to work at raising your score, close those extraneous accounts slowly—one every six months or so. To learn how to do that, see "Breaking Up is Hard to Do" in the archives at *DebtProofLiving.com*.

Credit and the single woman

Q: I am newly widowed and my daughter is recently divorced. We are finding very little written about credit and single women.

We do not know how to establish ourselves in our newly-single circumstances. Both of us, as married females, had 800 ratings and now find our scores have dropped to 750, with very little explanation for why. Can you help?

A: Here are the basic rules that anyone in any season of life should follow to maintain a good credit score:

- Pay your bills on time

- Do not apply for new credit haphazardly

- Do not close accounts if you can avoid it

- Always maintain a large gap between the amount you owe and your total amount of available credit.

I highly recommend you read *Your Credit Score* by Liz Pulliam Weston (3rd Edition, Prentice Hall). In this book Liz addresses the kinds of life changes you and your daughter are going through. She will help you understand every aspect of the credit scoring system and how to maintain a high score.

When free is anything but

Q: Recently I went to *Consumer info.com* to get my free credit score. I did and was charged for things I did not ask for. Now they will not refund my money. What should I do?

A: It is very important that you read all of the terms carefully before agreeing to anything FREE, especially on the Internet.

If you go back to this site (which, by the way, is part of the Experian Company and you know they are in the business of selling credit reports and credit scores) you will see the "offer" is for a FREE credit report, not credit score. There's a big difference.

When you click on "FREE Credit Report" at *Experian.com* you are taken to a screen and asked to fill in your personal information, also giving them your credit-card number and expiration date. That should have raised a big red flag!

By giving them that information you agreed to the fine print which says, and I quote in its entirety:

"You will not be charged for your free credit report and free trial membership. However, valid credit-card information is required to start your free 30-day trial membership. You may cancel your free trial membership at any time. However, you must tell us during your free 30-day trial that you do not want to continue your membership past the trial period, otherwise, you are hereby authorizing the $9.95 monthly fee to automatically be charged to the credit-card account below." Bingo!

Let me warn you and all who read this that canceling is not easy. It's far more trouble to cancel than to try to get anything free out of this site. So consumers, beware.

You need to cancel your subscription now and consider it a lesson well learned. By the way, I know of no way to get a FREE credit score.

Playing with a full deck

Q: I just got my credit report and see I have many open accounts I haven't used in years. How do I go about getting those puppies off?

Also, I have several accounts that I stupidly opened just to get an extra 15 to 20 percent off on that day's purchase. Is there any risk to me closing all of these accounts, too? If I was carrying everything they show on my report, I'd have a full deck of 52 cards.

A: Wow, 52 credit cards? You've got me beat, my friend—a record I relinquish, gladly.

Seriously, this is not a good thing. You don't mention your credit score, which leads me to believe you don't know what it is. I'm guessing that your score has suffered from this heavy load of mindless credit gathering. You can use MSN's credit score estimator at *http://moneycentral.msn.com/investor/creditreport/main.asp* to get a rough idea.

The money you saved on "today's purchase" by signing up for all of those cards surely pales by what having a damaged credit score has cost you in higher insurance premiums and higher rates of interest on your mortgage and auto loans over the years.

Closing these accounts cannot undo the damage that has been done. In fact, that could make things even worse. Experts tell us you should close no more than three accounts per year, which in your case would take 17 years. However, carrying that 52-card deck is not a good idea, either.

The great credit crunch that began in 2008 as the U.S. tumbled into recession may solve the problem for you.

Right off the bat, it's likely that many in your deck are for stores that have gone out of business. Mervyn's, Circuit City, and Linen's and Things come to mind.

Credit grantors are on a rampage to close and cancel inactive and dormant accounts these days, so that may take care of a few more.

As for the rest, identify one or two of the bank cards (MasterCard or Visa) you've had the longest as the credit cards you will keep active, and close the rest at a rate of about one every six months.

As painful as it will be, I suggest you get your credit score now so you know where you are. Then, watch it like a hawk. With so much open credit you are very vulnerable to identity theft. You should think seriously about getting identity theft protection through a company like Lifelock.

When to hold, when to close?

Q: You were right. I have started receiving notices of changes to my credit-card agreements. These are paid-off accounts I've kept because I didn't want to trash my FICO score by closing them.

Should I make small periodic purchases with these cards and pay the balance immediately so credit agencies won't close them due to lack of use? Or would that open a can of worms?

A: This does present a dilemma. On the one hand, you need only one good, all-purpose credit card, either a MasterCard or Visa. If you are careful to never use more than 30 percent of your available credit, pay it off monthly and never pay late, you will maintain an excellent credit score (provided you are paying your other bills on time as well).

To maintain a bevy of additional credit cards just so you'll have them is unnecessary. Each one opens an opportunity for identity theft. Beyond that, it's just a hassle to keep track of so much plastic.

This is a decision you will have to make, but I would allow all of those inactive cards to expire as you are contacted. You don't want to accept new terms and conditions. No matter how attractive those changes might appear to be, I can guarantee they will not be to your advantage.

In these rough economic times banks are doing all they can to recoup what they've lost. Any drop in your credit score when an active account is closed will be slight and your score will bounce back quickly.

Husband? What husband?

Q: We cleared up all our debts about 15 years ago and have prided ourselves on having an outstanding credit record.

About a year ago we requested copies of our credit reports from Experian. They sent my report but informed us they'd never heard of my husband—after some 25 years of buying cars, homes and furniture. Here we've been such good "kids!" Where did his credit rating go?

A: Think about it: With all of the millions of consumers in this country, each with a slightly different Social Security number, countless numbers of credit cards, consumer account numbers and millions of transactions being posted every day—mistakes are bound to happen.

Think of how easy it is to lose something in your home or office through carelessness or an untimely computer crash. All it takes is one transposition in a Social Security number and there goes a credit rating or even the entire report.

When it comes to your credit history and current standing, don't assume anything! Look at your reports often and maintain your own independent records. I suggest that this time you contact all three bureaus. What one of them might have misplaced, the others may have readily available.

Go to *AnnualCreditReport.com* this time, where each of you can get free copies of all three of the reports—Experian, Equifax and TransUnion.

Credit scores all over the place

Q: A friend and I both got credit reports and our credit scores from *FreeCreditReport.com*. All three of his came in between 730 and 740, and all three of mine came in between 740 and 750.

We both refinanced our homes recently, and the credit score he was given by his lender was 690; my credit score turns out to be 805. Can you explain this discrepancy? It looks like the money we paid to get our scores was wasted.

A: The explanation is simple. All of the credit reporting agencies (Experian, Equifax, TransUnion) and FICO have their own scoring systems, meaning they use different methods to compute your score. And there are many scoring models other than FICO, too. Your lenders most likely do not subscribe to the same agency, although most lenders do rely on FICO.

Also, your credit score can change daily. Think of it as a snapshot of your credit and financial situation at the moment that score is ordered. Things can and likely will change tomorrow—not drastically, but perhaps enough to change your score.

Let's say that you make a giant purchase on your credit card for $5,000 because you want the points or miles. Five days later you pay that charge in full. Great for your determination to not create new debt, but bad for your credit score.

If your lender snaps the picture of your credit while you have the balance, your score is going to take a hit, especially if that purchase brought you close to your credit limit. The scoring model doesn't care if you pay it off during the grace period.

I find it troubling that this delicate balancing act called credit scoring can have such a significant financial impact. With most lenders your credit score will determine the interest rate you will pay on a new mortgage or refinance. Over the years that rate can make a huge difference in how much you will pay.

Bad to open, worse to close

Q: In a recent issue of *Debt-Proof Living* newsletter, you mentioned that closing credit-card accounts will negatively affect your credit score. Why is that the case? If I am the one to cancel it, why would it make a difference?

A: I agree that it makes no sense at all. The best I can tell you is that the computer scoring model wants to see a wide margin between the amount of credit that you have and the balances you are carrying. The smaller that gap, the lower your score. When you close an account, you reduce your available credit, so your existing balances loom larger and reduce the gap.

Another factor: The computer scoring model has been programmed to favor credit cards you have had longer over those that have a shorter history. If you close an account you've had for a long time and keep open one's that are younger, this too will adversely affect your score.

But here's the most maddening part of all of this: If you have too much available credit, that too will negatively affect your score. You need to decide which is worse for you: Too many open credit accounts or taking a hit on your score by closing them.

Personally, unless I was about to buy a house, car or get a new insurance policy, I'd close credit-card accounts that were at $0, keeping the one or two majors (MasterCard or Visa) that I'd had the longest, and which have the higher credit limits.

I would do that systematically over a six- to 12-month period to avoid one big hit.

If you are careful with paying your bills on time and are not going over your credit limits, your credit score will bounce back quickly.

It's good to keep in mind that even in these tough times, a FICO score of about 750 or higher is a great score, and high enough to get you more credit than you need.

Early terminator gets threatened

Q: My daughter was told by her cell phone company that if she cancels and pays an early termination penalty fee, it will be a bad mark on her credit rating. Is that true even if she pays for the privilege?

A: Many people have no idea that just like other creditors, cell phone companies report to credit bureaus.

Negative remarks from cell phone companies such as late or missed payments, account closures and account collection may reduce your credit score.

However, in your daughter's situation, buying out one's contract is not considered a negative remark. In fact I would expect this to warrant a "paid as agreed" entry on her account, which would show up as a positive mark, not a negative.

Sounds to me like a customer service rep crossed the line into intimidation in an effort to keep your daughter as a customer.

Checking score often gets expensive

Q: I was told by Bank of America, who holds my mortgage, that each time I request my credit score I actually am decreasing the score, because each inquiry lowers the total number. Is that true?

I know there's no damage done by requesting the annual copies of my credit report, but I hadn't heard that I can actually lower the credit score simply by requesting it.

A: You have received incorrect information. Requesting copies of your own credit report and or score do not affect your credit score, according to *MyFico.com*—the company that invented and now provides computer models for TransUnion, Equifax and Experian.

I will tell you, however, that requesting your score so often is affecting your wallet.

Unlike your credit report which you can get free each year, you have to pay to get your score.

Look, if you are paying your bills on time, not going crazy with new credit and keeping your unsecured debt to a minimum you shouldn't have to even think about your score.

Your credit score is going to take care of itself as you take care of your finances.

Disputes bring no response

Q: Because I found errors in my credit file I sent information to correct them, but Equifax refuses to respond. Please tell me what I should do.

A: Are you using the correct form? Are you sending your disputes to the correct address?

The Fair Credit Reporting Act (FCRA) requires credit reporting agencies to respond within 30-days of receiving your disputed information. You need to contact them again, sending copies of everything you sent the first time. I trust you are keeping a good paper trail.

If there are errors on your report, chances are a bank, mortgage company, credit-card company or department store furnished inaccurate information to a credit bureau. They will continue to report what creditors tell them.

It's up to you to work things out with the creditor that messed up your credit record in the first place.

To help you interpret and understand the FCRA, the federal government has prepared the *Consumer Handbook to Credit Protection Laws*.

A copy is available ($.50) from Publications Services, Division of Support Services, Board of Governors of the Federal Reserve System, Wash., D.C. 20551. Or, you can visit the U.S. Consumer Information Center website, *Pueblo.gsa.gov*.

To catch a snooping ex

Q: I have reason to believe my ex-husband is getting credit reports on me without my permission. He has access to the credit bureaus through his business. What, if any, recourse do I have?

A: How much recourse would you like? The law is very specific and if you can prove it, I would say he's in a world of hurt.

First, I suggest that you get current copies of all three of your your credit reports (go to *AnnualCreditReport.com* where you can get a free copy of your Experian, Equifax and TransUnion files) so you have proof of all inquiries that have been made. Inquiries will show up on the report, including the name of the entity that requested your credit report. It should be obvious where these inquiries are coming from.

The Fair Credit Reporting Act makes it illegal for anyone (individuals or companies) to obtain your credit report before getting your permission in writing.

If an inquiry was made without your permission (all inquiries must be noted on your credit report) you can sue the inquirer and the credit reporting agency for damages in state or federal court, and recoup court costs and reasonable legal fees—and collect punitive damages for deliberate violations, too.

You will cause additional grief for the unauthorized inquirer when you file a complaint with the FTC by phone: toll-free 877 382-4357; by mail: Consumer Response Center, Federal Trade Commission, 600 Pennsylvania Ave., NW, Wash., DC

20580; or make an online complaint at *FTCComplaintAssistant.gov.* Or complain to all three.

Bad stuff sticks around a long time

Q: How long are negative entries allowed to show up on a person's credit report? And what is the procedure to get negative items removed if they are still there past the maximum reporting time?

A: The Fair Credit Reporting Act provides that bankruptcy information may stay in a credit file for ten years, and all other negative information may be retained for up to seven years maximum.

If you believe negative items are being reported past the time they should have fallen off, dispute them using the form provided with your credit report.

If you would like to curl up with a copy of the FCRA, you can find it at *FTC.gov/os/statutes/031224fcra.pdf.*

Getting bad marks off credit report

Q: Late credit-card payments have negatively affected my credit report and credit score. I have now paid the negative accounts in full and closed them.

Can I request that the credit-card companies remove those negative items? How likely are they to do so? Do they have to by law now that I have paid them in full?

A: Your credit report should reflect that you paid those accounts in full and also that they were closed at your request. But there is no way to get the negative information off your report, unless that information is not true.

The law allows the credit reporting bureaus to continue reporting that you were late, for up to seven years. That seems unfair to me, too. I've heard of people serving less time than that for capital crimes. But, don't stress out too much. If you show a pattern of no more negatives, your credit score will continue to improve with the passing of time.

Monitor your own credit files

Q: We pay $99.99 a year to Privacy Guard, a company that monitors all three credit bureaus on our behalf. It seems to me that this may be a waste of money. What's your take on this?

A: Credit monitoring companies offer a viable service. So do butlers and chauffeurs, but most of us cannot afford them. If you can afford that level of luxury that's one thing, but I have a feeling you could put that $100 to better use elsewhere and monitor your own credit.

Take advantage of the opportunity you have to get one free credit report each year from each of the credit bureaus at *AnnualCreditReport.com* or 877 322-8228.

Space your free reports through the year, for example January, May and September. Make sure you are set up to check your credit-card accounts online and then do that at least once a week.

If your identity is compromised, you will catch it early. As for the reimbursement these credit monitoring companies promise if you are the victim of identity theft, most people are not aware they already have this coverage as part of their homeowner's or renter's insurance. Check your policy to see if you are covered. If not you should be able to add an identity theft rider for only a few dollars per year.

Bankruptcies are forever

Q: In 1994 we filed for bankruptcy, followed by the longest ten years of our lives with that negative black mark in our credit files.

Finally, 2004 arrived and we found ourselves on the other end of the spectrum—great job and income, and living the plan (as we DPLers call it). Our credit union gave us a credit-card account with a $20,000 limit.

Now the bad news. In attempting to refinance our cars at a lower rate through the credit union, our previous credit history showed up. The credit union refused to refinance the cars and closed all of our accounts.

We have excellent credit and are planning to apply for a mortgage soon. How much damage is this going to do to our credit? We've already suffered for over ten years. Is it legal for them to revive a bankruptcy after ten years?

A: I'm so sorry that you have had to go through this ordeal but proud of you for the dramatic change you've made in the way you now manage your money.

I am afraid, however, that you, like many others, believe that a bankruptcy is erased after ten years. That is so not true.

A bankruptcy filing is like a birth, death, marriage or divorce. It is a legally recorded event that becomes a matter of public record forever.

The Fair Credit Reporting Act says in Section 605 that credit bureaus must exclude a bankruptcy from one's credit report after ten years from the date of entry, unless the credit report is to be used in connection with

1) a credit transaction involving a loan of $150,000 or more;

2) life insurance involving a face amount of $150,000 or more; or

3) the application for employment at an annual salary expected to be $75,000 or more.

A bankruptcy is *never* expunged from the record. And I doubt if your credit union learned of your bankruptcy from your credit report. Lenders routinely check public records for past bankruptcy filings when considering loan applications.

It's likely they relied on your credit reports alone when they granted that credit-card account with the $20,000 credit limit.

And, you need to know that all mortgage applications include this question: *Have you ever filed for bankruptcy?* You must answer truthfully.

If you lie and the lender discovers the bankruptcy later it can call the loan, legally recover all of their losses and charge you with fraud.

If I were you I would voluntarily disclose this when you apply for a mortgage. Your pattern of recovery and years of financial responsibility will be evident as they review your credit history.

At the very worst you may have to pay a higher interest rate.

Hiring reputable credit repair

Q: Can you recommend a professional to help me clean my credit report? I know I can do this on my own, but there are so many inaccuracies that the challenge of doing it myself is daunting.

I have a common name which may be part of the problem. My

report shows inaccuracies like I was married (never was), lived in a town I have never even visited, owned a home and mortgage (have never even applied for a mortgage, nor have I ever bought a home)—that type of thing. Thank you for any advice you may have. You are the best!

A: I don't want to worry you needlessly, but I believe you have cause for concern that someone may have stolen your identity. However, if the inaccuracies are limited to identification data only and not numerous lines of credit that are not yours, this should be relatively easy to clear up.

You need to start working immediately and directly with the credit bureaus to make sure all of this erroneous information is corrected.

Although I do not have a source to recommend, I'm sure there must be at least one reputable credit-repair company in your area should you decide to hire someone to work with you on this.

Look in the Yellow Pages under "credit repair."

Do your homework before your first visit. Contact the Better Business Bureau to see if the firm has had any consumer complaints. Check with your state attorney general's office or other state consumer agencies to find out if there are any pending legal investigations.

The FTC (Federal Trade Commission) warns that there are lots of crooks out there posing as credit-re-

pair professionals. They're closing them down as fast as they can.

The FTC also warns against relying on chambers of commerce or other trade associations where membership is based solely on a fee as a reliable reference or source for finding professional credit repair.

Credit repair services must follow the Credit Repair Organizations Act (FTC.gov/ro/chro/credit.htm), which is intended to protect consumers. You should receive an explanation of these rights before signing a written contract with a credit repair professional that includes the payment terms for services, including the total cost and a detailed description of the services to be performed.

I would be remiss if I did not close by telling you that there is nothing that a reputable credit-repair company can do for you that you cannot do for yourself for free.

Unauthorized or simply forgotten?

Q: At your suggestion I have been keeping up with ordering and reviewing my three credit reports each year. What angers me is the reports show that companies have inquired about my credit without my permission.

I have opted out so I am not getting offers from credit-card companies. I thought that other than prospective employers or insurance companies, no one could pull my credit without my authorization.

So how does this happen, and do I have a right to contact the companies and ask why they are doing this? Can legal action be taken? I don't like a credit inquiry showing up on my report when it was not authorized by me. Any suggestions? Thank you and bless you for your website.

A: You can and you should dispute any unauthorized inquiries not only because excessive inquiries will bring down your credit score, but because this could be an indication of some kind of identity theft. But before you do that, make sure you know who these inquirers are.

Remember that on each of your credit-card accounts you gave the card issuer permission to check your credit, monthly. And they do.

Typically, these inquiries do not show up on the report, so I am curious to know what inquiries you are talking about.

They could be on some other person and in your file by mistake. It is illegal to pull a credit report on any person without their written permission.

You will find instructions with your credit report(s) for how to dispute erroneous information.

And when you do, keep a good paper trail so you can follow up.

One little error is a huge mistake

Q: After reviewing my credit report, the only thing that is incorrect is that they have an address listed for me in Dallas. I have never lived in Dallas. Is this worth the hassle of trying to correct this minor error?

A: It is very important that your address is correct on your credit report. Follow the instructions that came with your credit report to get it corrected. Then follow up in a few months to make sure it has.

Hold the wedding, fix the finances

Q: My fiance and I are planning our wedding. I am a little concerned about his credit. He has bad credit (530-550 score) and I have good credit (750-780 score).

I am worried about his bad credit affecting my good credit once we marry. I am also concerned that I will be responsible for half of his debt even though I am not a cosigner on any loans. Will this affect my credit adversely in the future? Any suggestions?

A: I am happy that you are concerned. You should be.

Marriage means what's yours and what's mine is now ours—the good, the bad and the ugly. Your beloved appears to have a lot of ugly going on in his financial affairs.

His bad credit score will affect a lot more than just your ability to get a decent home mortgage. It affects where he will work, how much his insurance will cost and even if he can rent an apartment.

Landlords, insurance companies and lenders are now relying on credit scores to weed out poor risks. You can try to keep everything separate, but that is nearly impossible to do.

If you try to buy a house, a lender will average your credit scores. A combined score of 640 is not pretty. I can only imagine that you believe he's going to change once you are married—that he will pay your bills on time, quickly pay down his debt and that he will stop spending money he has not earned yet.

I have a suggestion for you. Postpone the wedding so he can do now all of those things he's promising after you get married—before you make a life-changing decision.

Can't buy a better score

Q: My husband wants to pay a company $575 to improve our credit rating so we can qualify to buy the home we're renting. I want to use the $575 to pay off debts. We're in a mess. What should we do?

A: Every day, companies nationwide appeal to consumers with poor credit histories. They promise, for a fee, to clean up your credit report so you can get a car loan, a home mortgage, insurance or even a job. The truth is, they can't deliver.

After you pay them hundreds or thousands of dollars in fees, these companies do nothing to improve your credit report; most simply vanish with your money.

No one can legally remove accurate and timely negative information from a credit report. The law allows you to ask for an investigation of information in your file that you dispute as inaccurate or incomplete. There is no charge for this.

Everything a credit repair clinic can do for you legally, you can do for yourself for free. Go to *AnnualCredit Report*.com and order your free credit reports for both of you. Go over them carefully. If you see any information that is not accurate or that you cannot confirm to be true, dispute it, following the simple instructions that came with the reports.

The best thing you can do to improve your credit score is to pay all of your bills on time; do not apply for or accept any new lines of credit; pay down your debts. In time you will see your score begin to improve.

As for that $575, my advice is to use that to start building your Contingency Fund. You need to save enough money to cover at least three months of expenses. This will be there to keep you above water should you go through a season of unemployment or some other financial challenge. There is something nearly magical about having money in the bank. It improves your attitude and makes you more willing to live frugally. Then, you'll be ready to start saving the money you need to buy a house.

I know things are difficult for you right now, but once the two of you can get on the same track where you are pulling toward the same goal, things will change quickly.

Discrepancies in credit scores

Q: My husband and I requested our credit reports, as we are applying for a mortgage. We paid additional money for our credit scores.

The mortgage was approved, and in the package was a copy of the credit reports and scores obtained by the mortgage company. Both of our scores were different on the three reports obtained by the agency than on the three reports obtained by me.

I feel cheated out of $30 (we paid $5 per score per person per bureau). Is this difference normal? There were fewer than two weeks difference in the dates on the reports, and no changes in our credit activities.

A: Yes, it's normal and you'll understand if you realize a credit score is a snapshot of your credit situation on one day as taken and interpreted by a specific credit bureau.

There are many scoring 'models' used to translate the data in a credit file to a three-digit score. FICO is the commonly accepted model and likely the one your lender relied upon.

Out of the blue, a student loan

Q: My daughter is looking to buy her first home and applied for a mortgage. She was denied due to a student loan on her credit report. She has never had a student loan. What does she do to clear this up?

A: Well, this is curious for sure. Is it possible she took out a loan that you are not aware of?

Regardless, your daughter needs to get all three versions of her credit report, review them carefully and dispute anything on them that she does not know to be true and correct—including this student loan. There will be sufficient information on that item for her to check it out.

She should have done this at least three months prior to applying for that mortgage.

Estimates are that 80 percent of all credit reports contain errors. If that is true—I do not doubt it—all of us need to be reviewing our credit reports regularly to make sure they contain only factual information.

Now that you got 'em, better keep 'em

Q: My husband and I just bought a house and don't foresee any big purchases anytime soon. I thought it would be a good time to cancel some of our credit cards.

I have many store charge cards, some I didn't even realize were still open until we saw our credit report. Oops!

My husband says we need to keep the oldest card and the one's with the highest available balance to keep the best credit score. Is this true? We pay everything in full each month. I would love some advice before I start calling creditors.

A: Your husband is correct. Keep those valuable lines of credit actively pristine. I wouldn't cancel anything right now. Things are just too volatile in the world of consumer credit. You don't want to do anything that could make your credit score hiccup.

We're living in unusual times when credit scores are going to be more important than you ever dreamed they might be. If you have a great one (750 or higher) you'll be blessed with great opportunities in low interest rates, the best insurance rates, and

better consideration for job opportunities.

Let's revisit the subject a year or two after this global credit nightmare has settled down.

When it's okay to give information

Q: I requested a free credit report at *AnnualCreditReport.com*. I remembered that you once wrote that it would be okay to give them my Social Security number, which I did. Then they said I needed to call to give them more information.

They asked me which credit cards I have and the numbers. I refused to give them this information, and was told they cannot send my free report without the requested information.

Is this how all credit report companies work and is it legal?

A: Credit bureaus have a fiduciary responsibility to protect your identity and private information. They need more than your Social Security number to make sure you are who you say you are. Just so you know, they have all of your credit-card information already including your account numbers. They know more about you than you might even expect.

In the process of requesting your report, they will ask about recent transactions you've made or other identifying information that no one but you would know as a way of checking to see if you are an imposter. Until they are certain you are who you purport to be, don't expect them to release your credit report.

The reason you had to call the office is the information you gave online was either incomplete or you gave an incorrect response. This was a precautionary move. And when you refused to complete the process by phone, they did the right thing by not sending your report.

Remember, these bureaus manage millions of files. It's possible that many of those files are for people with the exact same name as yours. Because you initiated the contact and made the call, you have nothing to worry about when you give them the information they need to match you to your account.

Home and Family Situations

Financial disharmony

Q: I married three years ago. My wife has memorized my credit-card information.

This is a personal card, and she is not listed as an authorized user. However, she charges to it and I get hit. I took a loan out from my 401(k) last year and paid off the $15,000 balance, only to have her run it up again.

My question is, because she is not listed as an authorized user on the card, can I protest the charges, or am I still responsible for them because she is married to me? We just started reading your book *Debt-Proof Your Marriage*, a chapter at a time and then we talk about it. Thanks for your support.

A: Here's the problem: You would have to dispute all of those charges, which means you would be reporting unlawful activity on your account. That could lead to her being prosecuted and I have a feeling you simply do not want to go there.

I am impressed and relieved that you two are reading my book. Just keep going. You are about to discover this is not a money issue at all, but a matter of trust. Without trust, your marriage is in jeopardy. The credit-card situation is a symptom of a much deeper need—the need to be fully open and honest with one another. Without that you will never experience financial intimacy. I hope you'll write back when you've finished the book.

By the way, you can call your credit-card issuer, report the card lost or stolen. They will immediately void your current number and send you a replacement card with a new account number. Provided you retrieve the mail, she will have no way to discover the new number. Just a thought.

Teen girls and their clothes

Q: How do you buy clothes for teenage girls without using plastic when you are drowning in debt?

A: I don't and you shouldn't either. Get the idea of using plastic out of your mind. It is simply not an option when you are drowning in debt.

How much cash do you have for clothes? What can you sell to raise cash? Where can you slash your expenses to free up a few bucks?

Have a family meeting with your kids and lay out the situation. Then follow a plan.

Teach them about consignment stores and thrift shops and all kinds of places to get great clothes cheaply.

Then (this is the hard part, but the best thing you could ever do) give them the cash, no matter how little it might be. It's up to them to buy what they can that meets your dress code rules. When the money is gone, that's it until all of you can raise more cash.

If there's no cash right now, that means they'll have to wear what they have until things change.

Your positive "can-do!" attitude will be the most important ingredient in all of this.

Financial infidelity

Q: I secretly transferred some credit-card balances and charged $9,000 on my husband's credit card after he thought he'd paid them off. He got to the mail before me on that fateful day and is still steaming.

This is not the first time it has happened. I am a stay-at-home mom and I get a sizable allowance.

I need to get my husband's card paid off and his trust back. Is it possible? I can't eat or sleep knowing that he knows, and that he is so angry. Please help me.

A: Financial infidelity can be as serious and devastating to a marriage as sexual infidelity. And rarely are money conflicts only about money.

You might wonder what gives me any credibility to even address such a serious matter. The truth is I sabotaged my own marriage in much the same way. I destroyed my husband's trust. That's why I'm going to suggest there's something much more serious going on here for you.

I'm sending you my book, *Debt-Proof Your Marriage*. The first half of the book is about your relationship and will tell you what you can do to experience emotional intimacy, which is the key ingredient in achieving financial harmony. You'll also read my story and I hope it will encourage you to know that this does not have to signal the end of your happy marriage. It didn't end mine.

In the meantime, here are the steps I offer to anyone in this situation.

1. Acknowledge. This is flagrant betrayal and deceit. Financial infidelity is not occasionally forgetting to record a check or an ATM transaction. Financial infidelity is consciously and deliberately lying about money, credit and or debt.

2. Show remorse. Your spouse needs to know that you are truly, sincerely sorry for what you have done, not just that you got caught. You probably can't apologize often enough. Authentic remorse doesn't include "Yes, but ..." or any other attempts to justify. True remorse says, "I was wrong and I am so sorry."

3. Understand. Remorse, as necessary as it is, doesn't take away the pain, but it does put the recovery process in motion. Only time and rebuilding of trust will do that. Understand that your spouse may need time to process.

4. Promise change. If you can honestly say you are now committed to total financial honesty, let your spouse know that in no uncertain terms.

5. Share details. Your spouse has every right to know the full extent of your financial indiscretions (not only what he discovered on his own). Come clean. Share your specific plans for recovery. You may have to get a job or sell assets to pay back the debt.

6. Offer reassurance. Even though you have decided to reform, your husband may be reacting for some time. Your first reassurance needs to be that this activity has stopped. Then understand that the rebuilding of trust takes time. Your actions will speak louder than your words.

7. Commit yourself fully. One of the keys to financial harmony is mutual respect and accountability. Let him know that you are 100 percent committed to change, recovery and restoration.

8. Consider counseling. There are times, although rare, that a spending problem signals something much deeper like addiction or serious depression. If you suspect this may be true, you should seek help from a qualified professional who specializes in such disorders.

Compromise negotiation needed

Q: I am completely dedicated to getting out of debt, but my husband does not fully cooperate. He loves to spend money on little things but they add up to big things.

That keeps us from reducing expenses and contributing to our Freedom Account and Contingency Fund. He says he wants to be debt-free, but he won't work with me. Any suggestions?

A: Sounds like it's time for a partner's compromise negotiation meeting. Let me caution you that it would be easy for you to take on the role of a stern parent to this "errant child," but don't let yourself go there.

It is not reasonable to think that either of you will never spend money again, so how about this: Each of you gets $100 cash a week (or an amount you determine) to spend as you like. When it's gone, it's gone until next "payday."

All plastic goes into a secret hiding place both of you know about and you pledge to the other that it's Hands Off! unless both of you are present and in full agreement.

If you back off a bit and begin living what you believe instead of talking about it so much, you may get his attention more effectively. Is your RDRP hanging on the 'fridge? Even if you've not started your Contingency Fund, you could draw up a projection for how 10 percent of your income could grow if you socked it away. Regardless of what you decide to do, make sure you always remain a fragrance; never become an odor.

Bailing out the 'rents

Q: Thanks to *Debt-Proof Living*, my husband and I have been debt-free for three years.

My father has recently been very ill, and my mother spilled the beans about their debt. They have two credit cards and several store cards with balances. They also have a mortgage and a car payment. I'm frustrated, disgusted and heartbroken to find out they have so much debt at their age.

My husband and I paid off one major credit card for them that had several thousand dollars on it. Afterwards my mother went out and ran the account right back up to the limit.

I'm not willing to go into debt to pay off their debt. I explained to her that with that kind of debt they will never retire. Am I wrong? I would appreciate any advice you might have for us.

A: I am sorry to hear about your father's illness, but that doesn't change my response: You are not wrong. You shouldn't bail them out by going into debt. I think you've discovered why

paying their debts isn't such a hot idea, either.

I would say the same thing if your mother were writing to me about you: You cannot fix anyone by making them comfortable in their misery. That only enables them to stay there. And buy more stuff.

I suggest you diligently save and invest now because the day may come that you decide you want to contribute to their day-to-day care. But even then you will not be responsible for their debts and should not feel guilty for that.

I hope everyone reading this—regardless of age—will take stock of the way they are managing their finances and preparing for the future. The best gift we will ever give our kids is our own solvency. In that way we will not become a financial burden to them.

Ack! Cheapskates everywhere

Q: I have cheapskates in my life. My father is one. My boss, my boss's mom and my boyfriend's mom—all cheapskates.

All of these individuals have the following in common: They are unhappy individuals. They avoid birthday parties, anniversaries or any type of holiday that requires gift-giving.

Often times they choose to be by themselves rather than to have people at their houses. I don't mean that they are unhappy because they avoid gatherings. They are unhappy because they are grumpy. They don't smile and they are afraid of their own shadows. They feel that somebody might steal from them, so they're always guarded.

These cheapskates all wear the same clothes over and over again, no matter the occasion. For example, my boss still wears his 1980 shirts.

I've known my boyfriend's mom for over a year. She always wears the same black pants, white blouse, black sweater. And yes, it is the same exact outfit.

My dad doesn't buy clothes. We have to buy them for him with our money. All of these cheapskates in my life have money. Lots of money. They are financially well off.

My dilemma: I want to have the kind of money they have when I retire. But, I don't want to be grumpy or unhappy. I am afraid of becoming one of them.

They all have all the money in the world, and don't enjoy it. Am I overreacting?

A: I once shared your attitude and determination. I went to extreme measures to make sure no one mistook me for a "cheapskate!"

I bought nice things, drove fabulous cars and bought lots of clothes. Our kids went to private schools, dressed well and had most everything they wanted. And I ended up in terrible—worse than horrible—debt.

Thankfully, I reformed, repaid all the debt, and have gone on to call myself a cheapskate, simply because it's a fun way to point out how far I've come from the credit-card junkie I once was.

I suppose there is a chance that the cheapskates in your life are happy, but I wouldn't count on it. For sure that's not what I want for my life. That's why I advocate a balanced lifestyle where you give away 10 percent of your income, save 10 percent for the future and then live the best life you can on 80 percent of your income.

The 10-10-80 formula works because it prevents the kind of extremes you cite. When you are giving, saving and then doing all you can to live an abundant life, you simply won't be grumpy.

I suggest you set your own agenda for your life and begin managing your money in such a way that you stay out of debt, are prepared for the future and are blessing others less fortunate by being a giver.

That's the secret for a happy life. And may your joy be infectious to all those grumpy people around you!

Partners pulling against one another

Q: My husband and I both work, but we literally have $150 in our checking account and no savings to speak of. The problem is, my husband is a spendaholic.

He bought a plasma TV without even telling me, and he owns every video game known to man.

When I try to talk to him about curbing his spending, he gets mad and says I don't seem to mind when he spends money on me! I'm really worried. We have two young children to support. How can I get him to change his ways?

A: Let me assure you this is not an uncommon situation. Most marriages attract one spender and one saver. And, that's a good thing because your differences can create balance—provided you're working together, not pulling apart.

To help your husband see your point, lovingly show him on paper that if the two of you saved only $50 a week, at the end of one year you would have $2,600 in the bank. In two years you would have more than $5,300.

I know from personal experience that saving money is as gratifying as spending with abandon, but with a much better payoff. If he's resistant to saving you should go ahead and start saving as much as you can on your own. One day he'll be grateful you did.

Also, I suggest a plan where each of you gets an allowance—a set amount each of you can call your own with a promise that you will limit your non-essential spending to that amount.

To understand how you and your spouse fit together financially, I'm sending you my book, *Debt-Proof Your Marriage*. You'll learn how much easier it is to talk—not fight—about money.

Come clean, tell husband now

Q: My debt is huge and my husband does not know the extent. This has happened before, and each time the debt has gotten worse. I have a problem with being honest about money.

Instead of telling him we are in trouble, I take out another card and get a cash advance to pay bills. Shopping is not the problem. The problem is that I look at available credit as available cash.

Why my husband hasn't left me is a good question. He is a very honest, loyal and moral person and I don't deserve to be with him, or raising our daughters.

His company (he's worked there for 15 years) is about to do a credit check on him. If he loses his job because of me, I don't know what I will do.

I feel at this point the only option is to confess and leave. I will get a better job and give him money towards the bills. Thank you for listening.

A: Tell him everything (and I mean all of it), but don't leave. You need to stay and take full responsibility with no expectations of his forgiveness or help with the debt.

If you get either, that is mercy, which you do not deserve. You need to devise a plan for how you are going to right this wrong. You have a problem, and it goes much deeper than what you've written here. That doesn't mean there is no hope.

I believe you and your husband could benefit greatly by seeking professional help with a good, reputable, compassionate counselor who deals with issues of addiction.

If I were you, I would find a Celebrate Recovery group (CelebrateRecovery.com). These groups meet in churches. At one of these groups you will find compassionate people who share your addictive personality and struggles, people who have found the help, hope and the forgiveness they seek. Celebrate Recovery is a wonderful organization and I hope you will check it out.

Your situation, while grave, is not hopeless. It's just that until now you have never wanted to change badly enough. Your love of credit outweighs your love for your husband.

Those pesky in-laws

Q: My in-laws have been deeply in debt and in poor health for years. When they pass on, will their children be expected to absorb their debt?

How should we plan ahead for this? They have refused all offers of counseling or help with budgeting.

A: Generally speaking, unless your husband and his siblings are cosigners on their parents' mortgage, credit-card accounts or other obligations, they cannot be held liable for those debts.

Upon the death of the first parent, the joint debts and assets, if any, will pass to the surviving parent. And when he or she dies, the creditors will look to whatever remains in the estate to satisfy all outstanding debts through a process called probate.

If there are not sufficient assets to satisfy their debts, the creditors lose. They cannot go after relatives or children.

Of course, the creditors get paid before children when it comes to handing out inheritances. In your case it sounds as if your husband is not counting on an inheritance anyway.

So, love them, do what you can for them now, but don't worry about getting stuck with their debts.

When adult children boomerang

Q: Our 25-year-old son is moving home (after five years of being on his own) with few possessions and an unbelievable amount of debt.

My husband and I don't know how to guide or support him through this period. We do not plan to assist him outright with money, and we definitely have a plan for the living situation. But what steps should he take so we know he is heading in the right direction financially?

We aren't sure what financial recovery looks like.

A: I suggest you create a list of House Rules, like those below, which he must abide by if he moves back. Failure to do so means he must leave.

Rule 1: He must enroll in credit counseling with a reputable organization (find the closest to you at NFCC.org) that offers a debt management program.

Rule 2: He has to enroll in that debt management program.

Rule 3: No credit cards, no debit card. One ATM card only. This will force an all-cash lifestyle. Money orders will accommodate bills to be mailed.

Rule 4: All adult children must pay reasonable room and board.

These four rules will force him to live a cash lifestyle and get him onto a debt repayment path that is being monitored and managed by someone other than his parents.

Last, make it very clear that you are not going to bail him out with any loans, advances or other forms of aid.

That's what I would do. As a mom, I know it will be harder for you to follow the House Rules than for him. But that will be the key to his success.

Inheriting parents' debts

Q: If my parents are in debt and they die, who pays the bills? I am terrified of inheriting my parents' debts.

A: When a person dies, creditors can only look to his or her estate (the assets that person owned upon his or her death) for the payment of debts.

If the debts are shared legally with another person still living, as in the case of a spouse in a community property state, or someone else who can sign on the account, that person may be responsible for part or all of the debt.

Call the Consumer Protection Division, Office of Attorney General in your state's capitol to find out the specific laws governing your state.

It is my opinion that unless you are a cosigner with your parents on their debts, you could not be held responsible in the event of their death. And their creditors could collect only to the extent your parents left assets in their estates.

And now for the bad news. If your parents do leave assets that you will inherit, creditors get to stand in line ahead of you. Let's say your parents leave a home, cars, personal property, stocks, bonds or other items of value. The estate would be required to liquidate them to pay creditors. Then if there's anything left, it is distributed to the heirs according to the terms of the deceaseds' will and or trust.

So, while you would not have to pay your parents' debts directly to their creditors, what you might have otherwise inherited will be reduced by what they left owing and from what you would have otherwise received.

Ultimate deceit

Q: My wife passed away recently. I'd trusted her to take care of our bills.

Shortly after her death, I began receiving bills for a bunch of credit cards I didn't even know we had, all of them in both our names. We were retired and, I thought, debt-free.

Now I am left owing thousands of dollars, and it is taking almost all of my retirement just to pay the minimum payments.

The companies are charging 21 to 24 percent interest, leaving me barely enough to live on. I don't want to file for bankruptcy and lose almost all of what I worked hard to own.

I would like to be debt-free again one day. Your advice would be most appreciated.

A: As a wife who hid credit-card bills from her husband (I do have a bit of a dark financial past), your letter sent chills up my spine but also made me grateful that those days are behind us.

I am curious to know how your name got on those credit-card applications. If forged, you may not be a legal cosigner and therefore may not be liable for the debts. You need to speak with an attorney who deals with consumer issues and is familiar with your state law.

If you are legally responsible for these debts, contact Consumer Credit Counseling Services (CCCS) right away. They may be able work with your creditors to get those interest rates reduced significantly and also set up a payment schedule you can handle.

I wish you well and hope your story comes as a wake-up call to anyone reading this who is hiding debt from his or her spouse.

Without trust you have nothing

Q: I have been dating a woman for about two years. Getting to know her, I have learned that she has significant financial problems that she has not told me about. I have found out by doing a little research on my own (public records etc.).

This is a serious relationship. We are both divorced with children. Money issues were one of the things that led to the breakup of my first marriage and hers, also.

I am recovering from my past mistakes and well on my way to living debt-free.

What is the best way to approach this with her?

A: First, let me say that the single most important factor in marriage is mutual trust. Regardless of everything else you love about this woman and her kids, without trust you have nothing. It's all emotional.

If she will mislead and lie to you about this most important issue, can you trust her in any other area?

I am not saying that she hasn't confronted her past financial problems and made a successful change. However, in that you put this in the present tense ("...she has significant financial problems ...") I'm going to assume that hasn't happened.

I can tell you from my own experience that your beloved is afraid that if you find out who she really is—warts and all—you will reject her. She's trying to present the best package possible to assure a future with you.

Can broken trust be restored? Yes, absolutely it can, but it is a process that takes time and two individuals, not only one, who are totally committed to fidelity and the restoration of that broken trust.

If you have never had a completely honest relationship with this woman, you may have little, if anything, to restore. You are trying to build this relationship on the equivalent of quicksand.

I suggest that you trade credit reports before you invest any more time into the relationship. A credit report can be an amazingly accurate character report. Granted, credit reports can contain errors and she may be able to explain an item or two. But outstanding balances, judgments, liens, collections, and patterns of behavior cannot be hidden or explained away.

If she agrees and then comes clean with her situation and problems with money, you should consider investing in couples counseling.

If she refuses to show you her credit report you should see that as more than a caution flag. That's when I would tell you to grab the kids and run, not walk, away from this relationship.

Mind your own business

Q: How does one go about telling a loved one she is ruining her financial life? I have an older sister who is a spendaholic; her husband is co-dependent and they have a spoiled brat for a daughter who gets everything she wants.

They are at least $25,000 in credit-card debt, have a car loan and other debts and bills, yet continue to spend like they have money. Recently she picked up a $10,000 bonus check. She told me she was going to "knock down some of the balances." This week they are shopping for a hot tub to put in their back yard.

A: I know how difficult it is to stand by and watch those we love make serious financial blunders. But these are not your dependent children. It is really none of your business what they do with their money or the way they raise their child.

The way you conduct your financial life will speak much louder than anything you could say. Keep your unsolicited advice to yourself and your nose out of their financial lives.

In the meantime devise a plan of recovery you would recommend just in case they come to you and ask for your advice. They just might.

A lesson from Judge Judy

Q: A year ago, I made a loan to a friend who quickly became unfriendly, acted rudely when we would meet and then became hostile when the money issue was mentioned.

Within a few weeks after making the loan, contact between us ceased. We had no formal agreement and the certified bank check that I gave to this person didn't even have a memo note that it was a loan.

I did make the loan from my Merrill Lynch business cash management account. What are my options? How can I get my money back? Thanks for your help. Your books and newsletter have been extremely helpful to me.

A: I'm not going to beat you up by pointing out that unless you can see it as a gift, never lend money to a friend or family member. And I won't give you a hard time about not reducing this matter to a written agreement. I'm sure you've already punished yourself more than adequately.

Based on a recent episode of the TV show, "Judge Judy" (I am not kidding), I think you should file in Small Claims Court to recover this loan. You have no contract, and no proof at all that this was a loan and not a gift. In fact, you have very little except your memory and a copy of a cancelled certified check (you can get that from the bank for a small fee).

But neither did the plaintiff on the show. And she prevailed simply because the judge believed her. So I say, go for it.

It costs very little (maybe $15) to sue in Small Claims Court. Of course you'll need to visit your local courthouse to find out the limitations and procedures. At that point it becomes your word against that former friend. If you win either by decree or default, then you'll have to learn how to collect on judgments. I doubt if this creep has the cash.

You may be able to deduct this as a loss when you file your income taxes (consult your tax professional).

In any case, don't underestimate the value of having learned a very difficult life lesson.

Teaching kids to manage money

Q: My husband and I are trying to teach our 12- and 13-year-old daughters about money.

The girls get a weekly allowance and we've agreed that if they run out of money before the week ends, that's it. We won't give them more.

When they do run out my husband slips them cash when he thinks I'm not looking. How can I make him understand he's hurting them in the long run?

A: Approach your husband in a way that will not put him on the defensive. Say something like, "Do you think we should reconsider the kids' allowances and maybe give them a raise?" If he says yes, do it.

If he says no, say you're tempted to slip them extra money during the week, but worried about the message that will send. Either response will initiate a conversation and opportunity to revisit your shared objectives, such as:

Why are the two of you doing this and what do you hope the kids will learn from it?

Right at the top of your list should be to teach them about real life. Once adults, they cannot expect to run to the boss for a handout to tide them over until the next payday.

Good luck. You are to be commended for teaching your kids to manage money. Any effort will come back to bless them, and you—many times over!

Include taxes and insurance, or not?

Q: Is it better to have my homeowners insurance and property taxes included in my monthly mortgage payment, or should I pay those items separately?

A: Opt to have them included in your monthly payment. Sure your monthly payment will be higher, but you will soon get used to it. Then you won't have to worry about quarterly or semi-annual property tax and insurance payments.

Here's the problem if you do not have them included: You forget they're coming and that always means for a big surprise.

If you are not prepared, you might find yourself running to the credit cards because you have not been setting money aside each month in anticipation.

Down payment on a home

Q: Will I have to come up with a big down payment now that the real estate market is in such bad shape?

A: Yes, I believe we are about to see a return to the days when 20 percent down payments were standard. But look at that as a good thing. You will start out with equity.

Because many lenders are now requiring borrowers to qualify for a mortgage based on their debt and income, you'll be less likely to get into a situation you cannot afford.

NYC renters need parents to cosign

Q: My son recently graduated from college. He and his two roommates are moving to New York City.

I've been informed that for them to rent an apartment, each parent must submit a current W-2, the last two years' tax returns and a verification of employment from the parent's employer.

The total annual income of all three must be at least $200,000 in order for the boys to qualify.

I am reluctant to release my personal info for this. I can understand the owner's desire for qualifying renters, but I thought the use of Social Security numbers and other personal information was restricted by law. Is this a common practice?

A: The law does not restrict a potential landlord from checking a prospective tenant's credit history.

The law does, however, require that it be done only with the prospective tenant's written permission. That's why your son, his friends and all guarantors (parents) will be required to sign a rental or lease application that gives the landlord permission to pull copies of your credit reports as part of a background check. There is nothing untoward about this.

If these boys turn out to be deadbeats, the apartment owner wants to know he'll be able to collect from the guarantor, which would be you and the other parents.

Landlords these days have to be very careful to whom they rent. Not paying the rent is not necessarily all it takes to evict a tenant.

Eviction requires court filings and attorneys and all kinds of crazy processes just to get the non-paying renters to move out. It's not easy!

I believe the prospective landlord is doing his due diligence on the front end to reduce the chances of ending up with occupants who won't pay, but won't get out either.

Debt and that squished feeling

Q: We would like to enlarge our small two-bedroom Chicago bungalow. Our kids are reaching the teen years and we need more space. We have always budgeted our money.

We have $6,000 in our Freedom Account, drive two paid-for cars and our only debt is our mortgage. We have college savings accounts for our kids and tithe to our church. Our annual income is about $130,000.

We have five different bids and they all came in about the same at $160,000 to add three rooms upstairs plus a stairway. Even though I know adding 900 square feet will increase the value of our home, I feel queasy about increasing our mortgage debt. What is your advice for us?

A: I can understand that you are nervous about taking on a new monthly payment. Here's a good way to find out if you can reasonably afford to do this:

Figure out what your new monthly payment will be using any mortgage calculator you can find on the Internet or at *DebtProofLiving.com.* Starting now, live as if you have already taken on this new expense. Start making the payment to yourselves every month, on time and without fail. How does that feel? Can you sleep? Stressed out

of your mind? You'll know in a few months if you can handle this.

It seems to me that you are in a good financial situation. You have no unsecured debt, you are preparing well for the future and you have a substantial income.

Provided you have at least three months' of living expenses put away in your Contingency Fund (six is better) and if you can continue to live on 80 percent of your income, this sounds like a reasonable risk that will improve your lives and increase your net worth, too. This is exciting!

Housing dilemma

Q: The rent on our three-bedroom house went up from $850 to $1,000. We were struggling before, so we really can't afford the increase. We have looked in an apartment community where our rent would be around $750 a month.

I found another home that could be a great permanent family home. This one is a rental, with the option to purchase. The monthly rent on this is $1,000.

We have huge student loan balances and our credit isn't that great.

Should we move to the cheaper apartment, into the house with the higher rent and option to purchase, or should we just stay where we are?

A: Okay, now I am really confused. If you are already struggling to make your $850 rent each month, how are you going to handle $1,000 a month—with or without an option to purchase clause?

Have you looked carefully at the conditions and terms on that option? Typically, what that means is that a portion of the rent you pay will be credited against the purchase price, if and when you are able to buy. That could be a small amount, like $25 a month. Given the information you've given me—even if that option to purchase is very favorable—I would advise you to go with the $750 apartment.

You need to cut expenses, not add to them. Lower rent plus a strong commitment to go on a spending diet should give you the boost you need to get your debts paid in the next two or three years. Then you'll be ready to start looking for a home to buy.

Home protection warranty limitations

Q: Last year, we purchased a 100-year-old house that came with a one-year home warranty, protecting items such as the electrical, heating, appliances, roof and siding.

During our first year the heater failed and was repaired under the warranty. We paid only the $100 deductible. Should we renew the policy? The premium is $385 for another year. The roof is 25-years old and in bad shape. We're sure it would cost considerably more than the $385 annual premium to replace it.

A: Before you make a decision, take a close look at the policy. What does it cover specifically? There's a big difference between repairing a furnace and replacing a roof.

Typically, a home protection warranty covers repairs necessary to bring the item to the condition it was on the day you became the owner. I could be wrong, but I don't think you will ever get a new roof from this policy.

There's only one way to find out for sure: Read the policy. If you can get a new roof for $385, that will be the deal of the century, in which case you'll know what to do.

Overwhelmed by Costco

Q: I am new to Costco, having dragged my feet to join because our budget really doesn't allow for anything past our normal grocery bill.

My friends go WILD and shop at rates that take my breath away. I believe I can save on particular items, especially paper products.

Any suggestions on how I can navigate such an overwhelming shopping experience?

A: I'm not convinced you will save on paper products at Costco. You'll get high quality and huge quantities but you can beat Costco's prices if you buy your paper products on sale at the supermarket when you also have a coupon—or at a discount department store like Target or Wal-Mart.

Some things are cheaper at the warehouse clubs (milk, cheese, frozen chicken breasts, for example). The problem is that you have to buy a lot in a year's time to save enough to break even on your membership fee.

I suggest you never take a checkbook or plastic to Costco. Take only a written list and cash. You will not be so tempted to buy things you didn't even know you needed until you wandered up and down the aisles. Like 50 pounds of onions or a plasma screen TV you simply can't live without.

Doing right by the kids

Q: What is the right thing to do when you honestly cannot afford to put your kids in sports, like Little League baseball, but you know it is such a good thing for them both physically and socially?

A: The right thing is to live within your means and not go into debt. That's the underlying principle that should guide all financial decisions.

If this is a high priority as you look at your total financial picture, decide what you will sacrifice to free up the

money for childhood enrichment activities.

Think about reasonable alternatives. Does your Parks and Recreation Department offer organized sports? What about the YMCA or a local church?

If there are other parents in the same situation, perhaps you could organize a neighborhood league of some kind. If your kids really want to play as much as you want them to, get them into a serious savings program now so they can help pay their fees next season.

Skimming funds from partnership

Q: My wife has always insisted on balancing our joint checkbook and I recently found out why.

The bank statement came yesterday while I was home so I decided to open it. I was shocked to see a check to her brother for $350.

I went through a couple of prior statements and found the same thing. I figure she's been doing this since her parents died several years ago.

We're not exactly rolling in dough. We have three kids and a big mortgage and money is tight. If she'd asked or at least discussed this with me, I would not have refused to help him, but this is way out of line in my opinion. How should I broach the subject with her?

A: Skimming money is a real problem for any partnership, especially a marriage. But money problems in a marriage are rarely only about the money. There's usually an underlying issue.

If she'd asked me, I would have told your wife that as noble as her intentions might be to help her brother, her commitment to you and your marriage trumps everything. It's wrong to do this behind your back.

Since you wrote, let me ask you: Why do you think she felt compelled to deceive you in this way? There was a time she told you everything. Maybe she believed you'd hit the roof if she brought it up.

I suggest that you go to her as a loving husband and partner, not a raging foe. Tell her how hurt you are that she couldn't talk to you about this.

Assure her that you are willing to talk now. Tell her that if you are going to enjoy financial harmony in your marriage, everything has to be on the table, her spending and yours too. Talk it out. I'm sure you can negotiate a compromise you can both live with.

A mortgage quandary

Q: I am retired and have a mortgage of $89,000 at 5 percent interest. I have enough money in my 401K to pay off the mortgage. Should I do this?

A: I don't have enough information to begin to advise you on this because it depends on your age, the total amount in your retirement account and how you have those funds invested currently. I can give you some ideas to consider.

Like all investments, money in a 401(k) is money at risk. Even if you have selected low-risk investments, you could lose it.

Your debt, on the other hand, is a sure thing and investing in it will give you a guaranteed return of 5 percent (the exact rate you are now paying). This is how that works:

Let's say you are currently paying $1,000 a year in interest on your mortgage. If you take $89,000 from your account and pay it off, you get to keep that $1,000 every year going forward. That is your return on the $89,000 investment you made in your debt. It's a sure thing regardless what happens to the market or real estate values and a wise move if you have sufficient money in the bank.

Knowing your home is paid for offers a certain amount of security in the face of a changing economy.

However, if doing this would deplete your retirement account and you have many years ahead of you, it may not be wise for you invest your money in this way at this time.

Especially in retirement, you need the security of readily available cash. I recommend you get sound advice from a counselor you trust who knows all the details of your financial situation.

Biweekly mortgage payments

Q: I recall my father paying his mortgage twice a month and saving a lot of interest. How does that work?

A: The theory is that by paying one-half of your mortgage payment every two weeks, in one year you will have made 26 half-payments or the equivalent of 13 monthly payments.

Using this tactic it is possible to pay a 30-year mortgage in about 22 years and avoid paying a lot of interest. The theory is great but there are a few pitfalls to consider.

First, mortgage companies will not accept half-payments unless you have enrolled in their biweekly mortgage payment programs. And they charge fees for that—$400 or more to enroll and then an additional fee is tacked on to each biweekly payment. Once enrolled, you're stuck with that plan, too. You can't go back to monthly without a hassle.

There is a clever way you can do this on your own—without your mortgage company's permission or approval while keeping your options open to go back to your regular payment schedule whenever you like.

Do this: Each month when you make your regular mortgage payment, write a second check equal to one-twelfth (1/12) of one payment. Clearly write in the memo area: "Principal Prepayment Only."

Because this second check will arrive with your regular payment it will be seen and credited as an over payment, not a partial payment.

Repeat each month. At the end of one year you will have made the equivalent of 13 monthly payments. Bingo! You have paid exactly what you would have with a biweekly plan without the fees and obligation to continue.

If things get tight you can always stop sending that extra check each month. Then start again as you are able.

One note of caution: Your mortgage is the last debt you want to pay off because it is a low-interest obligation that gives you a modicum of tax relief.

If you are carrying credit-card debt, student loan debt or other high-interest, unsecured debt—you need to pay those debts in full before you accelerate paying your mortgage.

Interest-only mortgage

Q: I have an interest-only mortgage which was the only way I could keep my house after a divorce. My plan is to put any extra money (gifts, rebates, etc.) on the principal and refinance in a few years. My rate is 6.375 percent for the entire length of the loan.

Is there a way to figure out how much to add to the payment each month to make it like a conventional loan?

A: You have a terrible—worse than horrible—mortgage. I wouldn't be surprised if it contains a prepayment penalty clause which could preclude you from making principal payments at this time. But you need to check that out, and I mean do it now.

I am hoping that since you wrote, you have already refinanced this into a 30-year fixed rate mortgage. Mortgage rates are way down so now is the time to do this.

Okay, back to your question. What you need is a mortgage calculator with an amortization schedule.

Do an Internet search or use the one at *Bankrate.com*. Click on "calculators." Find the Mortgage Payment Calculator and input the amount of your principal balance, the interest rate and the number of years.

When you press "calculate" you will get a figure that is the payment you need to make every month so that by the end of the term you have reached $0 and you own your home outright. The amortization schedule will show how each payment is divided between interest and principal.

Because so much of one's payment goes toward interest in the early months and years of a mortgage, the difference between interest-only and a fully amortized payment is not that much. For example a loan of $165,000 at 6.38 percent for 30 years has fully amortized principal and interest payments of $1,030. In the first month $877 of that amount is for interest, $153 is principal.

If you choose to pay only the $877 each month you will never get started paying off your mortgage. No matter how long you make those interest-only payments, you will still owe $165,000.

I hope you'll find a way to get started with amortized payments as soon as possible, unless you have already refinanced. Which I pray you have.

First-time home-buying teacher

Q: I'm a teacher and want to buy a house. I have heard of programs to help teachers purchase homes with little or no money down.

Recently I read that you don't recommend "no-down" mortgages. Why not?

A: I hope I did not discourage you from buying a home. That would certainly not be my intent.

The problem with a nothing-down transaction is that the interest rate is typically adjustable. And without a down payment the payment will be high from the start.

For someone who is strapped for cash already, this can easily put a new homeowner in over her head.

Now, having said that let me be quick to say that if your state has special programs for teachers or other plans for first-time home buyers, they may have caps on interest rates or other safety measures. It will cost you nothing to find out and I encourage you to do that.

I would speak with an experienced Realtor in your area. He or she should be especially knowledgeable about all of the loan programs available in your state and also about special loans for teachers.

Be realistic about what you can afford and should there be provisions for the monthly payment to increase, you can be sure that it will. I wish you well in going after your dream.

Haunted by her financial past

Q: My husband and I are looking to buy our first home, and I'm a little nervous about applying for a mortgage. During my single days, I got into a heap of trouble with credit-card debt and filed for bankruptcy.

Since then, I've been extremely careful about spending and saving but I'm still worried about what my past recklessness has done to my credit.

Even worse, I haven't been able to bring myself to tell my budget-conscious husband about it. What can I do to make sure this doesn't ruin our chances of getting a home?

A: You've been hiding a very important part of yourself from your husband. Had you asked me before you married, I would have strongly suggested that you and your beloved bare your financial souls by trading credit reports. Of course it's not too late. But it will be if you don't do this soon.

Talk to him about this, order your individual reports and then review them together. He loves you, remember? By opening the part of your life you have been hiding you will free yourself to love and to be loved even more deeply.

Many lenders look at patterns of behavior, so if you can show at least six months of on-time payments, you may be in a lot better shape than you think.

Check out the website *My Fico.com* and click on "Credit Education" to learn how credit scores are determined and what you can do to improve yours.

The sooner you and your husband see this challenge as "us against the problem" not "us against each other," the sooner you'll be sending out change-of-address notices.

Moving? Take your equity with you

Q: I hear that making mortgage prepayments in addition to regular monthly payments can save a lot of money in the long run. But the qualifier always seems to be, "...if you plan to stay in your house." Why is this?

We move every two to four years so what options would be the smartest for us?

A: I don't know the reasoning behind that "qualifier" you've heard, but I do not agree with it.

Prepaying your principal is like adding money to a savings account called "equity." When you sell this house you should move all of your equity into the down payment on the next one. The more money you have to put down, the less money you'll need to borrow for the mortgage.

If you are diligent to move your equity in its entirety into the next home and the next and continue to make principal prepayments, your equity will grow more rapidly and that means your mortgage requirement will continue to shrink until that blessed day that you own your home free and clear.

Selling one house and buying another does not have to interrupt the equity-building process.

One cautionary note: Whenever you make a principal prepayment, write a separate check and clearly note that the money is meant to prepay the principal. If it's not noted, your mortgage company could hold it and apply it to your next monthly payment, which will have almost no positive effect.

Negotiate Realtor fees?

Q: Recently, my husband and I have started house hunting. A very nice Realtor took us to see three homes. We loved one of them except it was a few thousand dollars out of our price range— just enough of a difference to break the deal. My husband had the bright idea of asking the Realtor if she would take less of a commission.

I was really embarrassed. I thought you could only negotiate on the price of the house, not haggle over the Realtor fees. Am I right?

A: It is illegal for the industry to set one commission rate, so real estate commissions are negotiable. For a $176,500 median-priced house in America, a 6-percent commission comes to $10,590 or $5,295 to each of the agents—your Realtor and the one who listed the property. Then both of them split 50/50 with their respective brokerage firms to cover overhead and expenses.

In that scenario your agent will earn $2,647. If this house has been on the market for a long time and she needs to close a deal, she may be motivated to contribute part of her fee to help you out. It would be appropriate for you to ask, especially if she knew that this property was out of your price range before she showed it to you. And it would be perfectly appropriate for her to decline, which she may if she has plenty of clients in a buyers' market (when there are fewer homes for sale than people who want to buy them, which sadly is not the case at this writing).

I am concerned however, that you may be flirting with trouble. Let's say she agrees to give you $500 or even $1,000 of her commission. If that's enough for you to make this deal you may be setting yourselves up for disaster if that is not enough to bring the sale price into your price range.

The worst mistake home buyers make is getting in over their heads. My best advice is to look at homes that are priced below the most you can afford. You can always upgrade in a few years.

Nothing-down? Nothing doing!

Q: What do you think of $0 down home mortgages? We have no money for a down payment and both the seller and his lender are trying to get us to go for this nothing-down conventional loan. Would you do it?

A: I wouldn't touch that with a ten-foot pole, and neither should you. What you are considering is a "sub-prime" loan. It's called that because you as a consumer fall beneath the traditionally acceptable qualifications for a mortgage-holder. You have a

high failure rate, which can only be spelled one way: Foreclosure.

If this is a variable-rate loan, you must expect that the interest rate will increase dramatically over the term. With nothing down, your payments are going to start out large and go up from there.

Should real estate values drop, you could end up owing more on your home than it's worth and then you'll be stuck.

My advice is to stay where you are but live as though you have that big new house payment. Just stash the difference into a savings account. Before you know it you'll have a down payment and you'll know if you can handle a big house payment.

Use savings to pay mortgage?

Q: We have $62,000 remaining on our home mortgage. We have the money sitting in our savings account and I'm just itching to pay off the house. Is this the wise thing to do?

A: I wish I knew how much you have in the bank. If it's exactly $62,000 and paying off your mortgage would leave you with nothing in the bank, it would not be advisable.

You need to have enough money in the bank to cover all of your living expenses for at least six months. You just never know when your income stream will be cut off or if you will have some other major emergency. You want to be in a position to fund your own emergencies.

However, if you have no other debts, enough in the bank for a six-month Contingency Fund, plus enough to pay off, or even to pay down your mortgage, paying off your mortgage would be highly advisable.

You are in an enviable position to have this option.

The magic of making double payments

Q: Would you please explain how making double mortgage payments works to reduce the principal?

A: Sure! Let's say you have these loan terms: $150,000 principal at 6 percent interest for 15 years. Your monthly payments are $1,265.78.

You are about to make your first monthly payment. If you asked for an amortization schedule you know that payment will be allocated $750 to interest, and $515.78 to the principal.

After you make your first double payment, your new principal balance is $149,484.21, because the entire $1,265.78 of your second payment went toward reducing the principal balance or for "principal prepayment."

You can make any amount of additional principal payment during the month once you have paid the pay-

ment and interest due—it doesn't have to be a full payment.

Just for fun, I ran the numbers with you making double payments every month using the example figures above. You might think that cuts everything in half. But the results are far more dramatic than that.

You would pay that 15-year mortgage in 6 years 11 months and slash the total interest you would have paid over 15 years ($77,841.93) to only $28,336.77. That's the power of prepaying the principal.

I suggest when making a principal prepayment that you write a separate check and write in the memo area: "Principal Prepayment Only."

Should you ever want to make several regularly scheduled payments ahead of time because you'll be going out of the country or for some other reason you need to pay your bills in advance, be sure your mortgage company knows without any doubt that you are making your payments "ahead." Otherwise they could use them to prepay the principal, leaving your regular payments due while you are gone.

You don't want to arrive home to a foreclosure notice.

Mortgage protection insurance

Q: What are your thoughts on mortgage protection insurance? We just bought a home and received a letter offering this to us. It would pay our mortgage if either of us dies. Thanks.

A: I think it's a bad idea. Mortgage protection insurance is a very expensive life insurance policy with a diminishing face value. Generally this kind of insurance is tied to mortgage and pays the remaining balance upon the death of the homeowner.

As you pay down your mortgage, the face value (the amount the survivor would receive) decreases too, while the premiums remain high. Wouldn't you expect that as the principal balance remaining shrinks, the cost of the insurance to pay off that balance would shrink proportionately? But it doesn't work that way.

In the event of a claim—let's say your husband dies—the company will pay off your mortgage.

That might sound great now, but years from now when your mortgage is very low and your situation has changed, paying it off might not be advisable.

I suggest you forego the mortgage protection insurance (not to be confused with private mortgage insurance or PMI which is another topic altogether) and buy term life insurance instead.

Now you'll have a low premium, fixed coverage and options in the event one of you dies. The survivor will get a check in the mail, not a paid-in-full mortgage. Paying off the mortgage with the life insurance money will be one of your options but not your only option.

A mortgage is a closed-end contract

Q: It takes about two weeks after I mail my mortgage payment for the check to clear my bank. My sister says my lender is making me pay more interest by delaying depositing my check. Is it true?

A: No. Your sister may be confusing your mortgage, a "closed-end contract," with an open-end contract like a credit-card account or other debt where the balance fluctuates up and down depending on how much of your available credit you are using. The law treats the two differently.

A closed-end contract has a fixed payment schedule. The interest portion of your monthly mortgage payment is the same whether you pay it early in the cycle or at the last minute.

A credit card or revolving open-end contract works differently. Making your payment early in the cycle allows more of it to go to the principal because interest is figured on the average daily balance.

Federal law as stated in The Fair Credit Billing Act (FCBA) requires open-end lenders to credit all payments to your account on the date they're received, "unless no extra charges would result if they failed to do so."

With your mortgage payment it doesn't matter on which day during the month it is processed, provided any delays do not result in a late fee. In fact, tell your sis that a delay could be to your benefit if your money is earning interest while it sits in the bank.

If you'd like to read highlights of all of the provisions of the FCBA go to *FTC.gov* click on "For Consumers" and then on "credit."

Tax deduction is a consolation prize

Q: I have heard from a number of reputable sources that having a mortgage is very good for one's financial situation. Would you explain why?

A: I'm assuming these "reputable sources" (probably mortgage lenders if my experience serves me well) are referring to the fact that the interest you pay on your primary residence is deductible when you itemize on your federal tax return.

What that means is if you are in the 28 percent tax bracket, for every $1 you spend in mortgage interest you can reduce your tax bill by 28 cents.

Who in his right mind would chose to have a mortgage just so he could pay 72 cents to get back 28 cents? Is that just incredibly stupid, or what? The truth is if you have a mortgage you still have to pay that interest and you will never get back anywhere near all of it.

For me getting a deduction for our mortgage interest is like a consolation

prize. Until I can pay off my mortgage in full, the deduction eases the pain of having to pay interest.

The truth is I don't want the deduction. I cannot wait until I don't have to pay any interest at all and claim absolutely no mortgage interest on my federal and state tax returns.

If you are choosing to keep your mortgage to protect your deduction, I'll make you a better deal than the IRS: You send me all your $1 bills and I promise to send back 50 cents for every single one. Guaranteed. I'll be watching my mail.

Use inheritance to pay off mortgage?

Q: Soon I will receive an inheritance that is almost equal to the amount remaining on my mortgage. I am a widow, age 55 with no dependents.

I have 25 years with the same employer and have been participating in the company's 401k plan for the past 15 years. I plan to work until I am 65.

Should I use the inheritance to pay off the mortgage or, as friends suggest, invest it and keep my mortgage because the interest is tax-deductible?

A: You need to check with your tax professional (a little something my attorney likes me to mention, as I am not a CPA nor am I an attorney), but if I were you, I'd pay off that mortgage so fast the lender would get dizzy.

Investing in your debt is always a wise decision because you cannot lose. If you pay off your mortgage, no matter what happens to the economy you'll enjoy a rent-free retirement.

As for the deductibility of mortgage interest, it is highly overrated. Your friends are not the only one's who don't get that a tax deduction for mortgage interest is a consolation prize for those of us who have no choice but to pay on a mortgage. I know, I just explained this to another reader, but let me do that again in a slightly different way. Let's say you pay $1,000 a year in mortgage interest and you are in the 15 percent tax bracket. By deducting $1,000 from your taxable income, you realize a $150 reduction in the tax you owe.

Does that make sense to you, to choose to pay $1,000 so you can get $150 back? If so, I have a better deal for you: You send me $1,000 every year and I promise to send back $500 every April 15, no questions asked. In fact, you don't even have to fill out any forms or prove a thing.

Please be sure to run this past a tax professional to learn what kind of a taxable event, if any, this may trigger for you.

How long to retain records and receipts?

Q: How long should we keep personal financial records like receipts and canceled checks?

A: The Internal Revenue Service usually has three years to audit your return, so you should keep all the relevant records at least that long. But it's important to keep some records longer.

• Most records of income and expense: At least three years, seven if possible.

• Property or investment: Until you sell.

• Real estate (initial cost, improvements, costs of selling): Until seven years after you sell.

• Tax returns: At least six years, ideally forever.

• Keep receipts attached to the owner's manual or warranty information for appliances or other durable goods for as long as you own them.

Yes, you need a Freedom Account

Q: I have no unsecured debts, only a mortgage. Do I still need a Freedom Account?

A: Yes. One hundred percent, absolutely and without a doubt.

Your Freedom Account—which you create yourself by opening a second checking account in the same bank or credit union where you have your household account—is a management tool into which you put money each month in anticipation of irregular, unexpected and intermittent expenses.

These irregular, intermittent and unexpected expenses have a tendency to take us by surprise because they do not recur on a regular monthly basis—things like taxes, vacations, car repairs, gifts, summer camp, and Christmas.

A Freedom Account has nothing to do with unsecured debts or even your mortgage.

Your Freedom Account will help you become a savvy money manager. That will bring to you great confidence and personal security.

Should I buy the extended warranty?

Q: What do you think about extended warranties offered with just about anything you buy these days?

Recently we bought an adding machine. It came with a one-year warranty and for $5 more, we got two years. Did we do the right thing?

A: Here's the scoop on extended warranties, generally: They represent a very low risk for the "insurer" and thus a high profit center for both the company and the salesperson. That should tell you that the chances of

you ever needing that extended warranty are very low.

Retailers use extended warranties as sales incentives. That salesperson who talked you into the $5.00 extended warrant probably saw $4.00 of it in his next commission check.

Here's my advice generally when it comes to extended warranties:

If the product is going to fail, statistics say it will do so during the manufacturer's warranty period. Pass on the extended warranty and create a special savings account just for Repairs.

Sock away the money you would have spent on the extended warranty into this account.

If you do have to make a repair, you'll have the money all ready to go in your Repairs account. What you don't end up spending on repairs could go to pay for a great vacation. That's how sure I am you'll never use most extended warranties.

Three exceptions:

1. The first year after buying a home that is not of new construction (on a new home all of the construction elements, appliances and other systems will carry their own separate manufacturers' warranties);

2. A previously-owned automobile that has a history of breakdown; and

3. Anything else that your independent research reveals is historically problematic such as a treadmill that gets a lot of use or a laptop computer.

Should I rent
or buy a home?

Q: I am 74, a widow and in reasonably good health. I've been renting. My Social Security and annuity income is adequate to cover my living expenses.

Should I buy a home? I have enough money to pay cash so I would have no mortgage. I could always sell it if I needed the money quickly.

A: Given your circumstances my advice is to continue renting.

Becoming a new homeowner in this season of your life could be more of a headache than a comfort. You need to be concentrating on safety and liquidity.

I would rather see you put that money into a variety of safe investment vehicles like certificates of deposit, money market funds and U.S. Treasury securities. That way, should you need cash to move into assisted living or some other type of care facility, you would be free to do so without concern for selling your home to realize the cash.

How do I deal with
guilt and remorse?

Q: We have been in credit-card debt for as long as I can remem-

ber. I am getting really excited to finally see light at the end of a very long and dark tunnel. But I am scared.

It is hard some days to keep my attitude positive. How do I get past the guilt of bad choices and terrible mistakes that landed us in such a horrible place of debt?

A: Look at the fear and guilt as built-in motivators that will keep you from going back to your old ways.

The way you respond to your situation is your choice. You can wallow in self-pity and make yourself miserable or you can choose to set a tone of joy in your home.

What you've done by making this U-turn on the road to financial devastation is fantastic! Just keep going and don't ever give up.

Meet me at our website every day for a dose of encouragement and to renew your commitment to living within your means and getting out of debt. No matter what.

What if expenses
exceed income?

Q: How do you set up a budget when your expenses outweigh your income? What category should be sacrificed? Savings? Food? I'm too frustrated to begin.

A: If your outgo regularly exceeds your income you have a situation that is spinning out of control and tantamount to a medical emergency. Financially speaking, you are bleeding to death. Critical situations, both medical and financial, require drastic measures.

You didn't give me specific details of your situation, so I am going to assume you are behind in your rent, over-limit and past-due on several credit cards. And probably overdrawn at the bank, too.

Your first job is to figure out how much money you need to bring everything current. $450? $600? More? Whatever it is, that is a critical number. What can you do to raise the funds? What can you sell? Maybe it's that second car or other tangible possessions you need to unload so you can turn them into cash.

You need to prioritize and that's something that can be difficult when you are in the middle of what feels like a firestorm.

Your first priority are matters of life and death. Basic food, prescription medications and shelter are at the top of the list—even if you have creditors breathing down your neck. You must pay your rent or mortgage or you will be out on the street.

Immediately stop all non-critical spending (read: life or death), even at the grocery store.

Most of us have plenty of food stashed in the freezer, pantry and refrigerator to survive for awhile and I bet you do too. Use it up! No milk? Drink water. No one will suffer irreparable harm by not drinking milk

for a few weeks. No fresh vegetables? Fine, eat the cans of pumpkin that have been lining your cupboards since last Thanksgiving.

The money you might normally spend on food can go toward this emergency situation. Don't get caught up in the lie that $10 doesn't matter because you owe $10,000. It does matter. It all adds up and that's true when you're getting into debt, and when you're climbing out.

Utility company's level-pay plans

Q: My electricity company offers a Level Pay Plan. They take the average of my bills for the past 12 months to determine my flat monthly amount for each month in the coming year.

I've become very budget conscious and wonder if you would recommend that I accept this option?

A: Most utility companies give this option and I think it is a great idea. Knowing exactly how much your utility bills will be each month will help you plan your spending more accurately.

Just remember that once each year these companies will look at your actual usage and then adjust accordingly.

If you've used less than projected, you'll get a refund. And if you've gone over you will have to make up the difference.

The only disadvantage I can see is that you might not be so diligent in cutting back your usage in any single month because no matter what you do it won't appear to make a difference.

Feeling rich and living it up

Q: My husband and I have been out of debt for approximately five years. It's great. The problem is we seem to spend a lot of money needlessly just because we can.

We have so much money over and above our living expenses that it is easy to be reckless.

We keep just enough in savings ($2,000 or so) for emergencies but never get beyond that goal.

I feel guilty about this. In a way it seems like it's always harvest time for us but we're not gathering for winter.

I just can't seem to control my spending. Any advice?

A: Getting out of debt was a great accomplishment, but quite frankly that only got you to the starting line. You're stuck. Your wheels are spinning, but you're not going anywhere.

I suspect the two of you have not decided on the guidelines that will determine disposition of your impressive income. Whether you make $5 or $500,000 you need to know ahead of time exactly what you will do with the money that flows into your life (and seems to be gushing out as quickly as it comes).

The 10-10-80 formula, which is at the core of Debt-Proof Living, is the answer. You give away 10 percent, save 10 percent, and then live the best life you can on 80 percent of your net income.

I think you might have some errant belief that because you are well-off you can spend with abandon. That's not true at all. Even the most wealthy cannot live as though money is of no concern. If they do, they're not wealthy long.

The cold hard truth is that even in your cushy condition you are living paycheck-to-paycheck.

If your income were suddenly snatched away through unemployment, a health disaster or other calamity (you should read my mail), you'd be in a world of hurt with only $2,000 in savings.

You need at least three months (six is better) of living expenses in your Contingency Fund. That is your first goal.

As for your spending problem, put yourself on a strict allowance that you and your husband agree upon. Pay it to yourself, putting that amount of cash into an envelope you carry in your handbag. When your allowance is gone, no more spending until next month.

You are in a most fortunate position and I hope you will take immediate steps to get yourselves unstuck and into high gear with managing your resources in a much better way. You have all the tools you need to build a solid base and a bright future.

Believe me when I say this: More money will never be enough until you learn how to take care of what you already have.

Drive that car until the wheels fall off

Q: I got into financial difficulty prior to finding you, but now I am diligently working toward reducing my debt.

Here's my dilemma: In about six weeks, I will pay off a loan which will free up $320 each month. My car is 10-years old and is beginning to need repairs.

I have very little in the way of savings.

Do I take the $320 each month and save it for a down payment on a car, add this amount to my current payment on my largest credit-card debt, or save for emergencies?

Considering that my credit standing isn't wonderful right now, I'm afraid that if I don't have a significant down payment for my next car, I will have a high interest rate or not qualify for a car at all.

Subscribing to *DebtProofLiv ing.com* and your newsletter has been a lifesaver for me! Thanks for all your help.

A: Your instincts are right on target. You need to start saving that $320 every month in anticipation of replacing your car.

Think of this as you think of any mandatory payment you must make each month. You have no options. You must pay it. The only difference is you are directing it to the Bank of You.

Don't be late, and don't even think about missing a payment. If you do not save for your next car and for emergencies in general, you will never get out of debt because every time something comes up you'll keep running back to your credit cards.

I'm saying a prayer that your car will run for at least three more years with minimal repairs. Find a good mechanic.

By then you will have saved up $11,520—more than enough to buy a gently used car with cash (don't buy new). And even if you should have to spend $1,000 to keep your current car together until them, you'll still be in good shape.

I am so proud of you—for all the progress you've made. Be sure to stay in touch so I can celebrate with you on your journey to financial freedom!

Online auto financing

Q: We just purchased a new car, and have only a few days to line up our financng. The bank and dealership interest rates are high. What do you think about online auto loans? Are they safe? My husband does not want to put our personal information out there because of identify theft and other reasons. Any advice on new car loans?

A: I think it's safe provided you stick with a well-known reputable lender like Capital One (*CapitalOne.com/autoloans*) which has an aggressive online auto loan program.

As I write, their lowest rate for a dealer-purchase new car is 5.44 percent. Read the privacy policy at the website regarding encryption and how they handle applications and client information. Personally, I don't think this is any different than walking into a bank and handing a stranger your application. You could always call Customer Service and arrange to send your application by fax or Certified Mail.

Can I sell my financed car?

Q: I am wondering if it is ever OK to sell a vehicle before it's paid.

I own a 2001 mini van that is in great shape. However, I'm now a single mom of one child and really have no use for a roomy, gas-guzzling van. I could sell it for $10,000 and have only 17 payments left which I make to a family member.

I am debating whether it would be advantageous to sell it, and use the proceeds to pay off my last credit card ($5,000) and then use the remaining money to buy the best used car I can find for $5,000. I just can't figure out what is best long-term, so any guidance would be much appreciated.

A: I like your idea. But you need to think this through.

First, let your lender know of your plan and desire to sell the vehicle that now secures that debt and your assurance that you will continue payments until your debt is paid in full.

Second, plan on a $5,000 used car needing occasional repair. If you can see your way clear on both of these issues, I like your idea a lot. And here's another idea:

Since you are used to making the car payment and a monthly payment on the $5,000 credit-card debt, increase your car payment each month by the amount you've been sending to the credit-card company. This will pay your debt even faster. And once paid, immediately begin paying yourself each month the payments you've been sending to your lender.

When it comes time to buy another car, you'll have enough money in the

Bank of You to fund your next car purchase. And what a happy day that will be!

Can I put a car on my credit card?

Q: My son owes $3,000 on his truck at 8.5 percent interest. Would it be smart to transfer the balance to my 5.5 percent credit card? I just wondered if I would save enough money to make it worthwhile. Thank you for your help!

A: OK. I am confused. If your son has a truck loan why are you considering paying it off with your credit card? How would this save you money?

I am going to assume that you are offering to help him out in an effort to reduce his payments or finish paying the debt more quickly with the lower interest.

The way I see it you have two issues here—the 3-percent difference in interest rates, but more importantly perhaps is the idea of you accepting the legal responsibility for his debt.

Sure, I know you think he can just make the payments to you, but it's not the same as your son being personally responsible to the creditors.

I ran the numbers and if he repays the $3,000 over 24 months at 8.5 percent, he'll pay just $98 more in interest over the term than at a 5.5 percent rate. That's a small price for the self-worth and dignity he'll gain in the long run if he retains sole responsibility for repaying this debt himself.

If that does not convince you, consider that his truck loan is at a fixed rate while your low credit-card rate is variable and could increase dramatically over the coming two years.

Another consideration: If adding $3,000 to this credit-card account will mean you're using more than 30 percent of your available credit on that account, your credit score could take a beating.

If I'm understanding your situation correctly, my advice is to leave the debt where it is and encourage your son to pay it off as quickly as possible. Allow him the satisfaction of having done this on his own.

Upside-down and inside out

Q: After several years of trading our vehicles in and upgrading each time we now have a big 2003 Chevy gas guzzler. We owe $33,335.82 on a zero-percent loan.

The top value, according to the Kelley Blue Book site (*KBB.com*), is $22,930 if we sell to a private party; $19,510 as a trade-in.

My husband doesn't think we can get out of this. We really regret all the bad choices we made and would be willing to drive something much cheaper. We have only have $1,400 in our

Contingency Fund. What are our choices?

A: You are "upside-down" in your loan to the tune of at least $11,000, meaning you owe that much more on this vehicle than it is worth.

Unfortunately, this is a very common occurrence in these days of long-term 0-percent interest on new car loans. That low monthly payment is so attractive most people fail to consider they won't have the option to sell the car for four or five years at the earliest. And if they do, as in your case, they roll the shortfall into the new loan making the upside-down potential even greater the next time around.

One option for you would be to sell the car then get a personal loan through your credit union or bank for the $11,000 difference. The payments on that new loan would surely be less than the current car payment. Then you could use the $1,400 to buy a clunker for temporary transportation. If you decide to keep the Chevy and tough it out, double up on your payments to speed things along, if you can.

At least that will improve your chances of having a car that's still running once it's paid in full.

Clobbered by the deficiency balance

Q: Is it legal for an auto finance company to make us liable for the cost of the vehicle after it was re-possessed and auctioned off at a fraction of the cost?

A: I am not an attorney and not qualified to offer you legal advice. However, you should be able to find the answer to this specific question by reading the fine print in your original loan document. What you are referring to is called the "deficiency balance" and it is my understanding that in most states lenders do have the legal right to hold a borrower responsible for that amount, provided the lender attempted to get the best price possible for the car.

I suggest you contact the lender right away to work out some kind of a payment schedule that both of you can live with.

This is not likely to go away on its own. If you do not pay they will sue you. And without any doubt in my mind they will get a "deficiency judgment." That means they can use any lawful means to get that money out of you, and probably all the court and attorney fees as well.

If you fail to take care of it now it will become a big black eye on your credit report and that could severely impact your ability to borrow, get a job, buy insurance, open a bank account or rent an apartment in the future.

An all-cash mini van

Q: We have saved $6,000 to buy a mini van but that's only enough for an older model.

Do you think we should buy the older model we can pay for in cash (and hope we don't have to do any major repairs right away), or use that $6,000 for a down payment and see if we can get a loan for $4,000? I'm thinking we could have a newer and nicer van for around $10,000.

A: It does seem logical in our credit-driven society to think of the cash you have as a down payment on what you want.

My advice, however, is that you not do that. Instead purchase the best car you can find for $6,000 including tax and license.

Each month instead of paying $200 to the bank (the way you would have if you'd gone for the $10,000 vehicle with a $4,000 loan), make those $200 payments to yourselves.

In a year you should be able to sell that $6,000 vehicle for at least $5,000; add to that the $2,400 you've saved and buy the best $7,400 vehicle you can find.

Keep making those $200 payments to the Bank of You and in another year upgrade to the best $9,000 vehicle you can find.

With each upgrade you will increase the quality and reliability of your transportation.

Keep making payments to yourself and routinely upgrading and you will be much farther ahead in five years than if you go into debt now and get stuck with a high-interest rate loan.

If you keep making payments to yourselves and routinely upgrade, in a relatively short time you will be able to buy a brand new van for cash. And I bet you won't.

There's something satisfying in buying a late model used vehicle on which someone else took that big depreciation hit.

Counter the insurer's offer

Q: I totaled my new vehicle after only eight payments. My insurance is not offering enough money to pay off the loan. My husband and I have excellent credit and do not want it damaged if we choose to default on the remaining balance of $2,500.

We have already purchased another vehicle and now have a new set of payments. What is the best way to handle this?

A: Most people don't realize that an insurance company's "offer of settlement" is just that—an offer. You do not have to accept it. You can counter their offer. Remember they want out of this claim as cheaply as possible.

You dare not walk away from this auto loan, which remains a legal obligation and separate from the insurance claim.

The bank or finance company that lent you the money to buy the car didn't say it would be okay to not repay the loan if you crashed your car. You have a moral and legal obligation to repay what you owe.

Unfortunately, it appears that you're going to have to fight this one out with the insurance company. You'll need to do some homework. Find out what that car would have been worth on the open market the day before you totaled it. Look in the classifieds and visit used car lots to find the same make and model with similar mileage and options.

Go back to the insurance company with a counter-offer along with proof of what that car was worth and then start negotiating. Do everything in your power to get them up to at least an amount equal to the balance owing on the loan.

Under no circumstances should you walk away from a deficiency if you do end up owing. That lender will turn around and sue you for the difference and you don't want that.

I am certain you can figure this one out and in a way that your insurance company steps up and covers this loss. Good luck!

Split the family?

Q: We have health insurance through my husband's company. The cost for our family of five has risen dramatically in the last six months.

We have been researching whether or not we could save money by obtaining our own insurance directly with the insurance company for myself and three children. My husband would continue to be covered by his company's plan.

It appears that we could get the same insurance coverage with the same insurance company for much less than we would pay through my husband's employer. Is this a good idea? Are there any risks?

A: It never hurts to compare and shop your insurance coverage and I suggest you do that. Just make sure you don't cancel what you have until you have something better in place. You don't want any gaps in coverage.

Make sure you are comparing like-for-like, paying attention to every aspect of the coverage.

You could find a cheaper premium but end up with a huge deductible, a long list of exclusions, or a weak list of service providers. Just keep in mind it is usually pretty difficult to beat a group plan.

Health insurance options

Q: After ten years at the same job, my husband was recently laid off. I'm a freelance writer. I work mainly from home so I can be with our three-year-old son. We've always relied on my husband's company for health insurance.

Now we're faced with paying for our own health insurance through

COBRA, and the cost for a family of three is outrageous.

We have no choice but to keep our coverage, but we also need to pay for other necessities like a roof over our heads and food. Are there any cheaper health insurance alternatives out there?

A: If you and your family are in good health I'm sure you can beat COBRA but you will probably have to accept a lower level of coverage. Start shopping.

If you belong to Sam's Club or Costco, both now offer health insurance for individuals in some areas.

Check out *eHealthInsurance.com* and then compare what you find with a quote directly from a company like Blue Cross/Blue Shield (*BCBS.com*), one of the nation's largest health insurance providers.

One good option you have is to accept a high deductible like $1,500 or more. While you'll have to pay for the routine stuff like office visits and prescriptions while you are between jobs, your monthly premium will be considerably lower and you'll have good coverage in the event of catastrophic illness or hospitalization.

Insurance scoring

Q: I recently renewed my auto insurance in New Jersey and was shocked to find out my insurance increased by $200 due to my credit score. Have I missed something? What does my credit rating have to do with auto insurance?

I've never missed a premium payment nor have I ever been late with my payments. I am truly befuddled. Doesn't past payment history with my insurance carrier count for anything?

A: Insurers have been using credit information since at least 1970 to price insurance premiums. They subscribe to the theory that poor credit indicates a person is at increased risk for accidents.

Using credit scores for insurance decisions is not only legal in most states, in recent years it has become quite the norm.

Curiously, the way insurers use credit information can differ from the way lenders use the same data. You could have a good credit score and quality for the best interest rates but get slapped with higher premiums.

The way to reduce your insurance premiums is to understand that insurance is meant to protect you against the kind of disasters that could wipe you out financially—not to pay for the little stuff you could easily cover out of your own pocket. Raise your deductibles and you'll lower your premiums.

Become diligent about improving your credit score by paying your bills on time, keeping your balances low on credit cards and lines of credit and not applying for credit you don't need.

Difficult Dilemmas

Credit counseling gets a bad rap

Q: I know you recommend debt counseling, but don't you think Consumer Credit Counseling Services (CCCS) is a racket? I've heard they get a kick-back from the credit-card companies.

A: I absolutely do not agree with your accusation that CCCS is a racket. Individual CCCS offices do collect and distribute funds that people owe to creditors through their Debt Management Programs (DMPs) and creditors do contribute to the organizations so they can stay in business. But so what?

The point of the program is not only to get money for the creditors, but to help people learn to manage their income and expenses so as to become financially stable.

Here's how CCCS works: Many people have difficulty with money management or have overextended themselves with credit. Others may need coaching on how to set up a budget. Some attend educational workshops while others receive confidential free counseling by phone or in person.

About 25 percent of those who go for counseling elect to participate in the DMP. This is a service for consumers who have enough money to meet their living expenses but not enough money to cover all of the payments to their creditors. CCCS contacts creditors on behalf of their clients and suggests alternative payments.

The creditors most often agree because they know that if the client doesn't get help things could get worse with the client filing for bankruptcy. Many, but not all, creditors even reduce interest rates for clients who stay on the program.

The CCCS DMP serves the dual role of helping clients repay their debts and helping creditors collect the money owed them. CCCS is indeed a non-profit agency. Those who enter the DMP pay a monthly fee of about $10 for disbursement of their funds. Most of CCCS's funding comes from voluntary contributions from creditors who participate in DMPs.

Since creditors have a financial interest in getting paid most are willing to make a contribution to help fund the CCCS agencies which are located in all metropolitan areas. These contributions are usually calculated as a percentage of payments clients make through their DMP—up to 15 percent of each payment received.

However, clients' accounts with creditors are always credited with 100 percent of the amount they pay through CCCS regardless of whether the creditor contributes to the agency.

CCCS has been responsible for helping millions of people get control of their finances and become debt-free and I cannot recommend their services highly enough. CCCS is a non-profit organization with branches in all areas. I am not familiar with each branch office of CCCS, but have had excellent feedback about the office in Atlanta which can help people in many states because they offer counseling by phone. That office's number is 888 771-HOPE. Or visit their website at CCCSAtl.org.

In search of a quick fix

Q: We are thinking about filing for bankruptcy. We owe $30,000 in credit cards, plus $1,000 in outstanding medical bills.

Every month we are falling farther behind because we have a $1,500 mortgage payment, monthly bills, babysitting, groceries, gas, etc. I know things are not going to clear up overnight, but can you please help us get some relief—quickly?

A: My heart goes out to you—I've been in financial trouble, too. You need to know that your problem is not the result of medical bills or a high mortgage payment. Your problem is credit-card debt. It may appear that the medical bill has pushed you over the edge, but it's the credit-card debt that is such a problem. You are ad-

dicted to spending money before you've earned it.

Bankruptcy won't address this problem. Quick fixes don't teach us much. You borrowed the money, spent it freely and now you have a moral obligation to repay it. I believe you are ideal candidates for credit counseling.

If it's any consolation, my credit-card troubles at one point were more than three times yours. It took 13 years, but I repaid every dime—no inheritance, no lottery.

What is debt consolidation?

Q: Should I consolidate my debts? What does that even mean?

A: Lots of people confuse debt consolidation with credit counseling and debt management. They are quite different.

Consolidating your debts always involves a new loan of some kind to pay off all your smaller debts, so you come out with one new, smaller monthly payment. Or, you might consolidate your numerous smaller debts into one new credit card, which would then become the new loan with a single new monthly payment.

Should you do that? No. New debt is not the solution for old debt. Unless you take care of the problem that got you into so much debt in the first place, a new loan will just make things worse.

If you consolidate, more than likely you will start using the credit cards again. Then you'll be in twice as much trouble.

Credit counseling and debt management are something altogether different, and highly recommended if you are having difficulty managing your unsecured debt.

Through counseling and education, a good credit counselor will help you find the root of your problem. And if you qualify for their debt management program, they will go to your creditors on your behalf to set up a payment plan you can handle. You will make your monthly payment to the DMP (debt management program), who sends the money to your creditors.

Just be careful. There are lots of wolves out there posing as credit counselors, debt consolidators, and debt negotiators.

The Federal Trade Commission at FTC.gov, is warning that many are imposters and scam operators. A good place to find a reputable credit counselor is at the National Foundation of Credit Counselors, NFCC.org.

Bankruptcy may be unavoidable

Q: My husband and I have really gotten ourselves in deep this time. At the time we thought it was a good idea. We started a franchise using our personal credit cards.

The manager we hired was inept and untrustworthy. Now we are in credit-card debt to the tune of $250,000.

We are trying to crawl out from under this problem and are out of working capital to keep things going.

We can't find anyone who will make us a consolidation loan. Please respond quickly we are sinking fast!

A: I wish you'd written before you headed down such a dangerous path. Instead, you violated nearly every rule of self-employment: You went into business with borrowed funds. You hired employees before you were profitable. You thought of credit as "working capital." Need I go on?

I will say that if there's one thing you did right it was not taking out a home-equity loan to fund this nightmare.

As much as your unsecured creditors may scream and yell, hassle and harangue, they cannot take your home. And they cannot eat you. But they can sue you if you are unable to keep up with your monthly minimum payments, and that would be awful.

Bankruptcy may be your only recourse. And while you might be relieved of the burden through bankruptcy, discharged debts don't disappear. The rest of us pay them through increased prices.

It pains me greatly to suggest it's probably time for you to consult with a bankruptcy attorney.

Life after bankruptcy

Q: Please give me some pointers on bouncing back from bankruptcy. Will this have any effect on future employment opportunities?

A: Pay your bills on time—never be late. Do not run up big balances. Do not apply for a lot of credit. Never use more than 30 percent of your credit limits. Let nothing prevent you from saving 10 percent of your income.

Many employers now require credit reports from prospective employees—it's the new character reference. Your bankruptcy could adversely affect your job opportunities.

If you are diligent, your credit report will soon reflect a definite change of behavior and your new lifestyle. This will be evident to anyone looking closely at your credit report.

Only time can neutralize the effects of bankruptcy. And once ten years have passed, it will be much better. Unfortunately, the sting is not likely to ever go away completely.

Forget debt consolidation

Q: My husband and I are able to pay at least the minimum amount on our consumer debts each month. In fact, we are using your Rapid Debt-Repayment Plan. It's working and it feels great to be making progress. But it will take 30 more months to be debt-free.

We want to start a family and buy a house. Would you recommend we find some kind of debt consolidation to speed this up? Thanks and keep up the good work

A: I am mostly opposed to debt consolidation, which means getting a new loan to pay off debt. Theoretically, it's trading in a bunch of debts and coming out with one debt and one monthly payment that is smaller than the sum total of the monthly payments from the consolidated debts. Got it?

Here's what usually happens—and we have statistics to prove it:

You transfer balances on credit cards A, B, C, and D to New Card E. You "wisely" trade in 18 percent interest for just 3.9 percent. You make the switch but don't exactly get around to canceling A, B, C, and D which you toss in a drawer (a nice "cushion" just in case of an emergency, and besides closing those accounts could be really bad news for your credit score).

Emergencies happen, I guarantee it. In a very short time (the average is about 24 months) not only have you visited the drawer a few times, cards A, B, C, and D are back where they were and now you are stuck with double the debt.

How did THAT happen? you ask yourself in a rare moment of lucidity.

Truth is, it happens all the time and the credit-card companies count on it. It happened to me countless times and statistics say it will happen to you, too. Until you've conquered the debt-monster's death grip on your life, new debt will never be the answer for old debt.

You are doing well with your repayment plan. Concentrate on that and stop looking for shortcuts. Add a booster amount to your monthly RDRP payment (you'll see that option on the RDRP Calculator at *Debt ProofLiving*.com). Pay more than the amount required each month and you'll avoid paying a ton of interest. I know you can do this. Get tough! Get angry that debt is controlling your lives. Be outraged that your desire to have children is taking second place to the demands of a merciless credit industry. And for heaven's sake, don't take on new debt to "fix" old debt. It doesn't work.

Become your own credit counselor

Q: I am wanting to know what you think about using a credit counseling service to help us get out of debt? We have $17,000 total in credit-card debt. Any advice would help. Thank you so much

A: Credit counseling can be a real life saver when it appears that bankruptcy may be your only other option.

Generally credit counseling would be indicated if you have fallen behind and are simply not able to catch up with your credit-card payments.

It can be a severe remedy with long-lasting side effects for people who have not fallen behind, but are sick of their big balances and high interest rates.

Your best bet is to become your own credit counselor using our Rapid Debt-Repayment Plan (RDRP) as your coach and guide.

Here's the "Cliffs Notes" version of the RDRP:

1. No more new unsecured debt.

2. "Fix" your monthly payments at their current amount.

3. Arrange your debts so the shortest payoff is at the top.

4. When you pay off the debt at the top, take its payment and add it to the payment of the next debt in line. When the second debt is paid take the payments from the first and second and add them to the third.

5. Continue doing this until all debts are paid.

The RDRP is an amazingly simple plan that will put you into the driver's seat with your debt situation. You keep all of your options and you do not blow a seven-year cannon ball through your credit report. (Most creditors report negatively for debts that are being managed by a credit counseling organization.)

Learn more about the RDRP: *Debt-Proof Living* (book), Chapter 7.

While the RDRP calculator is an Online Subscription benefit for members of *DebtProofLiving.com*, anyone can see the details and a demonstration on the home page of the website.

Considering the choices

Q: I am finally recognizing how much in debt I am. I need to make changes yet I have many bills to pay. Some are medical and dental bills that were not covered by insurance.

I am tempted to declare bankruptcy so that I can concentrate on medical bills, my rent and car payment and not get to this point ever again. Please advise and give me some hope of coming out on the other end.

A: Facing your situation and assessing the damage is the first and often most difficult step. You've just done that, so you've taken that difficult first step.

It is not uncommon to experience a wave a panic that screams "Get out of here! Run the other way!" But that is the coward's way out so don't give those thoughts space in your brain.

Bankruptcy might be legal, but it should never be your first option. And as long as you have a choice, I believe it would be a horrible mistake for you to even think about filing.

There are times (rare) when bankruptcy is forced on a person in such a

way that there is no other way out. You are not at that point because you say you are tempted to file—like that is one of the items on your menu of choices. Cross it off, take bankruptcy off your menu for now.

The choices that remain:

1. Seek credit counseling if you are behind in your payments, your creditors are hassling you and you have no way to bring your payments current.

2. Become your own credit counselor by developing your Rapid Debt-Repayment Plan, RDRP.

I'm hoping you will take the second choice. You'll finish up with an excellent record instead of a seven or ten-year black-eye on your credit report, depending on if you go with counseling or bankruptcy. And, you'll always know that you did the right thing.

Beware debt-settlement scams

Q: I contacted a company I saw advertised on the Internet because I have a mountain of debt.

They said they would help me negotiate down my unsecured debt to 40 cents on the dollar, maybe even less.

Is this for real? Will it harm my credit rating for years to come?

A: Settling your debts is not as easy as it might sound in that slick pitch. Assuming that is possible for you, do you have 40 percent of your total debt in cash to make such an offer? If this were to happen, those debts will show up as "settled" on your credit report.

A settled debt is just one step above bankruptcy, it's that horrible. It will stay on there for seven years. And that entry will come on the heels of staggering late-payment entries because this brilliant debt-settlement company will instruct you to stop making payments on your debts, so they can take that money and save it up for you for when they negotiate your settlement. Argh.

Trust me. Debt-settlement is not the same as credit counseling where you repay all of the principal on a mutually agreed and negotiated payment schedule.

By the way, did these folks mention fees? They can be very high. Or the IRS? The law requires each creditor who settles for less than the amount borrowed, send you a Form 1099 for that amount because it's money you received but did not pay back. It will be taxed the same as income.

You think you have problems now? Add the IRS to the mix.

Which bills to pay first?

Q: Our mortgage payment was due on the first. It is now the 21st. We have the money to pay it now, but we don't have enough to pay all of our bills that are due.

My husband thinks it would be better to pay our credit-card bills that are due and allow our mortgage to go 30-days behind.

What do you think and who should be paid first?

A: Allowing bills to become delinquent is wrong, but available cash can be stretched only so far. That doesn't mean you are excused from payment, just that you need to know how to prioritize in a way that will cause the least amount of long-term damage and keep you in the best position to eventually catch up.

Here is the rule to follow when you cannot pay all of your bills: Prioritize and pay them according to the severity of the consequences you will suffer for non-payment.

If you do not pay your mortgage or rent on time you have to assume your mortgage lender or landlord will proceed against you to the full extent of the law. The consequence for non-payment is eviction and that is severe!

On the other hand, if you are late with credit-card bills the consequences will be unpleasant but not as severe. You'll get a late fee, an interest rate increase (ouch!), perhaps a phone call after 30 days, and for sure a blemish on your credit report if they go past the 30-day mark. But you won't find yourselves on the street with the kids and your big screen TV.

All that to say my advice is that you should always pay your mortgage or rent ahead of other debts. It should be at the top of the list with food, medication and child support. Other bills can slide for a while.

Credit counseling is good when necessary

Q: What do you think of enrolling in CCCS, (Consumer Credit Counseling Services)? Would it be better for me to go through them to get my interest rates and payments lowered or do it with your Rapid Debt-Repayment Plan?

A: Think of credit counseling for your financial situation as you would chemotherapy for a life-threatening health condition. Things would need to be very serious to even consider such a severe remedy—even one that has the potential of saving your life.

Credit counseling has considerable side effects. It's a commitment to accountability and to counseling sessions. Creditors who agree to concessions requested through the counseling process will likely report this to the credit bureaus. Because you will be restricted from using credit while enrolled in counseling, your credit score will likely be impacted negatively. This is not something you would opt for if there was any way to avoid it.

You should not opt for credit counseling just to get your interest rates reduced. But, if your situation has deteriorated to the point that you cannot manage your own debt and you need professional intervention, you want the best—not some fly-by-night bogus organization that's trying to make a buck off the misery of others.

Consumer Credit Counseling Services (CCCS) sets the standard for non-profit credit counselors. They've been around for a long time and are not among the dubious counselors the IRS is currently investigating.

Generally speaking, if you are behind on your credit-card payments and are consistently unable to meet even the minimum monthly payments, you've reached the place that you should consider credit counseling. And at that point it is something for which you will be very grateful.

Credit counseling will not destroy credit

Q: The author of a personal finance book I read recently says that enrolling in credit counseling will destroy your credit. He says NOT to do it whatsoever.

Reading that, I panicked! My husband and I chose credit counseling and we are 14 months from paying off a whopping amount of consumer debt. Now I am wondering what horror is before us.

Consumer Credit Counseling Services (CCCS) has been a salvation for my husband and me. We felt that it was better to pay the debt than to claim bankruptcy.

What now?

A: In fairness I have not read the book or even know what book it is, so I do not know the context of the comment. If the author says that when you have three choices—getting out of debt on your own, entering credit counseling or claiming bankruptcy—then I agree that credit counseling should be the second choice. If you can do it, becoming your own credit counselor is the best option.

However, "NOT to do it whatsoever," suggests to me that the advice is that even bankruptcy would be desirous over credit counseling. I totally disagree.

I don't know your specific situation, but you mention bankruptcy as if that would have been your only other choice.

That being the case you have done exactly the right thing. And I'm proud of you for making the choice to enter credit counseling.

When I refer to becoming your own credit counselor, I refer to situations where a person has debt, has the ability to pay those debts but doesn't like the high interest rates. Or, just feels weary of having such big bills. In that case, even credit counseling is not warranted. That person needs to buckle down, wise up and get those debts paid.

The next scenario is the case where a person has fallen behind. Creditors are calling, threats are being made about turning the accounts over to collection. Now the situation has become serious to the point of requiring intervention. A reputable credit counseling organization, such as CCCS, acts as an intermediary between the consumer and creditor to set up a reasonable repayment plan. As you have discovered, credit counseling can be a godsend for the person who otherwise would have had no option but to file for bankruptcy.

Bankruptcy may be legal, but it is not moral. It can be life-altering, taking a terrible toll on relationships and one's self-esteem.

For a personal finance expert to recommend bankruptcy over credit counseling because of how it might play out on one's credit report is misguided.

There is no way to guarantee that your debt management choice will not affect your credit scores in the future. But that's secondary in my mind.

You felt a moral obligation to keep your word and when you found yourselves in trouble, you sought help. Repaying all of your debts 14 months from now will give the two of you a sense of joy beyond description. Doing the right thing is always the right thing to do.

Experian, one of the major credit bureaus, has this to say: "Accounts you pay through a credit counselor, including CCCS, typically are reported by lenders as paid through a debt management program. Most credit risk scoring systems now disregard that status. That means your participation in a counseling program would not be viewed negatively by most lenders."

CCCS of Atlanta says: "Even if you enter a CCCS Debt Management Program, CCCS does not report your participation in our Debt Management Program to credit bureaus. Some creditors may report that your account is included on a debt management program.

Creditors may report your account as current when they receive our proposal, while some wait until they have received three consecutive payments through CCCS. They appreciate that you are honoring your debts rather than running from them through bankruptcy, and after seeing a consistent payment history through CCCS, may look at you as a better credit risk than the typical consumer."

Get a load of this

Q: I recently found a website that promises to take our credit-card debt and have it erased.

They can do this because it is technically illegal for banks to issue credit cards. So this company takes your debt and challenges it in court, legally dissolving the credit-card debt.

I am skeptical, but hopeful. Do you know, is this truly legal?

A: I don't know which is more shocking: That anyone would suggest such a thing, or that you would entertain

for even a moment that it might be legitimate.

Of course this is not legal. Don't believe it for a second.

It is another in the long list of Internet scams that will hit you up for a big fee and leave you holding the bag. By the time they've fleeced your finances, you'll be in default on your payments and then you'll be in worse trouble than ever.

My best advice is to stop looking for loopholes and shortcuts. Get busy getting out of debt—the right way.

Education

Student loans: Good or evil?

Q: Is it ever wise to borrow money to go back to college?

A: Well now, that's a very broad question! I'll try to narrow my answer:

You have to weigh the risks: Realistically, what are the chances that once you graduate (if you graduate might be a better question), you will find gainful employment in that field of study? It's one thing if you will come out with a nursing degree or as a credentialed teacher, and it's quite another if you'll be really good at playing the lute.

If you are already employed in an industry that rewards a college degree with a guaranteed increased salary, borrowing the money to get that degree would be a wise choice. However, you should borrow only if you are unable to pay as you go.

For example, if you are a school teacher in a district that has an automatic pay increase for teachers with masters' degrees, the increase in salary will more than cover the cost of the education. In that case, I could support taking student loans to get the degree. Afterward, aggressively repay the loan with your increased salary before you get used to spending it elsewhere.

If, on the other hand, you have no assurance of a job in your field of study, it's risky. I'm not saying there's anything wrong with being a fabulous lute player—only that while your mother will be proud as anything, there aren't many jobs in that field that would make it possible for you to repay the loan.

Trust me when I say you will greatly improve your future if you do everything you can to pay as you go so you come out as close to debt-free as humanly possible.

No turning back on student debt

Q: Years ago my ex-husband and I had consolidated our student loans, so we now share this very large $100,000 debt. Is there a way we can have this divided into two separate loans?

A: I don't have good news. You are both responsible for the loan in its entirety. You cannot reverse or change that. State divorce courts cannot override or alter a federal loan, nor is it dischargeable through bankruptcy.

I wish you'd written before you consolidated because I would have advised you to not combine your loans if for no other reason than if one spouse dies, his or her student loans are forgiven.

As of July 1, 2006, spousal consolidation was no longer allowed as legislated in the Deficit Reduction Act of 2005. However, you do have the option of paying this consolidated student debt off early without penalty.

Theoretically you and your ex-husband could each borrow half from a new lending source, pay off this debt, then go on to pay off your respective new loans.

If you were to do that, make sure you are both doing this in good faith. The last thing you want is to pay off your fair share of the current debt, only to find your ex-husband didn't carry through by paying off his half.

In that case you would have your new debt and still be responsible for the old one, too.

Never ending student debt

Q: Twelve years ago my husband finished medical school with $70,000 in school loans. While in forbearance, when we couldn't afford the payments, it grew to $75,000.

We're back on track now and have paid the student debt down to $60,000. That's progress, but still so far to go.

We have $40,000 equity in our home. Should we use that to pay the student debt faster? We have no other debts.

A: Oh, those rascally college loans—so easy to get, so difficult to get rid of. Happy to hear that you've paid down $15,000. That's a big chunk, so give yourselves a tiny pat on the back.

I see no good reason to transfer your student debt to your home. You wouldn't want to do this for tax reasons (student loan interest is already tax deductible within certain limitations, so that wouldn't play into your decision).

By going this route you would not be eliminating any debt, just moving it from an unsecured position to one that is secured by your home. But worse, you would put your home at risk.

Mortgage lenders don't hesitate to foreclose when borrowers fall behind. The way it is now if you fall behind for some reason on your student loan payments, the lender will hassle you and make your life miserable, but cannot take your home.

I would rather see you forget that you have that $40,000 equity. It is an appreciating asset and possibly your only investment at this time. Leave it alone and let it grow to the glorious day that you have 100 percent home-equity.

On cosigning: Don't do it!

Q: I recently re-married after being divorced for seven years.

With three kids the credit-card bills have climbed and it seems like I'm always a month behind on the utilities.

My credit score is not very good even though I've always paid my mortgage and car loan on time.

My son is going to college and now my credit score isn't good enough to cosign for his loans. Any suggestions for us slow payers?

A: I cannot imagine how difficult it must be to parent solo. But you did that for seven years while keeping the mortgage and car payments current. You deserve a round of applause.

What I'm about to tell you, I'd say even if you had the best credit in the world: Never cosign a loan for anyone for any reason. Ever. And especially not a college loan.

As for helping your son pay for college, it seems to me that you are not in a position to do that. You cannot even keep your utility payment current.

Your first priority is to get caught up. Then you need to pour every ounce of your financial energy into building a Contingency Fund to three months (six is better) of your living expenses. Then, you need to get out of debt followed by making sure you will be financially set for retirement.

Nowhere is it written that parents are required to fund college educations. It is not cruel and inhumane treatment for a young adult to work

and to pay for his own college education.

The pay-as-you-go method is tough, but much easier in the long run than graduating with $50,000 or more in student loans to carry through life. I guarantee that if your son has to earn the money first and pay for his own education, he'll treat the process with a great deal more respect and appreciation. And, he'll show up for classes. Introduce to him the benefits of community college for the first two or three years. Or, the military.

Check your library for the book, *How to Go to College Almost for Free*, by Ben Kaplan (Collins Publishing). This will introduce you and your son to the idea of debt-free education and the specifics for how to do that.

In the meantime I'm sending you a copy of my book, *Debt-Proof Your Kids*.

You can't depend on schools to teach your kids how to manage money and live without debt. That's your job, and I want to teach you how to teach them.

Signing parent on a Parent PLUS loan

Q: My husband took out Parent PLUS loans to help our kids pay for college. I did not sign for these loans; only he signed.

Subsequently, he consolidated them with the U.S. Department of

Education. Will I be responsible for those loans if he dies?

A: Built into all federally guaranteed student loans, which includes Parent PLUS loans, is a 1 percent default fee. If the borrower—in your case your husband—dies or becomes totally and permanently disabled, the guarantee agency reimburses the lender for the balance remaining on the loan.

Since you did not sign the PLUS loans, you are not liable for the repayment.

Pay unsubsidized interest as you go

Q: My husband and I have a combined annual net income of $48,000. I am currently in college on student loans.

Should I start paying off my student loans now, even though I'm still taking them out? Or should I be saving that money to pay for school in cash next year, even though I have student loans this year?

A: You should be doing both. The loans you have already are more than likely unsubsidized.

Because you are not paying that interest (and are not required to), it is tacked onto the loan amount, causing your loan to grow month after month. Think: compounding interest.

I recommend strongly that you begin paying the interest on all your unsubsidized loans. Most student loans are unsubsidized. Subsidized loans are granted on the basis of financial hardship. In that case, interest does not begin to accrue until you have graduated, or you are found to not meet the minimum standard required for your loans to continue to be subsidized.

It shouldn't be much, but this will keep your principal balances at no more than the amount you borrowed.

You also need to be saving cash, as you suggested, so you can start paying as you go.

You don't want to come out on the other end with a degree and so much debt that you're worse off for having gone to school. I hear from many for whom that has become the situation and it is downright heartbreaking.

I'm happy to know you are thinking about these things now while you still have options. Good luck!

Can I pay for college with a credit card?

Q: My husband's consolidated student loan is fixed at 8.25 percent interest with a monthly payment of $177.

Would it be a good idea to pay this off with a low-interest credit card? I've been offered a new one with 4.9 percent interest, fixed.

I am very disciplined, so I know nothing else would go on the card and payments would be made on time.

Is this a good idea? Any help would be appreciated!

A: I know that looks tempting, but there are several things to consider.

First, the interest rate on the credit card is in reality, adjustable. Even if they are offering you 4.9 percent fixed, that means it is fixed until they decide to increase it. And by federal law a credit-card issuer can do that even if they advertised it as "fixed."

Any increase in interest will apply to the entire balance. Their only lawful obligation is to give you 15-days written notice (this will change in July 2010, but that is too late for you now). It's in the fine print in the terms and conditions: "You agree that we can change the terms and conditions at any time and for any reason."

(Note: Retroactive interest-rate increases on credit-card balances will be forbidden, but not until new Federal Reserve Board rules go into effect in July 2010.)

Another thing to consider: As it is now, this debt is legally your husband's, not yours even though you are married.

If you divorce, that student loan goes with him. If he becomes permanently disabled or dies before it is paid, the remaining balance is forgiven. But, if you've transferred the balance to a credit card with your name on it and any of those things happen, you remain legally obligated to pay.

When life throws a curveball ...

Q: My husband is an insulin-dependent diabetic. He has large student loans and we have an equally large mortgage. We are trying to respond to what life has handed us responsibly and realistically. If he dies before the student loan is paid, the outstanding balance is forgiven.

However, he has no life insurance and is no longer insurable. So, should we be working on paying off the mortgage before the student loans?

A: Under the circumstances it does make sense for you to concentrate on paying off the mortgage quickly, while staying current with the student loan payments. Once the mortgage is paid double your efforts on the student loans to pay them quickly.

You don't say if you are employed, but if you are and the loss of your income would place your husband in financial hardship, you need life insurance—not mortgage life insurance.

If his diabetes is well-managed, there's every possibility he will outlive you but his ability to earn enough to handle both debts could be greatly diminished.

Best way to prepay student debt

Q: I have not always been very good at paying my student loan on time, assuming it was better to pay something more urgent, say the electric bill, first.

I am in a better position now to get this paid off. However, I can't figure out the best way to do it.

My outstanding balance is $3,895. I pay 5.3 percent interest, compounded daily. My monthly payment is $56.11.

At this rate it will take seven more years to pay it off. I would like to make additional payments each month but the amount will vary. I'm not sure if it's better to make one larger payment each month, multiple smaller payments, or whether the amount saved in interest will be enough to make a difference.

I'm anticipating being able to send an average of $100 per month but want to send it in as soon as it is available so I won't spend it. Can you help?

A: Simply put, daily compounding interest means that at the end of the day the computer multiplies your outstanding balance by 5.3 percent and divides by 365. It adds the result to your outstanding balance. So, if you were to reduce the balance today, when they do this daily interest action tomorrow they will add on less interest because of the reduced balance.

Granted, it's a very small amount, but do that every day year round and you will see how it all adds up.

Student loans do not typically carry any type of prepayment penalty clause, so nothing prevents you from paying any amount at any time during the month. I love your idea of sending in what you can as you receive it so you are not tempted to spend it on something else.

Here are some rough figures: If you pay $156.11 per month (just $100 additional each month), you will have your entire student loan paid in just 27 months, rather than seven years. More than that, you will not have to pay $525.74 in interest which translates to a 19 percent return on the extra $100 you plan to invest in your debt each month.

Do it! And be sure to tell me when you get your Paid in Full notice so I can celebrate, too.

Cosigning parents caught in the middle

Q: Our daughter graduated from college with over $100,000 in student loans. Her first job did not pay enough for her to begin repaying the loans.

We cosigned one loan and the payment is $600 a month. We did not know that it was in default until she was several thousand dollars behind.

This came at us after a home remodel and a wedding. We are not prepared to pay this loan and we would like to give her advice but are at a loss as to where to start.

She just got a job with great benefits, but is still unable to begin paying her student debt. Can you give us any direction?

A: When you agreed to cosign that loan, you took on a legal obligation to repay it if she didn't. Whether or not you would be able to afford to do that was not part of the deal.

First thing: Call the lender and make sure you are receiving duplicate statements. Next, find out how much is required to bring this loan current. This deliquency is going on your credit report and trashing your credit score.

This loan is not going away. In fact, if it is in default it is in a state known as "negative amortization." This means the principal is growing every month because the unpaid interest is being converted to principal, which starts to accrue interest in the following month.

Ignoring repayment is possibly the most deadly of all responses one can have to student loans. Unlike other kinds of debt, federally guaranteed student loans cannot even be discharged through bankruptcy. They just go on and on and keep growing.

If this loans goes into default, all three of you will be in danger of having your tax refunds intercepted, your

property removed and even your Social Security checks garnished in retirement until payment is made in full. Ouch!

I wish that someone would have explained all of this to you before you agreed to cosign.

My best advice is that someone needs to get another job that nets at least $600 a month for as long as it takes to repay that debt. Doubling up on payments will help to knock it out sooner than later, too.

Debt payment part of a balanced plan

Q: My son graduated from college and will need to start his loan repayment plan soon.

He's thinking of paying the minimum required amount, and banking the rest of his salary to earn interest. I was under the impression it would be better to pay extra on his principal each month. What would you advise him to do?

A: I wish your son would have written because that would have demonstrated to me that he is taking his financial obligations seriously.

But since he didn't, I will trust that he will read this and take it to heart. The debt-proof living plan applies to every person in every situation at every income level. That he is just starting out does not put him into a different category with a different plan.

From each of his paychecks he needs to first give away 10 percent as an act of gratitude and for the purpose of bringing balance to his finances and to his life.

Next, he needs to save 10 percent in an account where he will build his Contingency Fund.

He needs to recognize that the future is unknown. That is why he needs to start building this pool of money that will be there to pay his bills when he goes through seasons of unemployment or other financial emergencies.

From the 80 percent of his net income that remains, he needs to pay his living expenses, which include his student debt payments. He must also begin to be prepared for his irregular and unexpected expenses that surely will show up from time to time (car repairs, clothes, entertainment, saving for a down payment on a house, engagement ring and so on). We call this a Freedom Account, and it will surely put him on the right path.

It would be foolish for him to see his student loan payment as the only or most important financial obligation. If he were to double up on payments to the detriment of being prepared for the future, he would be in a very bad way should he need tires for his car or should his rent increase tremendously.

If he discovers that after paying his monthly expenses, funding his Contingency Fund and Freedom Account, he has available cash—at that point he should consider increasing his student loan payment.

Doubling payments hastily, without making sure he is covered in other areas, could be a big mistake if that required him to live on credit cards to pay for other living expenses.

Hiding assets to get aid is a crime

Q: I have been told that if I have any "extra" money at the time my child is applying for college financial aid, I should take out cash and hide it.

For example, if my Contingency Fund is funded at $10,000 and my Freedom Account is fully funded at $9,500, it will look like I have about $20,000 at my disposal for college.

My friend says it would be better to get a safe deposit box and put the $20,000 in there in cash. She also says that if it is on your bank statement, then it will count against us as far as financial aid. What do you say?

A: I'm sure your friend means well, but if you follow this advice you might find yourself looking for Martha Stewart's name scratched in your cell wall at Camp Cupcake.

Hiding assets on a Financial Aid form constitutes fraud and is punishable by a $20,000 fine (bye-bye CF and FA), up to 19 months in federal prison or both.

There's a fine line between maximizing eligibility for college financial aid by sheltering assets, and hiding assets in order to qualify. One is legal, the other is not.

The children of people making $150,000 a year may qualify for financial aid while the kids of people making $50,000 may not. It all depends on how the rest of the parents' finances shake out and whether the school uses the popular "federal method" to determine financial aid (where home equity doesn't count) or the "institutional method" used by more elite schools, where it does.

College saving and asset planning has become so complicated, a professional organization was created in 2002.

The National Institute of Certified College Planners (NICCP) now offers a certification course in college financial strategies. You may benefit from consulting briefly with such a professional. Just be very careful. There are lots of financial aid sharks out there who will promise the moon then take your money and run.

Visit *NICCP.com* to learn more about the Institute and college planning, and to find a certified planner in your area for consultation. You can also do a great deal of research on your own at *Finaid.org* so you are more knowledgeable when you meet with a professional

Financial aid is needs-based

Q: We have set up a college fund for each of my kids through a national insurance company. We are not able to pay large amounts into the fund, but we figured every little bit helps.

My mother-in-law read that having college funds could cause problems for us getting financial aid once the kids get into college. Is this right?

A: She is correct in that student financial aid is needs-based, but so is most government assistance.

Is she saying that you should not be saving for your kids' college tuition, so you can qualify for aid?

I don't think you would ever say that getting a job could cause problems for you getting welfare or qualifying for food stamps. And I cannot imagine you searching for ways to hide your income or choosing not to save so that you could appear to qualify for assistance. Student financial aid is offered on a sliding scale according to need.

I believe you should save all you can, apply for financial aid and take whatever amount is offered based upon your true financial condition at the time.

Student debt dies with the debtor

Q: If my husband took out a student loan for college, would I be responsible for repaying this student loan in the event he died?

A: No, you will not be responsible, provided he doesn't do something "creative," like moving the debt to your home's equity, transferring it to a credit card or other form of debt you share.

You are not responsible for his student debt in life or death.

Uncle left holding the bag

Q: Several years ago I cosigned student loans for my nephew. He has been out of college and married for five years now.

He and his wife recently filed bankruptcy. I am now paying off his student loans. There are four loans, and the collective balance is just over $5,000. The monthly payment is about $100.

I could afford to pay them off in full, but am hesitant to take the money out of my savings. However, I'm thinking of retiring in the near future, and don't want the monthly debt. Would I be better off making the monthly payments, or paying the loans in full?

A: To answer your specific question, yes, pay those loans now. In full. Then, repay your savings account the $100 a month plus as much additional as you can. At least this way you are earning interest, not paying it.

While you didn't ask, I will add that I do not understand how you let your

nephew off the hook on this one. Federally guaranteed student loans are not dischargeable through bankruptcy, as you know because you are still paying them.

It was kind, perhaps, for you to accept the obligation, but since he's been relieved of other debt obligations, it seems to me he should be able to repay you. Approach him with a payment schedule that both of you can live with and then make it clear that you expect him to stick to it until you are completely repaid.

Doing the right thing will build character in him and it will be good for you, too.

Raid the kids' education accounts

Q: I have a lot of credit-card debt as a result of stupid overspending. I have set up a budget for the purpose of paying down the debt. But still, my income is short each month.

Since the birth of our children, we've been contributing to UGMA (Uniform Gift to Minors Act) accounts to help pay for college.

I have ceased the automatic investments, but realize there's a lot of money sitting in those accounts—enough to pay a few credit-card accounts in full.

Am I allowed to do that, legally or ethically? I just do not know what to do.

A: The laws that govern UGMA trust accounts vary by state. You need to speak with an attorney or CPA to learn if you have any options.

Frankly, I am not hopeful that there is any provision for you to use those funds for your benefit. The point of the Uniform Gift to Minors Act is to give an irrevocable gift to a child that he can use once he becomes of legal age.

However—and this may be the key for you—UGMA funds can be used to benefit the child while he is still a minor.

Are you paying for beneficial things like music lessons or school tuition?

You may be able to pay those expenses from the child's UGMA account. That would free up your income to increase the amount you have to pay your debt each month.

But, don't trust me on this. Check with an attorney or tax advisor.

The student loan debate

Q: I am a single parent with a child in college and I am going back to school myself. I have completed the majority of my general education classes at our city college and want to transfer to a university to complete my BA degree and hopefully my Masters.

You have advocated that one should not get student loans and should pay as you go. However, I'm 49 years old, I'm living with my mother in order to cut expenses so I can go to school, and I do not have the energy to get two jobs.

If I want to actually get my degree before I'm 80 and be able to use it, I need to get some type of student loan. Any suggestions?

A: I'm afraid I have more questions than suggestions.

What is your field of study? How certain are you that you will be welcomed into that field? What is the entry level salary in that career field? Will that allow you to live on your own and pay hundreds a month in loan payments for the next 15 years?

You say you do not have the energy to work two jobs now, but that's what you may be looking at if you run up tens of thousands in student loans and do not land some big fabulous salary.

While the education may improve your employability, the debt will take away many of your life options. Have you considered all of the non-debt options you have for going to school?

Perhaps you could go to work now for a company that offers tuition reimbursement. Does your state have grants for single parents, specifically women? Some do.

Have you searched for scholarships, grants and other forms of funding that do not require repayment?

Student loans are, in my opinion, way too easy to get. And that's the reason most students take the easy way out and just sign up for a lifetime of miserable student debt.

Student loans should not be your first option, but rather your very last— and then with the greatest amount of reluctance.

Should you end up borrowing money to finish school, please take the smallest loans you'll need to scrape by, not the most money the Financial Aid Office will hand to you.

You are a brave woman, and I wish you well.

Paid ahead but not paid down

Q: I've been paying extra on my student loan each month. Now I learn that instead of applying that additional amount to pay down the principal, they've been applying it to future interest payments. So I'm paid ahead but the principal hasn't budged.

I even wrote on the checks "apply overage to principal" and they still credited it toward future payments, not the balance.

I want to pay this off and send in extra but not if they are going to pay-ahead instead of paying it down.

I sent the lender an email but did not receive a reply. How should I go about handling this?

A: Email is not always the best way to deal with customer service issues, so pick up the phone and call (there should be a number on your statement). Then follow up with a letter sent by U.S. Postal Service Certified Mail with a Return Receipt.

Provided you have proof of your past payments and instructions to pre-pay the principal, insist that the lender go back and re-apply your payments as you instructed.

In the future write two checks, one for your required payment and the second for the principal prepayment.

The government has provided an ombudsman to solve problems like this for student loan borrowers. Go to *Ombudsman.ed.gov*, call 877 557-2575, or write to them at U.S. Department of Education FSA Ombudsman, 830 First Street, NE, Fourth Floor, Washington, DC 20202-5144 to get help in solving your problem if you are still unsuccessful.

Good luck with this. Prepaying your student debt is such a smart thing to do. You'll be so happy when your education is truly yours.

Save for college with UPromise

Q: I have heard about these college savings programs where you purchase things at regular stores and they deposit a portion into a child's college savings account. I'm wondering what you know

about this. Is it a scam? Thanks so much for all your wonderful information and support.

A: Joining *Upromise.com* is similar to earning frequent-flyer miles. You can save for a friend's child, a relative—even a child you hope to have in the future. You can save for your own education regardless of your age.

Upromise gives rebates of up to 4 percent from an impressive list of brands, including AOL Time Warner, AT&T, Borders, Century 21, Citibank, Coke, Exxon Mobil, GM, McDonalds, Staples, Toys R Us and online retailers, like *LandsEnd.com*.

These rebates are deposited to your child's 529 college savings account. Anyone can designate their rebates to your kids' college funds.

First, you open an account with *Upromise.com* and also a 529 state-sponsored college savings account through one of the Upromise approved investment companies like The Vanguard Group.

Then you register your credit, debit, grocery, and drug store cards. In addition to saving with your registered cards, there are many other ways to save for college with Upromise. It is very possible that a credit card already earning frequent-flyer miles could also earn frequent-tuition dollars. That's the upside.

The downside is that not all purchases at the stores you frequent will be subject to a Upromise rebate. Upromise makes sense if you would

have purchased these products anyway and you pay your account in full every month without fail. But if this program persuades you to spend more money or go into debt just to get the rebates, you'll cancel the benefits in a big hurry.

The Upromise concept is a great one, but it's not as simple or effortless as you might think.

First, the rebates you receive are tiny. It takes lots of rebates to add up to something significant. There are many limitations and exclusions. Face it, Upromise is not handing out free college educations.

Upromise is a for-profit corporation so you can be sure there's lots in it for them to have you sign up as a participating member. Still, every little bit helps when it comes to saving for the future. It all adds up.

If Upromise is right for you depends on your lifestyle, diligence and the number of people you can get to contribute to your child's Upromise account.

I have heard from people who found the program to be overly-hyped and more trouble than promise. Others have reported that saving $2,000 or more was quite simple and effortless. Clearly, this is an opportunity you must assess on an individual basis. Visit *Upromise.com* for more information.

Make sure you are clear on all of the exclusions, conditions and limitations imposed by the Upromise program. There are many. Read the fine print.

To learn more about 529 state-sponsored college savings plans, go to *SavingforCollege.com*.

Hiring help to borrow money

Q: Our son is filling out college applications, and we've also begun investigating financial aid options to help us pay his tuition.

A co-worker suggested that we pay a financial planner or some other "expert" to fill out the forms for us, since they'd better understand the ins and outs of it all.

It is a daunting task. I am wondering if it's really worth the money? And where can we go to find help even if we want to fill them out ourselves?

A: You could hire someone but you would still have to do the hard work of gathering all of your specific financial information. I think you will be way ahead if you do it yourself.

I highly recommend the book, *Taming the Tuition Tiger* by Kathy Kristof (Bloomberg Press) to walk you through the process. Check the library.

Another excellent resource is "The Student Guide," a comprehensive resource on student financial aid from the U.S. Department of Education. Grants, loans, and work-study are the three major forms of aid available

through the Department's Federal Student Aid office.

Updated each year, "The Student Guide" tells you about the programs and how to apply for them.

It is available free online in English or Spanish. Go to *Studentaid.ed.gov* to download the guide. Or call toll free 800 433-3243 to request a copy by mail.

Pay now, play later

Q: Here's the scenario: Someone in her mid-twenties is in debt (let's say a total of $30,000 between student loans, credit cards, and a car loan). She is considering pursuing a graduate degree.

Out of nowhere, she is offered two jobs! One is a higher paying job (not in the field of her intended study). The other is in a field more related to her plans for graduate school, but at a lower rate of pay.

Should she take the higher paying job to pay the debt off more quickly and then go to graduate school?

Or should she take the lower paying job that has more to do with her career goals?

It seems like financially it would make more sense to pay off the debt with the higher income job and then go back to school—the

"pay now, play later" idea. But, what do you think?

A: Yes, that is exactly how I would advise her. Taking on more debt now is too risky. For now, the job is a sure thing.

Tell her to work hard, live frugally and get those debts paid in record time. Then you ... uh, SHE will be in a much better position to consider that graduate degree.

Future

IRA maintenance fees are a given

Q: I am 24 and opened a Roth IRA account at a local independent bank one year ago. I deposited $2,000, and then much to my dismay received a $50 maintenance fee bill. I'm not sure I want to continue because of the fee. Are there banks that don't charge such high fees on IRAs?

A: Some banks and brokerage firms advertise no-custodial-fee IRA accounts, but believe me they are not free. Banks use those products for marketing campaigns so they can advertise "Fee-free IRAs!" Then they bury extra hefty fees where you probably won't notice.

Here's a rule of thumb: The more options and flexibility, the higher the fees. A $50-a-year maintenance fee is not bad at all on your Roth IRA. In fact, that is quite a good deel. It seems high while your balance is low. But as your account grows, the $50 annual maintenance fee will shrink by comparison to the growing balance.

You are smart to begin contributing while you are young. Once you retire all of the money in your Roth IRA will be available to you tax-free.

Matured U.S. Savings Bonds

Q: What can I do with three $50 Series E U.S. savings bonds I purchased in 1971?

I've heard that after 30 years they might not be worth much unless I turn them into another type of bond. Please let me know if you can. I appreciate all I have read and learned from your column.

A: You purchased those bonds for $25 each and after a number of years they reached maturity, meaning they earned enough interest to be worth their face value of $50 each. They continued to earn interest until 30 years from issue, around 2001. They are probably worth about $85 or $90 each at this time.

Of course you can just hold them until you die but I wouldn't do that since they have now begun to lose their "buying power" through inflation.

You could easily convert these bonds to new Series E or Series I savings bonds to get that money growing again. You can do this online or in person at most banks.

Information about savings bonds is available at the U.S. Department of the Treasury, Bureau of Public Debt's website at *TreasuryDirect.gov*. Or send a postcard requesting the "Earnings Report" to: Bureau of the Public Debt, 200 Third Street, Parkersburg, WV 26106-5312.

Invest in 401(k) or our debt?

Q: My husband contributes 8 percent of his gross income to his employer's 401(k) plan. Would it be wise to temporarily stop that contribution in that we have about $50,000 unsecured debt?

A: Yes, but only until your unsecured debts are paid. Putting your hard-earned money at risk while you are carrying high-interest consumer debt is not wise. No matter how you cut it, money in a 401(k) is at risk.

But, investing in your debt carries no risk and offers a guaranteed rate of return.

Let's say you have a $10,000 revolving credit-card balance at 18 percent interest. Each month you are paying $150 in interest ($10,000 x 18 percent / 12 = $150).

Great Aunt Gertie dies and leaves you $10,000. You can either pay off the debt or invest the money. Let's say you invest it.

Things don't go well and you lose some or all of it in the stock market. You still owe that $10,000 on the credit card and you're still paying $150 interest each month.

Now let's say you go the other way and use the money to repay the debt in full. Every month you get to keep the $150 you were sending to the credit-card company. That is your guaranteed 18 percent return on the $10,000 "investment" you made in

your debt. It's a sure thing regardless what happens with the economy. Now that's a good deal.

Caution: Even though you stop making contributions for a season, do not cash in his 401(k) account. The penalties and tax consequence are too severe.

Pay debt or build retirement?

Q: I have been on my Rapid Debt-Repayment Plan now for three months. I read in your book, *Debt-Proof Living* that there is no surer investment than a repaid debt.

I am thinking about redirecting my 401(k) contributions toward my debt to speed the repayment process. Is this a wise move even though I would be missing my employer's match? I am determined to get this debt out of my life forever.

A: Boy, this is a tough one. On the one hand it seems ridiculous to leave "free money" on the table (your employer match). But I agree that until you are free of your unsecured debt, you have no business putting precious income at risk in a retirement fund like your 401(k).

A reasonable compromise would be for you to reduce your contribution to be just enough to get the match, and to direct the balance of your current monthly contribution to boost your RDRP.

No matter which way you choose to go, do not cash in or take any money out of your 401(k) account. The penalties for doing so are just too great. Leave it alone to grow during this season of "redirection." Knowing it is there working for you will help you keep a positive attitude.

I wish you well in making the best decision for you. And if you decide to stop all contributions for a season, I would certainly understand. The drive to finally get out of debt can be very strong once you've had a taste of how great it feels to be moving in that direction.

Invest in your debt for a sure return

Q: I have been reading *Debt-Proof Living* newsletter for the past two years. We began our Rapid Debt-Repayment Plan (RDRP) at that time and we're doing really well. We have about $7,000 unsecured debt remaining.

We will be getting a $3,500 tax refund and it's presenting a problem. I want to funnel it into our RDRP to pay off our debt.

My husband wants to invest it in the stock market. He says now that the market is on sale and stocks are so cheap he can make a lot of money quickly and then we'll have enough to pay the en-

tire amount with some left over. I said no.

Mary, you have brainwashed me to pay off that debt! My husband is hard-headed. He wants to win this argument. I need more ammunition. We have never argued about money before. What should I say to him?

A: Well now, I'm flattered you think I could persuade your husband to your way of thinking. I'm not sure I can do that, but given my newly discovered brainwashing skills, who knows?

Show him that you can invest $3,500 completely risk-free with a guaranteed double-digit rate of return in the first year.

Here's how: If the interest rate on that $3,500 debt is 16 percent (you didn't say, but it's probably at least that high) and you pay it off, you can pocket the $560 interest ($3,500 x 16 percent) you won't have to pay the creditor over the next year.

If, on the other hand, your husband invests the $3,500 in the stock market, he puts the money at risk. I guess he could beat all of Wall Street and earn 16 percent, but I think we all can guess the chances of that happening. He could also lose some or all of the principal during the year, and you would still owe the $3,500 and the annual interest of $560.

Investing in your debt is a sure thing, the stock market is not.

No matter what happens, remember your marriage is a more valuable investment than anything money can buy. Don't let this drive a wedge between the two of you. I couldn't handle the guilt.

Finding a financial planner

Q: My wife and I have been members of *Debt-Proof Living Online* for years. We've completed our RDRP, have our Freedom Account well-funded and now we're ready to move to the next level. We want to begin investing and building wealth for our retirement years.

Should we hire a financial planner? Where would be a good place to receive this kind of advice?

Many thanks for your books and website. It has and continues to save us money and we will continue to be online subscribers, forever.

A: Thanks for your kinds words. I am knocked out by the progress you've made. Congratulations!

I agree that it may well be time for you to consult with a professional planner. Here's the challenge: Finding one you can trust who will not charge a fortune.

Anyone can call himself a financial planner. If you are ready to seek the services of a financial planner, and to avoid an amateur, you want one who has earned the special credentials of Chartered Financial Consultant (ChFC) or Certified Financial Planner (CFP).

These professionals make a comprehensive analysis of your entire financial life, identify your goals and then create an investment and insurance strategy to achieve those goals.

Generally, but not always, a professional financial planner will have minimum standards for new clients that have to do with net worth. Financial planners are not typically debt counselors. If you are deeply in debt, a financial planner is likely to tell you to come back once you are out of debt.

Planning means more than investing. Not all planners offer comprehensive services. Some give investment advice or focus on one aspect of planning like insurance or taxes. Estate planning is often offered by a credentialed financial planner or consultant and includes wills, trusts, tax-planning, legacy and end-of-life planning.

Fee-only financial planners are paid only for the advice they give. Typically they charge by the hour ($200 to $250), like an attorney. They do not earn commissions by selling financial products like life insurance and mutual funds. You can find fee-only planners at *NAPFA.org*.

Fee-based planners earn fees plus commissions. Like a fee-only planner, you pay for the advice and financial plan. The planner also earns commissions if you purchase products recommended in the plan.

Commission-based planners make money from the products they sell. Typically this type of planner does not charge for his or her time, but has a big incentive for you to purchase the products they recommend.

Not ready to meet face-to-face with a professional planner, but still anxious for a professional plan to follow that will address all areas of financial planning, including investing, insurance, college savings, wills and trusts? Then *eFinPLAN.com*—the first do-it-yourself financial planning website—has created a unique service.

With eFinPLAN you just sign up and start creating your plan by inputting information and answering questions from the privacy of your home or office, for less than $100.

Converting 401(k) fund to Roth IRA

Q: I am 60 and employed, making regular contributions to my 401(k) plan. Can I roll over the money in my account to a Roth IRA? A friend says that I can't take the money for any reason as long as I'm employed. I plan to work until I am age 66.

A: First you need to find out if your 401(k) plan allows for in-service distributions. If not, you cannot roll your account over to an IRA as long as you are employed with this employer. However, you may have another way to do this. Your 401(k) should have

something called a *Roth Deferral Account* that gives you the option of making future contributions to a Roth.

If your plan does allow for in-service distributions you can roll over the eligible amount into a regular IRA and from there convert it (subject to income limitations) to the Roth IRA you desire, paying the income taxes as required.

Unless you anticipate the taxes on your income to be the same or higher during retirement than they are currently, you probably want to take advantage of the pre-tax savings your 401(k) offers versus paying the taxes in your current (likely higher) tax bracket to make Roth contributions.

Because you are over 50 there is a provision in the law that allows you to open and contribute up to $6,000 annually into a Roth IRA in addition to your 401(k) contributions, provided your current annual income is less than $105,000 as a single taxpayer or $166,000 as a joint taxpayer. If you are over those income limits, your contribution becomes limited and eventually eliminated.

Please discuss this and any tax or legal information with your tax and legal professionals. Stuff changes all the time so you want to make sure you have the latest information.

Lost savings bonds

Q: When I was a child my grandparents gave me quite a few U.S. Savings Bonds. Now I cannot find them. Is there a way to replace them or am I out of luck?

A: Good news! Provided you have a fairly accurate memory, you may be able to get the bonds replaced.

The Bureau of Public Debt, the branch of the U.S. Treasury Department that issues all the various types of bonds and treasury notes, has come up with a simple system for replacing bonds. First you will need to get Form PDF1048.

Fill in the approximate issue date along with your complete name, address and Social Security number and if possible the bond serial numbers. Your grandparents might have recorded those serial numbers, so do some checking. Once the form is processed the Bureau will issue you a new set of certificates.

You can get the form by writing to: Bureau of Public Debt, Parkersburg, WV 26106. Visit the Bureau's website at *PublicDebt.treas.gov* for more information. If you should find the original bonds in the future, don't try to cash them. When new ones are issued, those originals will be cancelled.

Wanted:
Financial advisor

Q: Help! What is the best way to identify a financial advisor who can help us with retirement planning?

A: First, decide what kind of planner you want: commission-based, or fee-based.

A commissioned planner will not charge you by the hour for his or her services, but instead earns a commission on the products he or she sells you.

A fee-based planner charges a flat fee to create a plan and then leaves you on your own to implement it. You pay an hourly fee similar to the way you would pay an attorney; $200 - $250 per hour is customary.

I prefer a planner who is part commission-based, part fee-based. Ours, for a nominal fee, created a complete retirement and estate plan then walked us through implementation with specific recommendations.

Once you know the kind of planner you want, look for a personal recommendation from a friend or relative you trust. Let someone else weed out the bad ones.

401(k) loan is
troublesome

Q: We're expecting our third child, and would like to add on to our home. My husband can take a loan from his 401(k) at 4 percent interest. Payments will be deducted from his paycheck every week to put the money back into his account.

It sounds too good to be true and that's making me nervous. I don't want to jeopardize our future for an extra two rooms.

He thinks I'm being too worrisome. Is he right?

A: Borrowing from a retirement account seems simple enough but most people don't realize the full ramifications of doing that.

First, there's the matter of that new payment every week. Do you really have extra money each week for that new loan payment? If so, what are you doing with that extra money now? Let's hope you are stashing it into a savings account.

Next is a little matter of double taxation. Let me explain:

The money in your husband's account is "before-tax" dollars. If he takes a loan, he will repay with "after-tax dollars." That means if he deposited $100 into his 401(k) and then borrowed that $100 in an approved loan, he will have to earn about $128 to come up with $100 for the loan payment because it will be paid with after tax dollars. That's the first taxation.

When he withdraws that same $100 dollars in retirement, he'll pay taxes on it again.

Then there's the matter of life's uncertainty—which, sadly, is pronounced during these current economic times. If he leaves his employer for any reason before the loan is repaid, the entire balance will immediately become due. If you cannot pay the balance in full within about three weeks, the loan balance will be

converted from a loan to a cash withdrawal. He'll get socked with a 10 percent penalty plus the IRS and state tax collector will be knocking on your door to collect taxes on that full amount. Want to know how much money you'll have to come up with right away? Multiply the outstanding balance by about 40 percent. Where will you get that kind of dough if he is unemployed?

And if that's not enough, you must consider the potential loss of investment growth during the period of time you've removed money from the account.

Overall, my opinion and resulting advice is that borrowing from his 401(k) is so troublesome, it should be seen as your last resort, not the first.

If you truly believe you can afford these weekly payments plus interest on your current income, prove it: Start making those payments right now—today to yourselves. Open a special savings account make that payment every week without fail. You'll have to wait a little while for that room addition, but you'll have the cash you need and without going into debt.

Let's see, pay off debt or invest?

Q: Is it better to pay off credit-card debt before enrolling in a retirement plan? My interest is 3.99 percent fixed and the debt is quite substantial—$12,000. Also, is it better to pay the minimum payment per month plus the finance charges for that month or should I just pay the minimum payment - how much sooner would I be able to pay off the debt?

A: It is not wise to put any of your hard-earned money at risk while you have this unsecured debt. So yes, I believe you should pay off that credit-card debt first and as quickly as humanly possible.

If you pay only the minimum on your $12,000 (typically 3 to 4 percent of the outstanding balance is the way they figure the minimum payment, which by design is usually just about the amount of interest you owe that billing cycle) even at 3.99 percent, it will take roughly 55 months to repay it in full.

If you pay the minimum plus $100 each month, you reduce the payback time to around 38 months. Better. If you can pay more, do it.

On a cautionary note, do not assume that when it comes to a credit-card account's "fixed rate" it means anything other than the rate is not tied to an index.

By federal law credit-card companies may increase their "fixed" interest rates by simply giving the card holder 15 days notice (after July 2010 that will become 21 days).

I suggest you do all you can to pay this debt as quickly as possible while the interest rate is low. Soon you'll be in a better position to participate fully in that retirement plan

Free loans to IRS: Call 1-800-IM-NUTS

Q: Each year we get a federal tax refund of around $2,000. Up to this point we have used it to do things like buy half-a-beef and put some into savings.

Should we change our tax withholding and have this money go into our pockets now?

A: Yes! Overpaying your taxes is not wise because you are in effect giving the government a tax-free loan that it doesn't need and you cannot afford.

I don't know many people who have so much money they can afford to do that. You might see overpaying your taxes as a kind of "forced savings account," but why let the government hold your savings for you. So they can use it to bail out the banks? Or fund some cushy congressional weekend retreat?

If something comes up during the year and you need that money, you can forget it. You can't apply for your refund until after January 1 of the coming year. Worse, you don't even earn interest on that money!

You should adjust your withholding now and immediately set up an automatic deposit so that the difference in your paycheck is diverted to a savings account you manage and control. Ask your employer for a new W-4 Tax Withholding form, then increase your number of exemptions.

Your goal is to fine tune your federal tax withholding so closely that come April 15 you neither owe nor are owed. If you can come within $100 either way you are doing well.

How many
W-4 exemptions?

Q: My husband is starting a new job. How can we figure out how many exemptions to claim to maximize our monthly income and also insure we won't have to pay when we file our taxes?

A: It's simple. Go to the IRS website at *IRS.gov* and look for the worksheet and withholding calculator. Fill in the basic information it asks for, which will be specific to your situation The calculator will suggest how many exemptions you should claim on your husband's W-4 so you neither owe nor are owed next year.

Actually, now would be a good time for all of my readers to review their withholding situations. Employees may change the number of exemptions on their W-4s at any time.

Innocent spouse
may get relief

Q: How does one overcome unfair taxes assigned from a divorce? My husband, an attorney and former Bar Association president, did the taxes during our marriage. I have returned to work now and only make $14,000 a year.

A: You may have a legal way out of what appears to be an impossible situation. I am not an attorney nor a CPA, so I cannot offer you legal advice. But I can give you some important information.

Several years ago the IRS adopted a new provision called "Innocent Spousal Relief," for situations not unlike what you have described.

To learn more and to discover if you might qualify for such relief, which may include forgiveness of the tax liability, interest and penalties as a result of joint tax returns you signed, go to *IRS.gov*. Click on "Individuals," then scroll down to find "Tax Information for Innocent Spouses." That will take you to "Explore if you are an Eligible Innocent Spouse" to find out if you qualify.

If you do, download IRS Publication 971, "Innocent Spouse Relief." At that point I would seek the advice and counsel of an attorney or tax accountant.

I hope this information will provide some hope for you as you are going through such a difficult time in you life. Never forget that what doesn't kill us, just makes a stronger. You will not die from this. So you can expect to come out of this much better for having gone through it.

Best way to pay the IRS

Q: This year for the first time ever I will owe a lot of money to the IRS for my federal taxes.

Should I use my savings to pay my taxes, or is there a way to make payments that is not overly, well, taxing? I've been planning to use the money in my savings to pay off my high-interest credit cards.

A: While the IRS purports to set up payment plans in certain situations, if there is any way you can avoid that, you should. The last person you want to owe money to is Uncle Sam. Your taxes should take top priority.

Yes, I recommend that you use your savings to pay your taxes, it is that important. Since you do not say if this will deplete your account, I am going to assume that it will not. Whatever amount remains, keep that stashed for big emergencies (like taxes).

I can only assume further that since you owe so much to the IRS, you had a pretty good year. You made more money than you've ever made before. So why all the high-interest credit-card debt?

You need to immediately put yourself on a spending freeze, buckle down and get those debts repaid. It doesn't take many double-digit credit-card balances to wipe out any additional profit you might have otherwise amassed.

Can I pay my taxes with a credit card?

Q: I'm thinking about paying my taxes with a credit card to get the miles. Great idea?

A: No, it's a terrible idea. Here's why: Unlike typical credit-card transactions where the merchant has to pay a pretty sizable merchant's fee so you can have the privilege to "charge it!," the government is precluded by law from paying such a fee for you.

Merchants cannot collect this fee from your government of choice, so guess who gets to pay it? YOU. They call it a "Tax Payment Convenience Fee," and it will be from 2.25 to 3.93 percent of the amount you charge. Do the math.

There is no way that the rewards you might earn could possibly counter the fee.

Bottom line: Yes, you can pay your taxes with a credit card, but since you asked me if you should, my answer is: No, you may not! Only a fool would do such a thing.

Your Turn ...

Dear Friend,

If you have a question about personal finance or money in general, I'd love to hear from you. I am as close as your computer keyboard, Blackberry, iPhone—your preferred method for sending email.

When you write, please include your first and last name, and your state of residence. Email me at *DearMary@DebtProofLiving.com*.

Because I get thousands of messages each week, please don't expect a personal response. Instead, watch for your answer in my newsletter, *Debt-Proof Living* (see page 225), daily email, "Everyday Cheapskate," (see page 227), blog, *MoneyRulesDebtStinks.com*, website, *DebtProofLiving.com*, or perhaps even in my regular column in *Woman's Day* magazine.

And who knows? If your question is entertaining and carries a high likelihood that others want to know the same thing, you just might see yourself in the next book. Anonymously, of course.

Thanks for buying and reading my book. At the very least I hope you were entertained and at the most are more financially confident.

DearMary@DebtProofLiving.com

Glossary

401(k) savings plan: An employee-provided, salary-deferral plan approved by the Internal Revenue Service that allows qualified persons to save and invest pre-tax dollars.

ACH payment: The process that turns a paper check into an electronic payment at the checkout or upon receipt when sent by mail. It works like a debit card taking the money from your account immediately. A process developed by Automated Clearing House.

adjustable-rate loan: Also called variable-rate loan. The interest rate fluctuates, adjusting periodically to the moves of a key rate, such as the prime rate or one-year Treasury bills.

adjusted gross income, or AGI: Used to calculate federal income tax, your AGI includes all the income you received over the course of the year, such as wages, interest, dividends and capital gains, minus things such as business expenses, contributions to a qualified IRA, moving expenses, alimony and capital losses, interest penalty on early withdrawal of bank CD certificates and payments made to retirement plans such as SEP and SIMPLE IRAs.

affinity card: A credit card marketed to a group of customers with a common bond, such as membership in an organization.

allocation: The way in which your savings are divided among the different accounts you have selected.

annual fee: The annual charge, from $35 to $400, paid by a cardholder to the credit-card company for the privilege of owning that particular credit card. Many credit cards do not charge an annual fee. The annual fee is billed directly to the customer's monthly statement.

annual percentage rate: The true cost of borrowing money, expressed as a percentage. Includes interest and fees on some loans such as an auto loan. The interest rate on a mortgage or home equity loan does not include fees however. Also called APR.

appreciating asset: An asset that has a reasonable expectation of increasing in value with time.

appreciation: An increase in value.

appropriate: To set aside funds for a specific use.

APR: See annual percentage rate.

asset: Anything you own of value.

ATM card: A plastic card that gives the owner access to the automated teller machine when used with one's personal identification number (PIN). An ATM card often doubles as a debit card linking directly with one's bank account.

attitude: A way of thinking or behaving.

austerity: A severely simple lifestyle.

authorized user: A person you add to your credit-card account who has charging privileges, but is not responsible for payment on the account. Credit information on the account is reported to the authorized user's credit report—both good and bad.

automatic deposit: A deposit that is made from one's account or paycheck into an investment or other account every month or at specific intervals as directed by the account holder. Authorization is made by the account holder and can be retracted or amended at any time. A painless way to get into the habit of saving or investing regularly.

automated teller machine (ATM): A convenient machine where you can deposit or withdraw money from your savings or checking account any time of the day or night. (Often thought of by children as a place in a wall from which Mommy and Daddy get as much money as they want.)

automobile loan: A loan from a bank, credit union, or finance company to purchase an automobile.

balance transfer fee: A charge by the credit-card company to customers for transferring an outstanding balance from one credit card to another.

bankruptcy: A legal declaration of insolvency. The bankruptcy law contains several types of bankruptcy. Chapter 7 is full discharge of all of one's debts except for student loans and obligations to the IRS. Chapter 11 (business) and Chapter 13 (personal) denote reorganization repayment plans set up and administered by the courts.

belief: A feeling of certainty about the meaning of something.

bill pay: See online bill pay.

biweekly mortgage: Another form of prepayment. If you make mortgage payments every two weeks—or the equivalent of thirteen payments a year, rather than twelve—you can reduce the term of a 30-year mortgage by eight to 12 years.

biweekly schedule: A method by which a person pays one-half of a monthly payment every two weeks. The net result is 26 half-payments each year or the equivalent of 13 monthly payments. A fairly painless way to pay more than is required and thus reduce the time and fees associated with the indebtedness.

boomerang kid: An adult child who leaves home and then returns for one reason or the other, which is most always financial, to live with parents.

budget: A formula for adjusting expenditures to income.

buying power: Worth determined by how much it will buy. For instance, the buying power of a dollar today is much greater than it will be 50 years from now.

canceled checks: Checks that have been paid by the bank as directed by the checking-account holder. Canceled checks are sometimes returned to the customer for record keeping, although most banks and credit unions return copies of the canceled checks to the customer.

capital gains: A profit that results from investments into a capital asset, such as stocks, bonds or real estate, which exceeds the purchase price.

card-hopping: The act of transferring your credit-card balances to a low-interest card for just the introductory period, then transferring again to another card for its introductory period. Card-hopping can be detrimental to one's credit score.

cash advance: A very expensive loan taken against a credit card's credit limit.

cash-advance fee: Charge by the bank to the customer using credit cards for cash advances. This fee can be stated in terms of a flat per-transaction fee or a percentage of the amount of the cash advance. For example, the fee may be expressed as 2 percent or $10. This means the cash advance fee will be the greater of 2 percent of the cash advance amount or $10. Banks may limit the amount that can be charged to a specific dollar amount. Depending on the bank issuing the card, the cash-advance fee may be deducted directly from the cash advance at the time the money is received or it may be posted to your bill as of the day you received the advance.

cash flow: Generally referred to in terms of the money that flows into your possession. Spending more than comes in produces a negative cash flow. A positive cash flow occurs where more comes in than goes out.

Certificate of Deposit: An interest-bearing receipt from a bank guaranteeing that upon deposit of a specific amount of money, at a specific point in time, a guaranteed amount of interest will be paid to the bearer along with the original deposit. CDs are available in a variety of denominations and for varying time periods. The longer you agree to leave your money on deposit, the greater the interest rate you will earn.

cheapskates: Those who give generously, save regularly, and never spend more money than they have; an endearing term to members of DPL.

Christmas Club: A savings program that was first offered by various banks during the Great Depression. The concept is that bank customers deposit a set amount of money each week into a special savings account, and receive the money back at the end of the year for Christmas shopping.

co-branded card: A credit card that is issued through a partnership between a bank and another company or organization. For instance, a large department store may co-brand a card with a bank. The card would have both the bank name and the store name on it. Some co-branded cards are also rebate cards that provide the consumer with benefits such as extra service, cash, or merchandise every time the card is used. Also called an affinity card.

collateral: An asset owned by the borrower that is pledged and held by the lender pending the borrower's faithful repayment of the debt. Something of value such as real estate, stocks, bonds, or other assets offered as security to encourage a lender to make a loan.

compounding interest: The concept that money makes money, and the money that money makes, makes more money. When interest is allowed to remain in the account rather than being paid out, it becomes principal. Now interest is earned on the interest. Compounding interest is what allows investments and savings to grow.

consumer credit industry: That segment of the business world that extends credit to consumers on an unsecured basis.

consumer debt: Unsecured loans offered to consumers to buy goods and services.

contribution: IRA contributions are limited to $5,000 for the 2009 tax year if you're younger than 50. If you're 50 or older, you can contribute as much as $6,000 for the 2009 tax year. Contributions are classified as either tax deductible or nondeductible.

contentment: Wanting what you have.

Contingency Fund: A personal finance tool unique to Debt-Proof Living; a pool of money that is readily available and very safe, held as a hedge against emergencies such as health and safety issues or the loss of one's income.

corporate downsizing: The process by which a corporation pulls in its belt by drastically reducing overhead and expenses. Corporate downsizing is often the catalyst for massive layoffs.

cosign: A contractual promise to pay another person's debt arising out of a contractual obligation if that person fails to do so.

credit card: A card authorizing the holder to buy goods or services on credit; a small piece of plastic that has the ability to make its bearer do strange things he or she probably wouldn't dream of doing with cash.

credit counselor: An intermediary who works with a debtor to set up a payment plan that his or her creditors will accept.

credit inquiry: A notation on one's credit report that indicates the person gave a company permission to look into their credit file.

credit insurance: Insurance that pays off all or part of a loan if the borrower dies or becomes disabled or unemployed.

credit repair: The process of improving, rehabilitating, or correcting one's financial reputation among creditors.

credit report: A report filed by subject's name, birth date, and Social Security number that gives an accounting of that person's credit activities and payment history. This report will help a new lender determine the credit worthiness of the applicant. Many prospective landlords and employers look at a person's credit report to get a true picture of the applicant's character. Major companies providing these credit report services include, Experian, Trans Union, and Equifax.

credit scoring: A point system lenders and credit bureaus use to assess your credit worthiness.

credit union: A nonprofit financial institution formed for the benefit of its members. Since there are no stockholders, profits are partially paid back to the members in the form of dividends. Offers checking accounts, savings accounts, and loan services. Generally better interest rates, lower fees, and personal service. Must qualify to join. Not open to the public.

daily spending record: A simple list of where you spent your money today. Should include every single expenditure, even the small ones.

day-trading: A form of investing that involves buying and selling stocks for a profit in the same day with no overnight holds. The chances of losing money are very high.

deadbeat: A term often used by a credit-card issuer to describe the cardholder who pays off his or her account each month, thereby not paying any interest or finance charges. A deadbeat is one who does not contribute to the bank's profitable bottom line. Can also refer to an adult child or grandchild who is irresponsible and financially immature.

debit card: A plastic card that gives you electronic access to your checking account. Often doubles as an ATM card, but can also be used like a credit card to make purchases from vendors.

debt: Something that is owed.

debt consolidation: A new loan taken to pay off a bundle of smaller debts, thus ending up with just one new debt with a payment smaller than the sum total of those just paid off.

debt management program (DMP): Usually offered in conjunction with credit counseling, this program requires the person in counseling to make one payment to the DMP each month, which in turn distributes funds to client's creditors. Many creditors require DMP involvement to accept a person into counseling.

debt settlement: An agreement by the creditor to take a smaller amount of money than owed by the debtor in full settlement of what is owed.

debt trap: That place one finds himself in when overcome by too much debt. A place of bondage.

debt, intelligent: That to which the borrower is obligated in a loan transaction secured by collateral that can be repaid anytime.

debt-proof living formula: Give away 10 percent, save 10 percent, and live on 80 percent.

debt, secured: A loan that is collateralized.

debt, stupid: A debt that is not secured, has no collateral attached to it, and can be incurred with your signature alone.

deductible or nondeductible: Contributions to a traditional IRA are tax-deductible if you are not covered by your employer's retirement plan. Even if you do participate in a company pension or 401(k) plan, you still may be able to deduct contributions to a traditional IRA depending on your income and filing status. Contributions to a Roth IRA are not deductible.

dejunk: The act of getting rid of all the clutter in your home, office, and life.

depreciate: To lose value simply because of the passing of time.

depreciation: A loss in value or efficiency resulting from usage and or age.

deprivation: The act of withholding, as in when I get a tax refund I am depriving myself of the use of my money for a whole year, while the government gets to use it interest-free until I get it back as a refund.

discontentment: Not being happy with what you have, as in that feeling of having to pay for something with a credit card because I just can't wait until I save the money to pay for it.

discretionary income: That which is left after all the bills are paid; money available for non-essential expenditures. This is for many people, something they don't know about firsthand, but believe me there are some people in the world who have discretionary income.

dislocated worker: Anyone fired or laid off due to downsizing or a self-employed person whose business failed because of a turn in the economy, not to be confused with a dislocated shoulder which is almost as painful.

displaced homemaker: A woman who has left the workplace to rear children, is single as a result of either divorce or death, and requires training to return to the workplace.

diversification: The practice of spreading investments among a number of different investments to reduce risk. It's the opposite of "putting all your eggs in one basket." A mutual fund is an example of diversification because it invests in many different securities.

dividend: A sum of money to be distributed to stockholders.

dollar-cost averaging: Investing the same amount of money in the same investment at regular time intervals.

down payment: The up-front money required to enter into a loan.

DPLers: People actively engaged in debt-proofing their lives.

durable goods: Things that have a life expectancy exceeding three years.

Education IRA: Renamed Coverdell education savings account, in honor of the late Sen. Paul Coverdell, is not strictly an IRA, since it doesn't finance retirement. Instead, you can make annual contributions up to $2,000 per child, to an account that's exclusively for helping to pay education costs. The money you put aside in a Coverdell account doesn't count against the annual retirement IRA contribution limits for you or your child. You can't deduct the Coverdell contributions from your income taxes, but earnings are tax-deferred and qualified withdrawals are tax-free.

entitled: Feeling that is the result of having an available balance on one's credit-card account.

equity: The value remaining in excess of liabilities or loans.

estate planning: The process of planning the transfer of all personal assets at death to chosen beneficiaries.

f (fixed): If the letter f appears after the annual percentage rate (APR), the interest rate is fixed and not subject to adjustment.

falling payments: Payments that fall in direct proportion to the outstanding balance, such as minimum monthly payments on credit-card accounts, as opposed to mortgage payments that remain fixed regardless of the current outstanding balance.

FDIC: Federal Deposit Insurance Corporation, which insures deposits in federal U.S. banks.

federal tax withholding: Money withheld by one's employer and sent to the IRS in anticipation of payment of federal income taxes and Social Security taxes.

federally insured: Money deposited into a bank or savings and loan that is covered by FDIC insurance. In the event the financial institution becomes insolvent, the insurance will reimburse the depositor.

FICO: Credit scoring model and software developed by Fair Isaac Company.

financial bondage: That uncomfortable situation where one owes so much money to so many creditors he feels like a slave.

financial calculator: A calculator that figures payment schedules and debt-payoff periods.

financial freedom: The state or condition of being free from financial pressures brought on when one lives from paycheck to paycheck and under the bondage of heavy debts.

financial planner: An investment professional who assists individuals in putting together a financial plan and coordinates various financial activities.

financial security: That point in time when you can live the lifestyle you have chosen, financed from the assets you have accumulated, without the need for additional income.

for-profit corporations: A corporation that has stockholders and the expectation of making a profit, which is then paid to said stockholders.

Freedom Account: A separate checking account into which you deposit monthly 1/12 of your known irregular expenses. A financial tool unique to Debt-Proof Living.

frugality: That which is necessary to keep your expenses less than your income.

gambling: Putting money at unreasonable risk in an effort to profit from the outcome of a game of chance.

grace period: The period of time the customer is allowed to pay the monthly bill before the account begins to accrue interest. Issuers determine a grace period based on different stages in the transaction. A grace period can begin based on one of the following: 1) transaction—the actual date you used your card for a purchase or a cash advance; 2) posting—the actual day the issuer received the charge and posted it to your account; 3) billing—the date that your bill is generated for mailing to you.

HEL: Acronym for home equity loan.

HELOC: Acronym for home equity line of credit.

hoarding: Saving to an extreme and to the detriment of your joy and ability to do good in the world.

home equity loan: A loan secured by the equity in your home. Also called a second mortgage.

home equity line of credit: A line of credit, similar to a credit card, secured by the equity in your home, accessible by a debit card or checkbook.

home mortgage: A loan from a bank or other lender that is secured by the value of the home.

income: The money that flows into your life.

identity theft: A crime where a thief assumes the identity of another for the purpose of opening lines of credit, stealing the contents of a bank account or similar.

individual retirement account (IRA): A personal savings account specifically designated for your retirement. The money placed into an IRA may be tax deductible depending on your income and participation in other retirement plans. Even if it is not, all money in your IRA account grows on a tax-deferred basis—taxed only when you begin withdrawing funds.

insurance premiums: Payment for insurance coverage.

intelligent borrowing: Borrowing only when the loan is secured and the proceeds go to buy something that will appreciate.

interest: A fee the borrower pays to the lender for the temporary use of the lender's money.

interest-bearing account: A savings or checking account that earns interest for the account holder.

introductory rate: Also called the "teaser rate," this is the rate charged by a lender for an initial period, often used to attract new cardholders. This rate is charged for a short time only and is used to entice borrowers to accept the card terms. After the introductory period is over, the rate increases to the indexed rate or the stated interest rate.

investing: The deliberate act of putting money to work in a commercial endeavor with an expectation of a reasonable gain and with the full understanding there exists no investment that is without some level of risk.

investment portfolio: The entire collection of one's investments. A portfolio should represent lots of different types of investments, including stocks, bonds, mutual funds, real estate, security, and cash. A well-diversified portfolio is one that offers the greatest security.

irregular expenses: Any expenses that do not recur on a monthly basis.

joint owner: Another person who shares all profits, liabilities and responsibilities equally on a line of credit, loan or ownership of an asset or liability.

laddering: An investment technique where you purchase multiple financial products with different maturity dates.

late fee: Charge to customer whose monthly payment has not been received as of the due date or stated deadline for payment as shown on the billing statement. Late fees are a serious indication of the borrower's lack of financial integrity and show up on one's credit report for future lenders or others assessing borrower's character for up to seven years.

leasing: Renting for a specific number of years. Leasing carries a legal obligation on both the part of the lessor (owner) and lessee (renter).

liability: A financial obligation.

lien: A legal right to claim or dispose of property in payment of or as security for a debt.

line of credit: A preapproved loan where you can draw down as much or as little of the line as you want and pay interest only on the amount you actually use. A credit-card limit represents a line of credit as does a home equity line of credit where the loan is secured by the equity in the home. If the borrower defaults, the lender can foreclose on the property.

liquid cash: Money that is available right now in spendable cash. An investment in stock is not liquid. It would have to be sold to convert it to cash.

liquidating: Turning assets into cash.

liquidity: The ability of an asset to be turned into cash. Your checking account is very liquid because you can draw out the cash at any time. U.S. Savings Bonds are somewhat liquid, but it takes about three weeks to receive the cash once liquidated. The equity in your home is less liquid because of the time necessary to go through the sale and actually receive cash. Great Uncle Fred's stamp collection would have a low degree of liquidity.

living beneath your means: Spending less than you earn.

long-term investment: An investment you intend to hold for a minimum of five years.

lower-rate cards: Credit cards with amazingly low interest rates. Usually the low rates are limited to the first six months or so until the true rate kicks in.

means: Money or other wealth available to provide one's living.

minimum monthly payment: The least amount a creditor will accept as the monthly payment on your debt. Often the minimum payment represents only the creditor's profit and does not reduce the principal.

money leaks: The ways that money leaves your life unnoticed and unaccounted for.

money managers: Caretakers of money.

money market account: A savings account offered by a bank that pays better interest than a passbook savings account. Offers check-writing privileges and is guaranteed by FDIC up to $100,000. Not to be confused with money market funds that are not FDIC insured and issued by mutual fund companies.

money market fund accounts: Specialized funds sponsored by mutual fund organizations that take your money and make very short-term loans to big businesses, the U.S. Treasury, and state/local governments. A way of pooling your money with other small investors and getting a better deal on interest rates. A savings account disguised as a mutual fund. It is not insured against loss the way a money market account in a bank is insured by the FDIC.

monthly interest rate: The annual interest rate divided by 12. Credit-card companies use the monthly interest rate times the average daily balance to determine the monthly interest payment on a credit-card account.

Monthly Spending Record: Four week's worth of daily spending records blended into categories to reveal the money leaks and a picture of where your money goes.

MSRP: Manufacturer's suggested retail price.

mutual fund company: Corporation chartered by a particular state that pools the money from shareholders and invests in a portfolio of securities. It is "mutual" because the fund is actually owned by its shareholders who pay a pro rata share of fund operating expenses and receive a pro rata share of income earned and capital gains realized.

net asset value (NAV): The current value of a mutual fund share, stock share, or bond share. The net asset value of any mutual fund, stock, or bond changes daily.

net income: Your take-home pay reflecting what's left after taxes and other items are deducted.

net worth: The dollar value of your assets (what you own and what is owed to you) minus your liabilities (your financial obligations).

no-load mutual fund: A mutual fund whose shares are sold without sales charges of any kind. Some no-load funds charge a small fee, usually 1 percent, for investments held less than six months.

non-recurring expense: Any kind of expense that is a one-time charge. An appraisal fee would be an example of a non recurring expense of buying a home.

NSF: An abbreviation for "nonsufficient funds," which means the check bounced. It is illegal to knowingly write a check when there are not sufficient funds in your account equal to the amount of the check.

offers of entitlement: Preapproved or preselected credit-card applications or offers.

online bill pay: A service offered by most banks that allow an account holder to view daily activities online and also pay bills electronically.

opt-out: The act of requesting one's information to be taken off lists that are sold to banks and others for marketing purposes.

overdraft protection: A line of credit attached to one's checking account that kicks in $200 at a time to cover checks written in excess of available funds. High interest rates plus significant fees for accessing funds are charged to the account.

passbook savings: A regular savings account in a bank or credit union, the contents of which used to be recorded in a little book called a passbook.

paycheck-to-paycheck: Spending the entire amount of one's paycheck before the next paycheck is earned.

payoff plan: A specific written plan to pay off debt that lists payments, dates, and the date the plan will be complete.

Pell Grant: A gift from the government for one's college education that is not subject to repayment.

personal finance: One's money in one's personal life as opposed to a business.

PLUS loan: A loan made under the Federal Family Education Loan Program to an eligible parent or legal guardian of a dependent, undergraduate student.

points: An up-front fee charged by a lender which, in effect, lowers the nominal interest rate on the loan. A point equals 1 percent of the total loan amount.

portfolio: A collection of investments.

poverty: Living on less money than it takes to survive.

premium: The annual price you pay for an insurance plan as a whole is called a premium.

prepayment penalty: The amount of money (usually expressed as a percentage) a lender may require to be paid in addition to the unpaid principal balance when a loan is paid off ahead of schedule.

prime rate: The interest rate a bank charges to its best or "prime" customers. Each bank will quote a prime lending rate.

principal: The amount borrowed separate from interest.

private mortgage insurance (PMI): The insurance homebuyers must maintain until the equity in the property reaches at least 20 percent. This insurance protects only the lender in case the borrower defaults on the loan. Sometimes confused with mortgage insurance, which is similar to life insurance.

prospectus: A legal document that describes the objectives of an investment, such as a mutual fund, including risks, limitations, policies, services, and fees. By law a prospectus must be furnished to all prospective investors.

purchasing: Acquiring goods and services with a plan and purpose in mind.

purposeful giver: A person who does research and looks for needs so that his or her giving is directed purposefully and not in a haphazard or flippant way.

quitting points: Events or occurrences in our lives that weaken our resolve to never give up and tempt us to quit.

Rapid Debt-Repayment Plan: Also referred to as RDRP. A simple, powerful plan to repay rapidly your unsecured debts. A financial tool unique to Debt-Proof Living.

rebate cards: Cards that allow the customer to accumulate cash, merchandise, or services based on card usage.

rebate: Something given back. In the case of a grocery product, the rebate is the amount of money sent back to the consumer in exchange for a proof-of-purchase or some other qualifier.

repossess: To take back. Lenders repossess cars or homes they've lent money on when the borrower defaults or refuses to make payments as agreed.

required minimum distribution: Generally, if you have a traditional IRA, you must begin taking money out of the account by April 1 of the year after you turn 70½. The amount is a minimum distribution determined by your age and life expectancy. The IRS has established simplified tables that a traditional IRA owner can use to determine the required distribution. If required payments are not made on time, the IRS will collect an excise tax. Roth IRAs aren't subject to minimum distribution requirements until after the Roth owner dies.

resale value: The value of an asset determined by what it could bring if sold.

retirement nest egg: That money exposed to interest and growth during your working years that becomes the security of your retirement years.

revolvers: Credit-card customers who roll a balance over from month to month, pay interest faithfully, and never quite have enough money to pay the balance in full in any given month.

revolving debt: Debt that continues from month to month, year to year.

rollover: This is the term used when transferring assets from one tax-deferred retirement plan to another.

Roth IRA: The most notable thing about a Roth is withdrawals are tax-free if the account has been open for at least five years and you're at least 59½ when you start to withdraw money. Contributions to a Roth are not tax-deductible. You can withdraw your contributions anytime you want, no penalty or taxes. You can also withdraw earnings for a qualifying event if the account is at least five years old. Qualifying events include: death or disability of the account holder and a first-home purchase.

saving: Putting money in a safe place where it is not exposed to the risk of loss and pays only a pittance in interest—not enough to keep up with inflation.

savings bond: An IOU from the U.S. government in exchange for a loan. U.S. Savings Bonds are very safe but pay low rates of interest.

second mortgage: A second loan on a house or other real estate that is second in position to the first mortgage holder. If the homeowner gets into financial trouble and cannot pay, the lender in first position has first right to the property.

secured debt: A debt that is secured or guaranteed by something of value. A mortgage debt and automobile loan are examples of secured debt. If the borrower gets into trouble, the home or the car can be sold to satisfy the obligation. Also called a "safe debt."

Securities Exchange Commission (SEC): The governmental department that regulates the securities industry—the stock market, bond market, etc.

security deposit: Money given up front to a landlord or car leasing company as a promise of the lessee's faithful performance of the deal.

selective amnesia: That mental "condition" where you conveniently forget that Christmas (or other) is coming; then when you finally remember, it's too late to do anything but shop with the credit card.

SEOG: Supplemental Educational Opportunity Grant; $200 to $4,000 a year available to very low-income undergraduate students.

shopping: The activity of cruising through stores and shops with a credit card, checkbook, or cash.

signature loan: An unsecured loan that can be obtained with one's signature alone.

single-cycle billing: A billing method to determine interest owed on a credit-card bill by multiplying the monthly interest rate by the average daily balance of the past 30 days.

slippery places: Situations, events, or locations where you could easily trip and fall, financially speaking. An example might be the mall where you could easily slip into an old habit of shopping mindlessly and running up a lot of debt before you have time to analyze what's going on.

solvency: Having enough money to pay one's bills, debts, and obligations, with some left over.

speculation: Exposing money to high levels of risk with the expectation of a large return in a short period of time. Speculation should be left to highly experienced professionals.

spending limit: A term credit-card companies use instead of "credit limit" to soften the idea of a loan or debt being involved.

spending plan: A written strategy for how you plan to spend your money.

spending record: A detailed, written account of where your money was spent.

statement closing date: The date on which the credit-card company cuts off the billing cycle. Purchases made after the statement closing date will show up on the next month's statement.

stupid debt: A debt that is not secured, has no collateral attached to it, and can be incurred with your signature alone.

SuperNOW account: A type of checking account that requires you to maintain a higher minimum balance and in return pays you a higher rate of interest.

surplus: That amount of money over and beyond what is needed to pay all of your expenses.

teaser rate: A low introductory rate to entice a borrower to accept the loan or credit card.

thrift: The economical management of assets and resources.

transaction fee: A fee charged for the privilege of borrowing money through a cash advance.

tax and penalty-free withdrawals: You can take money out of your IRA tax-free and penalty-free as long as you repay the full amount within 60 days, but you may only do it once in a 12-month period.

Treasury bills: Government issued bonds that have very short-term maturities. Also called T-bills.

two-cycle billing: A billing method to determine interest owed on a credit-card bill by multiplying the monthly interest rate by the average daily balance of the past 60 days. To be banned by the Federal Reserve Board as of July 2010.

U.S. Treasuries: IOUs issued by the U.S. government in the form of Savings Bonds, T-Bills, T-Notes, and T-Bonds.

unclutter: To simplify your life by getting rid of the clutter and unused stuff.

underwater: A term used to describe the condition when the debt on one's home or car is greater than its current market value. Also known as "upside-down."

unemployment benefits: Proceeds of unemployment insurance available to someone who is laid off, but only for a short period of time.

unsecured loan: A loan not guaranteed by the pledge of any collateral.

upside down: Owing more money than the collateralized asset is worth. Typically used to refer to a car loan or lease where the car has a fair market value of less than the balance due.

v (variable): If this letter appears after the annual percentage rate (APR), the interest rate is variable and subject to change.

values: Specific types of beliefs that are so important and central to your belief system that they act as life guides.

windfall: An unexpected sum of money in any amount.

work-study programs: A federal program that provides on-campus jobs for students. Money earned from the job goes to the payment of tuition and is not subject to repayment.

Index

10-10-80 formula, 72, 125, 150
401(k), 102, 186
    borrow from, 64, 102
    hands off!, 93
529 college savings account, 181

A

AAA, 45
ACH, 7
activation sticker, 41
airline ticket, with cash, 31, 45
all-cash auto purchase, 154
amortization schedule, 139
AnnualCreditReport.com, 37, 42, 112, 116, 118
APR vs. APY, 12
Ask for ID myth, 32
ATM, 19, 64
    allows overdrafting, 13
    fees, 14
authorized user, 34, 35
auto financing, 152
    refinance, 152
    upside-down, 154
auto bill pay, 20
auto debt, 63, 87
auto loan, 83
auto loan, refinance, 82
auto purchase, all cash, 154
Automated Clearing House, 7
Automobile Club of America, 45
AV VO.com, 78
available credit, 103

B

bait and switch, 28

balance checkbook, 16
balance transfer nightmare, 48
balance transfers, 41
bank
    FDIC insured, 9
    for sale now what?, 12
    goes broke, what happens, 9
    online, 19
Bank of America, 20
Bank of You, 151, 153, 155
banking
    walk-in, 19
Bankrate.com, 6, 16, 139
bankruptcy, 65, 112, 160
    never expunged, 113
    recovery, 103
    unavoidable, 161
BCBS.com, 157
before-tax dollars, 191
Better Business Bureau, 69, 114
bill collectors, 96
bill pay, online, 5, 20
    auto, 20
bills, which to pay first, 165
biweekly mortgage, 138
Blue Cross/Blue Shield, 157
boomerang, 127
    House Rules, 128
broke, 97
Bureau of Public Debt, 190
Buxx, 45
buying power, 185

C

capital gains, 86
CapitalOne.com/autoloans, 82, 152
car debt, 76
car, rent with cash, 31, 45
Cardholder Security Plan, 37
cash, 31
    airline ticket, 31

T

U

V

W

Y

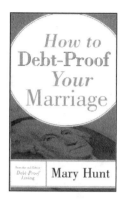
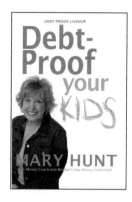